INDIAN CRICKET

Celebrating
30 Years of Publishing
in India

INDIAN CRICKET

THEN AND NOW

Edited by

VENKAT SUNDARAM

Harper
Sport

An Imprint of HarperCollins Publishers

First published in India by Harper Sport 2023
An imprint of HarperCollins *Publishers*
4th Floor, Tower A, Building No. 10, DLF Cyber City,
DLF Phase II, Gurugram, Haryana – 122002
www.harpercollins.co.in

2 4 6 8 10 9 7 5 3 1

P-ISBN: 978-93-5699-419-5
E-ISBN: 978-93-5699-416-4

Typeset in 11.5/16 Adobe Caslon Pro at
Manipal Technologies Limited, Manipal

Printed and bound at
Manipal Technologies Limited

To all cricket players and cricket lovers who have followed this sport avidly and seen in it a metaphor for life and fair play. They have been involved with the game in different capacities and popularized cricket in every nook and corner of India, making us a force to reckon with amongst the cricket-playing nations of the world. Our humble salute to each one for their contribution.

CONTENTS

Legends of the Past

Winds of Change

The Modern Age

Domestic Stalwarts

FOREWORD

Rahul Dravid

I am delighted that an anthology on cricket in India has been produced by several former cricketers and senior sports journalists. It is a laudable effort to inform the present generation of cricketers and fans about how the game started in the country and the magnificent contribution of so many luminaries over the years. I like this idea of players and journalists coming together to present stories of Indian cricket to help this generation understand and acknowledge the contributions of the past stalwarts.

I am happy to note that some of the finest names associated with the game are joining hands to bring out this book. I have always held cricket writers in high esteem. They do an excellent job of documenting local, domestic and international cricket and deserve the highest accolades for their contributions. This book is a must-read for young cricketers and avid fans, and it can serve as a source of inspiration to young boys and girls who are going to take up cricket as a career.

I have loved reading about the history of cricket and collecting books on how the game evolved and became so popular. Documenting history is important because you have to know where you came from and how you started. Even pictures of village cricket from the days of old excite today's connoisseurs of the game. It is always interesting to read about the players and officials who worked to support cricket over the years. In my case, there are many who made an early impression on me when I set out to pursue a career in cricket.

When I was growing up, there were many highly accomplished cricketers in Bangalore, including G.R. Vishwanath, Erapalli Prasanna, B.S. Chandrasekhar, Syed Kirmani and Roger Binny, among others. These cricketers, and many more before them, set the template for the excellence and class that defined Karnataka cricket. I made my debut in 1991, playing alongside the likes of Anil Kumble and Javagal Srinath. The former cricketers were always available with their insights and advice. In those days, cricket was more of a pastime as the commercialization of the game was still a decade away. I wonder what motivated the cricket legends of the past to keep going, as monetary rewards and career options in the sport were limited.

I am particularly impressed that this book has articles penned by greats such as Vijay Merchant and Vijay Hazare, among many other legends of the past. We can also learn about the role of the colonial administrators in the very early days, and later the maharajas who patronized the game. The book touches upon major events in Indian cricket, such as the victorious tours of the West Indies and England in 1971 and our maiden World Cup win in 1983. These are landmark moments that raised the profile of the game in every Indian's mind.

The popularity of cricket confirms it as the most inclusive sport in the country. It is heartening to see cricket being played in every nook and corner of the country and hearing about boys and girls from small towns claiming spots in the national junior and senior squads. It is a matter of pride that Indian cricket has emerged so powerful in today's times. The passion for the game was always there but there is a concerted direction to the progress with emphasis on providing quality support from the grassroots level to the international stage. We have come a long way as a cricket nation thanks to the professional set-up of the Board of Control for Cricket in India (BCCI). I am stunned by the sheer number of matches that the BCCI conducts in a season. In the process, there is employment generated for various stakeholders, other than the players, such as umpires, scorers, match referees, ground staff and administrators.

One of the reasons for cricket assuming such spectacular character is the development of the infrastructure. We are second to none and some of India's stadiums can match the best in the world. Now there are turf surfaces even in villages. The number of academies that have come up in small centres goes to prove that cricket is being administered well. The outskirts of little towns are dotted with cricket fields engaged in sporting activities round the year. Few grounds in big cities are vacant on weekends as the corporate world uses them for their cricket fixtures. Social cricket is immensely popular.

The incredible success of the Indian Premier League (IPL) has transformed the face of cricket. It has made the game far more interesting with teams playing to win in every format. There is no place for draws even in Test cricket because the approach to the game now is marked by a prominent bent towards aggression.

There are more results in Test matches and the fans enjoy the contests more. The IPL has made cricket self-sufficient, and the BCCI has set an example for organizers of competitions for other sports such as football, hockey, kabaddi, volleyball and badminton.

From a game once sponsored and nurtured by the royal class, cricket has come to be accepted as a game for everybody. It is the soul of our sporting society and the fact that India has won two 50-over World Cups and the T20 World Cup is a matter of national pride. Each era has its attraction and stories that capture the exploits of our players. It has been a privilege to be a part of this fabulous cricket journey and I am glad that we can now read the defining stories of Indian cricket in the form of a book.

PROLOGUE

Venkat Sundaram

It was a pipe dream born amongst a group of old friends. We had all played cricket at levels of certain distinction and now liked nothing better than to relive the days in the sun. We had the desire to give something special back to the great game that had given us so much joy, despair, pleasure, heartbreak, honour … and above all made all our lives worth living. Our group of friends wanted to produce something to celebrate the story of cricket in India, remembering the various twists and turns as our own paths intersected with that magnificent highway of dreams. It was a story waiting to be told.

But, as I mentioned, we were old friends—emphasis on the word 'old'. We had aged. Did we still have it in us to give that dream some shape and—more importantly—substance? The spirits, set on fire, were willing. The challenge lay in the actual act of producing something tangible.

Indian cricket has come a long way from when the patronage of maharajas and enthusiastic businessmen was required for the locals to emulate the British. Thanks to the vast following for the sport in India, the Board of Control for Cricket in India (BCCI) is now the envy of the cricket boards of other nations. Today, the Indian Premier League (IPL)—a BCCI creation—is the second-most valuable sports league in the world and is poised to scale even further heights.

As Indian cricket goes from strength to strength and virtually rules the cricketing world through financial power, skill and success, the paths and alleys traversed in the formative days to the years of coming of age—and the struggle to lay the platform on which the current success was built—are in danger of being deemed archaic and obsolete or simply forgotten. Not too long ago, a great Indian opening batsman was nearing the world record for the first-wicket partnership in Tests. When informed that he was within touching distance of a record held by the great Indian all-rounder Vinoo Mankad, he asked who Mankad was. Very few names in Indian cricket have been bigger than Mankad—yet this incident illustrates that even he is liable to be forgotten. We had to do something so that these names live on.

Thus, we picked up our pens and dipped them into our memories. We scanned the archives for forgotten accounts penned by names from the past. We reached out to formidable names in the world of cricket, and its chroniclers. People responded from around the world, bringing to life history both well-known and obscure with the aim of documenting it for posterity. Cricketers, writers and commentators contributed new articles while older ones were resurrected from long-lost journals.

You are holding in your hands the compiled volume that was a result of these efforts. In the following pages you will find varied voices on the game, from superstar international players and domestic heroes to veteran umpires and respected journalists. Nostalgia has thus been channelled into a reservoir of information that will always be available for every devotee of the game. Our dream thus found form, shape and substance, and emerged as this splendid book.

This is our tribute to the king of sports, which touched our lives in a special way—the passion of a country of over a billion. It serves as a wonderful window into the past, through which one can look back at the fascinating journey of Indian cricket.

THE EARLY YEARS

1

THE ORIGINALS

Raju Mukherji

This is a clarion call to all Indian cricket lovers to respect the heritage, traditions and spirit of our nation's cricket by expressing our gratitude to its pioneers for laying the foundation of the sport in our country. Here I pay tribute to three exemplary figures from India's cricketing past in the hope that their deeds will be long remembered.

Mehallasha Pavri

Mehallasha Edulji Pavri was born into the Parsi community in Navsari in 1866. He was a doctor by profession but was drawn into the cricket circles in Bombay at a time when the mercantile Parsis were more than eager to befriend the colonial British administrators. They saw cricket as an opportunity to socialize with the Britons, and learned the rudiments of the game from watching the latter play at the Bombay maidans. The Parsis eventually wanted to have their own teams to play against the white men on equal terms.

It was easier said than done. The Britons in India did play against the Parsis but were sarcastic, condescending and downright insulting towards their Indian opponents. The affronts made the Parsis more determined than ever. They resolved to get better at the game and become competitive as quickly as possible. It was 1886 when the first Parsis travelled to England to test themselves in the English conditions on their pitches. Only the senior cricketers of the community could afford to pay for the voyage and it was they who travelled. Unsurprisingly, the Parsis fared disastrously against the English, who were by far the best in the business in that era.

Pavri was not in that first Parsi team that travelled to England. But by 1888, when the team for the next tour of England was selected, he was an automatic choice by virtue of his stupendous performances against the British in the Presidency matches. On English wickets, Pavri was a man inspired. A natural athlete, he unleashed thunderbolts with nagging accuracy and regularly sent stumps cartwheeling. Pavri picked up skills from the masters of seam and swing, in particular Bill Lockwood. He added the break-back to his repertoire and felt equally at ease with the old ball as with the new.

In a match against the Gentlemen of England at Eastbourne, the Parsis set the Englishmen a target of 120 after being forced to follow on. However, Pavri came into his own and claimed 6 wickets with his whiplash action, bundling the Gentlemen out for 56. For Pavri, England was a revelation. In India, the colonials had scoffed at the Parsis' efforts, but in England the locals were genuinely generous with praise and guidance. Pavri's extraordinary haul of 170 wickets at only 11.66 earned respect and plaudits. By dint of his outstanding personal success, his team's profile improved by leaps and bounds. In 1886, the Parsis had won just one match, losing nineteen out of twenty-eight; two years later, they had eight victories and eleven losses from thirty-one matches.

Pavri's domination over G.F. Vernon's team that toured India in 1890 and Lord Hawke's 1892 touring side led to an invitation to play for Middlesex in the county championship in 1895. Thus, Pavri became the first Indian cricketer to have played county cricket in England. Ranji too first played county cricket for Sussex in the same year as Pavri, but the royal had learnt his cricket in England and had already represented Cambridge University by then.

Pavri played cricket seriously till 1912 before concentrating on the medical profession. He authored an excellent book on cricket in India at the time. Meticulous and methodical as befits a man of medicine, he was a rare deity in the pantheon of Indian cricket. His deeds proved that Indians could be as good as any cricketer in the world.

Palwankar Baloo

Among the first Indian cricketers of international eminence was a Dalit, an 'untouchable' from the lowest caste. His name was Palwankar Baloo and he was born in 1875 in Dharwad in present-day Karnataka. After his poverty-stricken family migrated to Poona, the young Baloo had to quit school to augment the family income. His first job was with a Parsi cricket club, where he rolled the pitch and swept the ground.

In 1892, he began working in the exclusive environment of Poona Gymkhana, where he was required to assist the chief groundsman. In his spare time, he bowled to the European players at the nets. A European priest known as 'Jungly' Greig was the first to discover his exceptional talent at left-arm spin. Word soon spread that the young Dalit groundsman possessed outstanding cricketing ability. But the high-caste conservative Hindus of Poona would not even contemplate giving him a trial. In the caste-ridden culture of the city at the time, a 'low-born' Dalit could get little sympathy and even less opportunity.

Eventually, Baloo's family moved to Bombay, where the cosmopolitan clime afforded him comparatively easier social mobility. Even in the big city, the more orthodox members of the Hindu Gymkhana were initially not in favour of playing with a Dalit. But regular defeats at the hands of British and Parsi teams compelled them to include Baloo in their side.

He was an immediate success in the local matches, which made him an automatic choice in the combined Hindu team for the triangular tournament in which the Hindus competed against the Parsis and the British. The Hindus began to win matches and titles almost immediately through the fantastic exploits of Baloo, the social pariah. From 1907 to 1920 he was the best bowler in the land, demonstrating phenomenal performances and remarkable consistency. However, even though he was winning them trophies, the upper-caste Hindus did not allow him to sit beside them at lunch.

Despite opposition to his leadership from his own community, Baloo had the satisfaction of captaining the Hindus to victory in the Quadrangular tournament of 1920. For a low-caste Hindu to be given leadership over the supposedly 'higher' castes was a major rip in the social fabric of the Hindu community at the time. The upper-caste Hindus accepted him more out of self-interest and convenience rather than any sense of camaraderie.

When the Maharaja of Patiala decided to take an all-India cricket team to England in 1911, Baloo was an automatic choice. In England, Baloo did not worry about the cold weather, nor was he bothered by the ever-changing conditions and the varying pitches on which he had no experience. He teased and tormented the English batters and created havoc, exhibiting to the world what a social outcast from an obscure village in India was capable of if given the right opportunities.

On Baloo's triumphant return from England, prominent social activists hailed his greatness in public addresses. B.R. Ambedkar, then a young student, became a self-confessed fan of his. Baloo was joined in the Hindu team by his brothers Shivram, Vithal and Ganpat. These four brothers made the Hindu team the best in the country. But whatever they achieved in cricket ended up being for the benefit of the upper-caste Hindus. The Dalit brothers were merely pawns to be exploited and forgotten.

Ambedkar called on Baloo to change his religion to Buddhism as he was convinced that the 'untouchables' had no future within the Hindu community. But Baloo did not heed the call as he felt that with Mahatma Gandhi's emergence and influence, the status of his community would improve and that they would become an important part of the mainstream. The contradiction in approach between the two friends drew them apart. In 1937, Baloo was coerced to fight an election against the formidable Ambedkar and lost.

Palwankar Baloo died in penury in 1955, forgotten by the men he had helped prosper. Every Indian cricketer owes him an eternal debt. He is the man who opened the doors for Indian cricketers to earn respect abroad. No national award or recognition nor any financial support was ever granted to this dignified genius. Indian cricket is guilty of having forsaken him.

D.B. Deodhar

Dinkar Balwant Deodhar was born in Poona in 1892. If Pavri and Baloo had fired the imagination of the youth of the time through tales of their exploits in England, it was Deodhar who allowed Indians to savour the taste of success first-hand at home. If any Indian player can claim to have lifted the country to Test status, it was most certainly the erudite Sanskrit scholar from Poona.

Deodhar's mission was to prove to the ruling Britons that the locals could surpass the best English players at their own game. On a winter morning in 1926, a representative India side faced the daunting task of taking on Arthur Gilligan's England (then MCC) team. This was the occasion for which Deodhar, then thirty-four, had been waiting for. The grassy Bombay Gymkhana pitch laden with fresh dew beckoned the great fast-medium bowler Maurice Tate to exhibit his mastery, but combining doggedness with exemplary strokes, Deodhar relentlessly kept piling up runs.

Only once the imposing MCC total of 362 was passed did Deodhar allow his stupendous concentration to flag. He had contributed a masterly 148 out of the team's total of 437, a lead of 75 runs over an England team comprising prominent Test cricketers. For the first time ever, a representative team of the colonial masters was subjugated by an Indian team on home soil in full view of their countrymen. No longer would the Englishmen in India make fun of Indian cricketers or dare to take them lightly. That day Deodhar was not only batting for his team but was also building self-respect among a people regularly subjugated to indignities.

Gilligan was enchanted by Deodhar's character and skill. Once back in England, he proposed to the MCC that India deserved to be among the nations playing official Test matches. This eventually led to India joining the Imperial Cricket Conference. Their first Test was played in 1932 against England at Lord's. But the irony is that the man whose innings was primarily responsible for elevating India to Test match status never got an opportunity to play Test cricket himself.

On India's inaugural tour of England in 1932, Deodhar's name was missing from the travelling party as by then the cricket crusaders had given way to cricket conspirators. The new breed of administrators declared that at forty, Deodhar was too old to play for the country. This might be true by conventional standards. But Deodhar did not confirm to such stereotypes and was physically fitter than most of the cricketers chosen—not only in 1932 but also for the second tour of England in 1936.

Even during the latter tour, he was a regular player for the Hindus in the Quadrangular and Pentangular communal cricket tournaments as well as for Maharashtra in the Ranji Trophy. His performance in first-class cricket in the 1930s was far superior to most of those chosen to play for India at the time. Even at the age of forty-eight, he scored 246 against Bombay and led his team to victory over Madras in the Ranji Trophy final. At fifty-two, he scored a century in each innings against Nawanagar.

Deodhar was a victim of selection politics. He was an educated, free-thinking and liberal man whose individualistic streak and love for his own province meant that he never played on the teams of the influential maharajas. His upright character became a noose around his international career's neck. However, it is to his credit that he took these rejections in his stride and kept playing for Maharashtra till the age of fifty-four. Even at that age his batting was prolific.

After retiring from playing, Deodhar became a national selector. Here too he left his imprint by not allowing Anthony de Mello, the BCCI president at the time, to meddle in the selection of the national team. Deodhar suffered for this courageous approach but he could not be enticed to compromise on his principles. He can be considered responsible for the rise of some of the legends of Indian cricket, including world-class players such as Vinoo Mankad and Vijay Hazare.

I met Prof. Deodhar just once. It was 1973 and Bengal had just been beaten by Maharashtra in a Ranji Trophy quarter-final tie at Poona. Bengal's captain at the time was Chuni Goswami—who had also captained the Indian football team to a gold medal at the Asian Games. It was his farewell match for Bengal and the last match of my debut season.

Inside the pavilion sat an elderly man with eyes glued to the match. Chunida—as we all addressed our captain—said to me, 'You always keep blabbering about cricket. Can you identify the gentleman sitting there?'

I took a good look and said, 'Isn't that Prof. Deodhar?'

'Good. Then come, I will introduce you to him.'

'But does he know you?' I asked.

Chunida gave me a sidelong glance. 'Everybody in India knows me.' A typical Chunida response.

As we approached him, the elderly gentleman looked up and recognized Chunida. He said, 'Chuni, happy to see that you are still playing.' Chunida nodded and shook hands with him.

As soon as I was introduced, Prof. Deodhar said, 'Good technique and temperament, but poor physique. Will never play for India.'

I was stunned by his assessment. I thought I had had a very successful debut season. In fact, I had played a responsible innings, albeit in a losing cause, in this match too. Yet, the professor was so downbeat about my prospects. However, if I was honest with myself, he was absolutely correct. My physique was never strong enough. I lacked stamina and suffered from a congenital heart ailment.

I said quickly, 'Sir, I do not crave to be a Test player. I want to be like you.'

'What do you mean? Like me in which way?'

'Sir, I want to be an academic first and only then a cricketer.'

The elderly gentleman smiled and grasped my hand. 'That's the spirit I like.'

That grasp was not the limp handshake of an eighty-year-old man. It was the steely Maratha grip that finished Afzal Khan.

The conversation with the living legend was enlightening. I did not want to let him go. He also seemed to enjoy my company. When I asked him about his cricket career, he merely said, 'It is for others to judge. I enjoyed my cricket as much as my academics. I was happy to have kept my backbone straight throughout.'

I responded, 'Sir, your protégés have answered the nation on your behalf.' He furrowed his eyebrows and nodded.

'Sir, please consider me to be your disciple, like Ekalavya was to Drona.' I touched his feet in pranam and he was visibly moved by the reference to the Mahabharata.

Prof. Deodhar was every inch a philosopher-warrior. The irony of destiny is that a man who was so successful and talented was denied his due because of the intrigues of his own countrymen.

Every Indian cricketer owes an eternal gratitude to these pioneers, who can be considered to be their 'cricketing grandfathers'. They laid the path and paved the way so that others could have a smooth journey. Let us not forget these immortal souls.

2

PRINCES AND MERCHANTS: THE EARLY YEARS OF INDIAN CRICKET

Arunabha Sengupta

We know how it went. On the morning of 25 June 1932, India entered international cricket with a resounding leap. However, the ensuing steps turned tentative, uncertain, faint. They played four series before Independence, all of them against England. One series was played at home and the others away. India lost six of the ten Test matches across the four series, and did not win even one. At first glance, the record looks dismal—and this does not change even if we look closer. We find a fightback here, a century there, a great bowling performance somewhere. We romanticize about them, as cricket fans are wont to do. However, success eludes the storyline, and the coffers are barren.

Yet, if we flip through the pages of history and scrutinize them in detail, further stories emerge and develop. These are stories of journeys made and not made, alliances forged and not forged, records jotted down on the front page and the back. We are left wondering what might have been if only some things had turned out differently. There are so many alternative stories that could have etched themselves in the annals of time. What if the Indian challenge did not fritter away after the great first day? What if they had been able to field the strongest team? Did the win column necessarily have to remain empty until 1952?

If the Merchants and the Princes …

The team that reached the shores of old Blighty in the summer of 1932 was called 'All-India'. The concept of 'India' as a country did not exist for the British overlords. A year earlier, Winston Churchill had declared in his speech to the Constitutional Club that 'India is a geographical term' and that it is 'no more a united nation than the Equator'. The known entities were British India and the Princely States, and they combined to form the All-India team.

The day before the only Test All-India would play on that tour, the English cricketers finished their county engagements and travelled across the country to London, many reaching the team hotel late at night. The idea was to roll out of bed, turn up and knock over a greenhorn side from an exotic faraway corner of the Empire. However, such thoughts were scattered by a flurry of wickets in the first twenty minutes. The excellent new-ball duo of Mohammed Nissar and Amar Singh, in combination with some electrifying fielding by the Malaya-born Lall Singh, reduced England to 19 for 3. The England captain, Douglas Jardine, and the wicketkeeper, Les Ames, led the recovery and they eventually scored 259. In response, All-India ended the day at 30 without loss. They were off to a rather good start in Test cricket.

The following day, however, they ran out of steam. From an excellent position of 110 for 2, the debutants collapsed to 189 all out. The rest of the Test was a saga of surrender. Only Amar Singh's half century from No. 9 in the second innings provided a bright spot. The batting lacked depth and class and was further hampered by C.K. Nayudu nursing an injured hand. But the bowlers matched their experienced English counterparts in potency and effectiveness.

It was the oft-heard story of a spirited but limited side. But did it really need to turn out that way? That very summer, two of the best batters in England were Indian. Only, they were not playing for India. At the same time, a classy young batter in India—who would go on to achieve greatness—had not travelled to England for political reasons.

The Nawab of Pataudi, Iftikhar Ali Khan, was named Wisden Cricketer of the Year in 1932 due to his exploits in the 1931 season, in which he had amassed 1,454 runs at 69.23 with six hundreds. That same summer had seen K.S. Duleepsinhji plunder 2,684 runs at 54.77 with twelve hundreds, including 109 at the Oval in the Test against New Zealand. He had already played twelve Tests for England, scoring 995 runs at 58.52.

In the 1928–29 season, Duleep—who was wintering in India after a successful summer for Sussex—had been approached by the newly formed Indian cricket board. He was requested to play a role in the development of Indian cricket. This included an offer to captain the side on the tour to England in 1932. Duleep had been undecided. He had turned to his uncle, the great K.S. Ranjitsinhji, for advice. Ranji had told him, perhaps rightly, that playing for

Skipper Mansur Ali Khan Pataudi introducing Queen Elizabeth II
to Chandu Borde, England, 1967.

Photo courtesy Chandu Borde

Ajit Wadekar, Bishan Singh Bedi and Sunil Gavaskar with Prime Minister Indira Gandhi after
the Indian team's victory in England, 1971.

Photo courtesy Bishan Singh Bedi's collection

Abid Ali being lifted by spectators after India won the Oval Test and the series in England, 1971.

Bishan Singh Bedi showing Alan Knott how to twist and turn in a yoga pose, Delhi, 1973.

Indian High Commissioner to Australia
K.S. Duleepsinhji with Sir Donald Bradman and
Indian captain Lala Amarnath during the Indian team's
tour of Australia, 1947.

Photo courtesy Inder V. Singh

Indian team captain Nari Contractor sharing a light moment with Salim Durrani,
possibly 1962.

Photo courtesy Nari Contractor's collection

(L-R): Yajurvindra Singh, Sunil Gavaskar and Bharat Reddy after the 1979 England and World Cup tours.

Sachin Tendulkar cutting a cake on his eighteenth birthday.

England would allow him much better opportunities. Duleep made his debut for England the following summer.

In the winter of 1931–32, Duleep travelled to India to spend time with an ailing Ranji. Drafted into the Indian selection committee, Duleep discovered the talented Amar Singh that season. Duleep also played for the Viceroy's XII against Roshanara Club, hitting 173 in the second innings. In the same innings, Pataudi scored 91 and the two shared a 189-run partnership.

Meanwhile, in India, a twenty-year-old Vijay Merchant was demonstrating his impeccable class with a serene 157 in the final of the Moin-ud-Dowlah Gold Cup. The match was played in December 1931, just before the Congress Working Committee took the decision to start the second phase of the Civil Disobedience Movement. On 4 January 1932, Mahatma Gandhi was arrested in Bombay and taken to the Yervada Jail. The Viceroy, Lord Willingdon, outlawed the Congress party. Protesting the arrest of Gandhi, the Hindu Gymkhana boycotted the 1932 cricket tour of England. That meant Merchant could not go, nor could other stalwarts such as L.P. Jai.

When All-India visited in 1932, it was Duleep who led Sussex against his countrymen in the opening first-class match of the tour. When the visitors beat Worcestershire by three wickets, Pataudi batted at No. 3 for the county, scoring 83 in the first innings. The following month, the all-important Gentlemen vs Players fixture was contested at Lord's. Duleep batted at No. 3 and Pataudi at No. 4 for the Gentlemen. The former scored 132 and the latter hit 165, with the two sharing a 161-run partnership. Nearly 2,400 runs were scored between the two that season, but not one of those runs was for India.

What if all three—Pataudi, Duleep and Merchant—had been playing for India on that tour? What if, upon the dismissal of

Wazir Ali to make it 110 for 3, it had been Duleep walking out to
join Nayudu at the wicket? What if Pataudi had been slotted to
come in after that and Merchant, who had not yet started opening
the innings, was to follow at No. 6? We can only speculate.

If Some Codger Had ...

In any case, in 1932 India did become a Test-playing nation—or
a Test-playing 'geographical entity', if Churchill was to be taken
seriously. England, Australia, New Zealand and white South Africa
had already entered the Test fold. West Indies too had started
playing Test cricket, always with a white man at the helm. India
thus became the first Test-playing side to be led by a non-white
cricketer. But that is also a story of what might have been, with a
happy ending for a change.

Test status used to be granted with arbitrary randomness,
characteristic of a game that was run for all intents and purposes
as an exclusive private club. That was what cricket used to be, with
the Imperial Cricket Conference continuing under that revealing
name until 1963. It did change its name to 'International Cricket
Conference' and eventually 'International Cricket Council', but
until 1993 England and Australia had veto powers as founding
members. Democratization of the game from stuffy Imperialist
privilege is still a work in progress. With the growth of the
subcontinent as the financial epicentre of the game, the power
dynamics have shifted. Not everything may be great about the way
the game is governed now, but at least cricket is becoming more
inclusive. It was very different for a long, long time.

In late 1889, a band of amateur English cricketers of
questionable pedigree visited India under the leadership of
Middlesex stalwart George Frederick Vernon. This tour has gone

down as the first ever made by an English cricket team to India. All but one of the matches played on the tour were against all-white teams. Three years down the line, the cricketing grandee Lord Hawke brought another team to India. He had been invited to do so by Lord Harris, then the Governor of Bombay. The side included the immensely gifted future England captain Stanley Jackson. The team played two well-contested games against the Parsis, losing the first and winning the second.

At the Gymkhana Ground on Boxing Day 1892, the visitors faced off against Bombay. The home team was all-white, with at least one important stalwart in Major Robert Poore. This Hampshire legend later played three Tests against Lord Hawke's Englishmen for South Africa. Apart from Poore there were a few other decent first-class cricketers in the Bombay side. A month after that, in Allahabad, Hawke's men squared off against a team that was actually called 'India' but was led by an Englishman. Apart from the Britons, there were a couple of Parsis, including M.E. Pavri. Another interesting personality playing for 'India' was E.H.D. Sewell, the cricketer who gained subsequent fame as a cricket writer.

A year before Vernon visited India, he had taken a motley group of cricketers to South Africa on the invitation of William Milton, the Western Province Cricket Club supremo. They had played two matches against an arbitrarily chosen white South African side comprising 'cricketers' with little or no skill, most of them expat Englishmen. The provincial-minded Milton, a former England rugby international, had excluded even the white Afrikaner population. The parochial team were routinely beaten in one-sided games, which were nonetheless recorded as the first Test matches played by South Africa. It is a poignant example of the arbitrariness of cricket's early days.

If we compare player by player, far better home sides took on the English team in India in 1892 than on their tour of South Africa four years earlier. I would say that Indians were distinctly lucky that some old codger fiddling with the scorebooks at MCC did not have a sudden moment of imperialistic inspiration to brand one of the games played by Vernon's side (or the two games played by Hawke's team) as Test matches. Instead, India made their official Test debut in 1932, appropriately led by C.K. Nayudu.

Commoners and Royals

Of course, the 'commoner' Nayudu was not supposed to be the captain. India, after all, was a land of maharajas. This had deep social implications. English teams, both Test and county, were led by amateur cricketers at the time and this practice would prevail for a few more decades. For the Indians, the social equivalent of an amateur was a prince. Therefore, Indian teams were expected to be led by princes.

The old scorebooks at the Sussex cricket museum reveal that Ranji had been listed as any other amateur cricketer, appearing as 'Mr K.S. Ranjitsinhji' in his first few games. After a few matches this changed, and for the rest of his career he became known as 'Kumar Shri Ranjitsinhji', after the realization that 'Kumar' denoted the title of prince in India. This allowed the Indian player to be accepted as an 'English gentleman'.

The 1932 tour was bankrolled by Vizzy, the Maharajkumar of Vizianagaram. The other great patron of cricket, the Maharaja of Patiala, was forty-one at the time. He had sponsored the training and selection and had been named captain before dropping out at the last moment. The official captain appointed was the Maharaja of Porbandar, who managed scores of 0, 2, 0, 2 and 2 in his first few games on the tour. Porbandar was too embarrassed to carry on after his string of low scores. The official vice-captain was Porbandar's brother-in-law, Prince Ghyanshyamsinhji Daulatsinhji of Limbdi, and he was expected to lead instead. However, he strained his back and was unable to play.

This fortuitous turn of events led to the leadership for the first-ever Test played by India being taken on by the most deserving commoner. Nayudu was deserving of the honour. His glorious innings of 153 for the Hindus against the touring MCC side of 1926–27 had led India to be considered as a worthy entrant into the Test world. Visiting captain Arthur Gilligan did not play that match but sat enthralled as Nayudu slammed 11 sixes and 14 boundaries in his 116-minute knock. 'His polished display of batsmanship was one of the best I have ever seen,' Gilligan said later.

Two months later at the Roshanara Club in Delhi, Gilligan had a meeting with the Maharaja of Patiala, English businessman Grant Govan, and Govan's Karachi-born Anglo-Indian employee, Anthony de Mello. This meeting laid the foundations for India's foray into international cricket. Gilligan urged the men to form an Indian cricket board. According to de Mello, 'Gilligan promised to state our case when he returned to Lord's.' The Board of Control for Cricket in India (BCCI) was formed in December 1928 with Govan as president and de Mello as secretary. Gilligan kept his word. Two years later, India gained admittance as a full member of the Imperial Cricket Conference.

Nayudu also led the side in 1933–34 when Douglas Jardine's men visited India to play the first Test matches on Indian soil. A new 10,000-seater double-decker stand was erected at the Bombay Gymkhana ground. On the eve of the match, a cartoon in

The Times of India depicted a lion and a tiger tossing a coin while a kangaroo in flannels watched from afar. The following day, 15 December 1933, the government declared a holiday to mark the first day of the Test. At the ground flew a Union Jack flanked by the 'rhubarb and custard' flag of the MCC on one side and the blue British Raj flag on the other. The band played *God Save the King* as the first Test Match in India commenced.

It was predictably one-sided. But in the face of inevitable defeat came the home side's hour of glory. It mattered little in the context of the match but was a spectacular moment for Indian cricket: debutant Lala Amarnath hit the first-ever Test hundred for India. He scored his runs in 117 minutes while hitting 18 fours. In the madness of the celebrations that followed, the centurion had to be escorted to the pavilion by police to guard him from the spectators who had spilled on to the ground. Upon arriving at the pavilion, he was garlanded by the mayor. The Maharajahs of Kolhapur and Baroda were among those waiting to congratulate him. Women supposedly tore off their ornaments to fling them at him and local jewellers competed to shower gifts on the new hero. Sewell wrote in *The Times of India* that he hoped Amarnath's head was screwed on firmly.

While the royal hand was missing in leadership during that tour, there was plenty of royal intrigue elsewhere. The Maharaja of Patiala ruffled a lot of important feathers by making passes at Viceroy Willingdon's unmarried daughter. Having earned the Viceroy's wrath, he responded by showering lavish hospitality and gifts on the English cricketers when they played at Patiala. This led to Jardine inviting him to play for his side against the Viceroy's XI, bringing Willingdon to the brink of apoplexy. Diplomatic pressure and good sense ultimately prevailed. Jardine relented and played the Maharaja in the game against Delhi and Districts instead. But the English captain unleashed his most ruthless self against the Viceroy's side and engineered a rout through Stan Nichols and Hedley Verity.

The Royal Hand Emerges

By 1936, when All-India (still known by that name) toured England, the royal hand was back in all its 'glory'. The notorious Vizzy captained the side and infamously fell out with Amarnath. What took place after that has oft been written about. Amarnath rebelled against the quixotic batting orders and Vizzy's ignorant obstinacy in not giving him the field placements he wanted when bowling. After receiving some choice Punjabi epithets from the all-rounder, Vizzy complained to the manager, Major Brittain-Jones. Amarnath was sent home on disciplinary grounds even before the first Test was played.

That was not Vizzy's only controversy during the tour. It was rumoured that insecurity about his own cricketing prowess made him goad Baqa Jilani into insulting the forty-year-old C.K. Nayudu at the breakfast table. The supposed promise made to Jilani, duly kept, was a Test cap. There was also the order he issued to Mushtaq Ali to run Merchant out. Merchant had openly backed Nayudu as captain in Tests, and Vizzy had not been amused. As they walked out to bat, Mushtaq spilled the beans. 'Try it if you can,' Merchant said and laughed. They ended up hitting centuries and adding 203—one of the rare bright spots of an otherwise miserable series that ended as a 0-2 loss.

Another bit of controversy was when Vizzy gifted a gold watch to the opposition skipper during a tour match and got a couple of long hops in exchange. In today's terminology, this would have gone down as spot-fixing. Less frequently recounted is the manner in which Vizzy was celebrated by the British top brass. At a dinner hosted for the All-India team at Lord's, Vizzy was elected as a member of the MCC. Just after the match against Essex, it was Vizzy who opened a new playground at the Hornsey YMCA Boys' Club at Tottenham Lane, Crouch End.

On 24 June, a couple of days after Amarnath had been sent home, members of the two houses of the British Parliament hosted a lunch for the Indian cricketers at the House of Commons. Presided by Lord Ebbisham, the company included, among others, Prime Minister Stanley Baldwin, former Viceroy Lord Willingdon and former England captains Stanley Jackson and H.D.G. Leveson-Gower. The prime minister proposed the health of the popular Indian team and toasted the name of 'their splendid captain Maharajkumar of Vizianagaram'. On 15 July at Buckingham Palace, King Edward VIII conferred a knighthood on Vizzy, who remains the only Indian cricketer to have been knighted.

In the three Test matches of the tour, the only ones he played in his career, Vizzy scored 33 runs at 8.25. What might have been if Amarnath had not left? What if Vizzy had had the sense to step down as captain? What if India had played with eleven cricketers instead of ten plus an inept royal?

When Gandhi had visited England in 1931 to attend a conference, Churchill refused to meet him. The King's first reaction to a proposed meeting had supposedly been: 'What! Have this rebel fakir in the palace?' He eventually relented, but during the meeting he took the opportunity to let his visitor know that civil disobedience was a 'hopeless and stupid policy'. 'Remember, Mr Gandhi,' he is supposed to have said, 'I can't have attacks on *my* Indian Empire.'

But the King had had no reservations in sharing a ride with the Maharaja of Patiala during his silver jubilee celebrations in 1935. This was despite a 200-page chargesheet having been submitted against this Indian royal—with witnesses—in 1929. The charges included several counts of murder, rape, assault, cruelty and misuse of power. He was a convicted criminal but was too important to the Empire to be put behind bars.

After the War

During the Second World War, 2.5 million Indian soldiers fought for the Allies. However, in his account of the war published in 1950, Churchill wrote: 'No great portion of the world population was so effectively protected from the horrors and perils of the World War as were the peoples of Hindustan. They were carried through the struggle on the shoulders of our small island.' By the time the next Indian cricket team—still called All-India—travelled to England in 1946, Churchill had been sent off smouldering and Clement Atlee had become the prime minister.

During the third Test at the Oval, Atlee watched with his wife as Merchant conquered the bowling and November-like conditions to score a sublime 128 in his final Test innings in England. The Test coincided almost seamlessly with the Great Calcutta Killings of 1946, with the massacre of some 4,000 people of both Hindu and Muslim communities. A young John Arlott asked Merchant whether India really deserved independence in view of the on-going religious riots. 'Shouldn't the white man stay on to secure the peace?' he asked. Merchant reminded his friend that the British had had to undergo a civil war to obtain their own political liberties. It was Merchant as senior statesman who spoke about the relationship between Britain and India at events.

From the start of the Second World War to the eve of the tour, Merchant had scored 5,003 runs in domestic cricket at an incredible average of 131.66 with 21 hundreds. In contrast, Pataudi had played very little cricket after 1934—only six first-class matches in eleven years. Yet, he resurfaced—scoring 7 and 1 in his two first-class innings in early 1946—and the captaincy was handed to him. He failed in the Tests, managing a mere 55 runs at 11.00, but did show form in the tour matches.

However, even if Pataudi had not reappeared on the scene, it was unlikely that Merchant would have been made captain. Instead, the Maharaja of Patiala—who had played a Test against Jardine's team as a prince—had a better chance of being named skipper. This was because of the English preference for princes as the natural leaders of Indians—a trait later termed 'Ornamentalism'. In any case, the three-Test series ended 1-0 in favour of a war-ravaged England. The coffers of Indian cricket remained without a win until four and a half years after Independence.

Could It Have Been Different?

There is no point questioning what could have taken place on the field of play as that cannot be altered. But were all the events that did take place on the field properly documented according to fair standards? At the time, Test status—now considered sacrosanct—was often handed out with a wink and nod after checking for the correct colour of tie.

In 1929–30, Arthur Gilligan fell sick at the last moment before a tour to New Zealand and his brother Harold led the England team he had assembled. Incidentally, Duleep toured with this side, rattling up 358 runs at 89.50 in the Tests, which were the first ever played by New Zealand. Apart from Frank Woolley, the rest of the English side were inexperienced youngsters. At the same time, on the other side of the world, Freddie Calthorpe led a second England side against the West Indies. With fifty-year-old George Gunn and fifty-two-year-old Wilfred Rhodes, the team that toured West Indies had the highest-ever average age of thirty-eight. Representative matches on both these tours were given Test status.

In 1935–36, an Australian side visited India for the first time. The captain, Jack Ryder, led some stellar but aging former cricketers such as Charley Macartney, Stork Hendry, Ron Oxenham and Bert Ironmonger. Alongside them there were a few promising young lads. It was again Patiala who bankrolled the tour. Four representative matches were played, apart from a few tour matches. Led by the Yuvraj of Patiala in the first representative game, Nayudu in the second and Wazir Ali in the final two 'Tests', the Indians came back from 0-2 down to square the representative series 2-2. There were some superb performances by Nissar, Amar Singh and Wazir Ali. The Australian touring squad was as good as those two English touring sides of 1929–30, if not better, and was definitely superior to some of the early Test sides that toured, or represented, South Africa. However, these matches were not given official Test status.

Two years later, Lord Tennyson brought a formidable fifteen-member side to India. It had stars such as Bill Edrich, Alf Gover, Joe Hardstaff Jr, Ian Peebles and Arthur Wellard. Thirteen of the squad had played Tests or would go on to do so. Five representative matches were contested, and Tennyson's team prevailed 3-2. A young Vinoo Mankad—yet another cricketer discovered and promoted by Duleep—scored more than 400 runs at 62.66 and captured 18 wickets at 14.56. Although illnesses and injuries prevented their best eleven from appearing in most of the matches, Lord Tennyson's team was arguably stronger than a lot of Test sides, including the two that travelled to New Zealand and West Indies in 1929–30. Yet, once again Test status was not granted to the matches.

Perhaps it is more difficult to make a case for the three representative matches played after the Second World War by an Australian Services side led by Lindsay Hassett. The team visited India on their way back to Australia after the much-celebrated 'Victory Tests' against England. Buoyed by a double hundred by Rusi Modi and some stellar bowling by Shute Banerjee, the hosts clinched the final 'Test' at Madras by six wickets and won the series 1-0. Merchant led India in this series, a few months before he would tour England under Pataudi.

Thus, in these three rather high-profile series, India won five and lost five 'Tests'. If any of these three series had been blessed with official status, India would have registered a mark in the 'wins' column way before 1952, when they eventually won their first official Test. Because Test status at the time was doled out according to the fancies of powerful men at Lord's, India was denied these potential Test wins. It is perhaps the saddest of India's sagas of 'what could have been' that the caretakers of history shoved these splendid performances into the back pages.

3

C.K. NAYUDU: THE FIRST ICON OF INDIAN CRICKET

Vijay Nayudu

Col. C.K. Nayudu (1895–1967)—known to most as 'CK'—can be counted among the legends of Indian cricket as the man who put Indore on the cricketing map. He was from the Cottari family hailing from Machilipatnam, a coastal town forty kilometres from Vijayawada in Andhra Pradesh. The family migrated to Nagpur later as CK's father, C. Narayanswamy Nayudu, and uncle C. Suryaprakashrao Nayudu—both of whom had studied law at Cambridge University—were practising law in Central Province and Berar.

CK picked up the game in Nagpur thanks to a local coach named Mr Bhide. The young Nayudu soon became known for his big hitting. In those days, cricket was played in Bombay between the British and the Parsis in what were called the 'Presidency matches' from 1892 to 1906. It became the 'Triangular' from 1907 to 1911 when the Hindus fielded a team, and then came to be known as the 'Quadrangular Tournament' from 1912 to 1936 after the Muslims joined the contest.

CK made his debut for the Hindus in 1916 in a match against the British. Former Ranji player and cricket historian Vasant Raiji wrote in his book *The Story of Bombay Cricket*: 'CK blocked the first three balls from Frank Tarrant and then lifted the fourth ball for a straight six. In later years, the crowd expected sixes from him every time he came to bat.' CK soon started dominating the tournament with his consistent big hitting.

Maharaja Tukojirao Holkar had brought J.G. Navle to Indore in 1915 as his son Yashwantrao was very keen on playing cricket. CK's father had been a judge in Indore in the early 1900s and thus the Maharaja knew about the Nayudu family. After Maharaja Tukojirao heard about CK's cricketing exploits, he invited the latter to Indore in 1923 and made him a major in the Holkar army. This marked the introduction of cricket in Indore and the rest, as they say, is history. Holkar played in the Ranji Trophy for fourteen seasons and reached the finals in ten of those campaigns, winning four times.

A lot has been written about CK's knock at the Bombay Gymkhana ground in December 1926 in the match between the Hindus—who were the winners of that year's Quadrangular Tournament—and the MCC, led by Sir Arthur Gilligan. CK scored 153 with the help of 11 sixes and 14 fours in less than two hours. The crowd had never seen such big hitting. CK's knock was regarded by many who watched it as the 'innings of the century', one that changed the image of India as a cricket-playing nation for good.

I have met a few Parsi and Maharashtrian cricket fanatics who had witnessed that innings by CK. They took pride in recalling every shot he played that day. A Mr Dabolkar, who was a teacher, recalled that he had climbed a tree adjacent to the ground to watch the match, like many people did those days. Those trees are still there, overlooking the ground. He added that a few sixes had landed on the trees near him, and he had shouted, 'Don't hit us, we are not playing!'

There is an interesting anecdote around this match that very few people know. The famous jurist M.C. Chagla wrote in his autobiography, *Roses in December*, that during the hearing of a case at the high court, word filtered in about what was happening at the Bombay Gymkhana. Even the judge was curious to know what the commotion was about, prompting Chagla to say, 'My Lord, CK is batting, and I appeal to you to postpone the hearing.' The judge agreed and the two of them headed for the Bombay Gymkhana to witness the hurricane batting. Such was the popularity of CK in those days that even the Bombay High Court stopped working for a few hours to watch him play!

Sir Arthur Gilligan was so impressed with CK's knock that he presented him with a silver-plated cricket bat signed by all the MCC players. This bat is presently in the proud possession of the Cricket Club of India (CCI). The impressive performance of the Indian players against the visiting MCC team in 1926–27 led to the formation of the BCCI in 1928 with the efforts of the president of Bombay Gymkhana Lord Harris, the Maharaja of Patiala and the administrator Anthony de Mello. It was decided that India would be granted Test status in 1931.

However, this was eventually delayed till June 1932—when, at age thirty-seven, CK led India in their first-ever Test match, played at Lord's. The crowed expected another brilliant knock from CK as he had scored 101 at the same venue the previous week against Middlesex. CK did get the top score for India with 40 but his team lost the match. However, they succeeded in earning the goodwill of the English people. CK had a successful tour of England and was named as one of the Wisden Cricketers of the Year, becoming the first Indian to achieve this distinction.

There was an interesting incident when he hit a ball from 'one county to another' while playing against Warwickshire at Birmingham. India were 91 for 7 when CK and N.D. Marshall put up a partnership of 217 in 140 minutes. During his knock of 162, CK hit a six that crossed the River Rea, which divides Warwickshire from Worcestershire. Thereby, he had hit the ball into the neighbouring county, prompting the headline.

In December 1933, an England team led by Douglas Jardine visited India to play the first Test match on Indian soil. The match was played at the Bombay Gymkhana and is best remembered for Lala Amarnath's brilliant knock of 118, the first Test hundred by an Indian. Amarnath put on a 187-run partnership with CK, who scored 69.

There was an incident narrated by Vasant Raiji, who saw that match as a young boy. When Lala Amarnath reached his hundred, the crowed invaded the ground. CK went to protect Amarnath without realizing that the ball was still in play. An English fielder was about to run him out, but Jardine signalled to the fielder not to do it. This was a fine gesture from Jardine, who had just returned from the infamous Bodyline series in Australia. India lost the match due to their poor fielding and Jardine's resolute batting.

The match is also remembered for another incident that led to the creation of the CCI. The Maharaja of Patiala went to watch the match along with de Mello and Maharawal Laxman Singh of Dungarpur (who was the father of cricket administrator Raj Singh Dungarpur). However, they were stopped at the entrance of the

Bombay Gymkhana as 'Indians and dogs' were not allowed to enter. Patiala was furious as he had funded the England tour to play this Test Match. He was made to sit in a tent erected by the ground.

Soon after the match, the trio went to the governor of Bombay with a request for land near Churchgate to be leased to them for building a cricket stadium. The governor was Lord Brabourne, who agreed to sanction the land on a long lease. The stadium—which would be named after Brabourne—was built in 1935 through funds raised by Parsi traders and industrialists. It became the home of the CCI, which was founded that year.

The visiting English team played a few more matches across the country against teams sponsored by local maharajas. Jardine referred to the tour as 'C.K. Nayudu's circus' because every team wanted CK to play for them to ensure a full house at every venue.

Advancing age did not affect CK's passion and fitness levels. He continued to play competitive cricket till he was sixty-three. I have heard many stories and anecdotes from former Holkar and Bombay players. Chandu Sarwate once told me that CK's captaincy style was unique. He used to plan how to dismiss the opposition's top batsmen using field settings. During a match, Polly Umrigar of the opposition came in to bat and CK immediately asked Hiralal Gaikwad to bowl a bit short of length with fielders at cover point and mid-wicket with two slips. Gaikwad asked for one more fielder in the covers but CK didn't heed his request. Umrigar hit two fours through the cover region. Then Gaikwad bowled one on the stumps. Umrigar went for an on-drive but edged the ball to cover point and was out for 23. CK then told Gaikwad: 'If we had not got him out, he would have scored 150 or more. He is a good back-foot batsman.'

Mushtaq Ali was playing a match for the Muslims against the Hindus at the Islam Gymkhana. CK came into the tent that served as the pavilion and was surprised to see Mushtaq sitting with his blazer on. Mushtaq told CK that he was not feeling well. CK responded, 'What nonsense. You must go to bat as your team needs you.' Mushtaq took his advice and went in to bat on the fall of the next wicket. He scored a brisk 36 to help his team win the match. Such was CK's commitment to the game that he would even encourage the opposition to put up a fight.

K.S. Bhatnagar recalled a time when Holkar was chasing a small target of about 180 on a dicey wicket to win the match. Someone suggested to CK that he should tell Mushtaq to play carefully. CK replied, 'No, don't tell him any such thing, otherwise he will not get the runs.' Mushtaq Ali played in his usual style and won the match for the team. It showed CK's confidence in his players.

There is an interesting story about Brian Statham, who came to India with a Commonwealth team in the 1947–48 season and played a match at Indore. The manager of the Commonwealth team boasted to CK about the exploits of Statham, who was a fast bowler. CK sent Gaikwad, a left-hander who was primarily a bowler, to open the innings under clear instructions to smash the bowler. Statham was hit all over the ground and went wicketless in that match.

Madhav Apte was in the Bombay side that played a Ranji Trophy match against Holkar at the Brabourne. It was the early 1950s and CK was about fifty-six at the time. When CK came to the crease, Bombay captain Vinoo Mankad told Dattu Phadkar to bowl a few bouncers. CK hit a couple of them to the boundary, but he missed one. The ball hit him in the mouth and broke his teeth. Blood was all over the place. The fielders rushed towards him, but CK signalled them to stay away. He picked up his broken teeth and put them in his pocket. Then he put his handkerchief in his mouth to stem the bleeding, refusing medical attention. He resumed his innings and went on to score 68.

There is another anecdote involving Khandu Rangnekar, who played for Holkar but was on an official tour to Calcutta during a Ranji Trophy match against Maharashtra at Indore in March 1953. When informed that Khandu was not available for the match, CK immediately sent him a telegram asking that he return immediately. Khandu replied: 'Can't come as there is no train or flight.' CK send a message back asking him to come by road. On the morning of the match, Rangnekar reached the Yashwant Club, which was the venue of the match.

He went to CK and said, 'Sir, I am very tired. I travelled by car for two nights without proper sleep.' He also said that he was running a fever. CK looked at him and said, 'Okay, you are batting at No. 8. Go and take rest.' However, wickets tumbled and Khandu had to be soon woken from his deep sleep. Pads were strapped on and he was pushed out to bat after the next wicket fell. Any other player would have returned to the pavilion in no time, but Rangnekar scored a brilliant 153 and Holkar won the match.

In the 1956–57 season, Salim Durrani was part of the Rajasthan team that played a UP side led by CK at Benares. By then, Vinoo Mankad was captaining Rajasthan and had the likes of G.S. Ramchand, Vijay Manjrekar, Subhash Gupte, Kishan Rungta and G.R. Sundaram. CK was about sixty-two at the time. When he came out to bat, Mankad told Durrani to stand at silly mid-on. He said in Gujarati, 'Don't worry, the old man can't hit now.' Durrani was hesitant but did as he was told. Mankad's first three balls to CK went for 6, 4, and 6. All the shots passed very close to Durrani like bullets, prompting him to go and stand at square leg for his own safety. CK went on to score 84 before getting run out.

There are numerous other stories surrounding CK's exploits on the cricket field. I never saw him play but have often heard stories involving him, because many of his former colleagues used to drop in to meet him at home. No subject other than cricket was discussed. I used to spend my entire summer and winter vacations at Indore. My duty was to serve tea, lunch or snacks to the visitors.

I remember one incident when I was returning home after playing a match. When I arrived, CK was standing on the porch. I had no alternative but to talk to him. He asked me, 'What happened in the match and how much did you score?' I answered that we won, and I had scored 132. He asked me how I got out and then demonstrated to me how I should have played that ball. No word about my having scored a hundred. He then told me, 'Go clean your bat and shoes, take a bath and come for dinner.' While speaking his cigarette slipped out of his mouth, but as it fell he caught it with two fingers and said, 'See? My reflexes are still good.' He was seventy-one years old then.

There are very few players who have left their mark on the minds of generations of people. C.K. Nayudu was one such individual, a man who personified the elegance and dignity of the gentleman's game both on and off the field. As Neville Cardus once said, 'We remember not the scores and the results after many years; it is the men who remain in our mind and the imagination.' Col. C.K. Nayudu will be remembered as long the game of cricket is played in India.

4

THE MANCHESTER DRAMA: 1936

Vijay Merchant

My most memorable Test match was played under the greatest mental strain that I have ever had to bear in first-class cricket. It was the second Test of the 1936 tour of England, played in Manchester—in which I played my finest innings, especially considering the stress I was under, the quality of the opposition and the adverse circumstances under which it was played. To provide you with a clear picture of the situation, I will have to take you behind the curtains and tell you what happened four days before that match.

Realizing that we were captained most inefficiently and by one who did not deserve a place even in an Indian second eleven, I decided to approach the captain—the Maharajkumar of Vizianagaram, known as Vizzy—directly with my concerns. We were close friends, and he would confide in me about most of the difficulties he faced. As a matter of fact, I spent an hour every evening with him, giving my humble suggestions as a junior cricketer of the party. This emboldened me to approach him with this very uncommon request: for the captain to sit out of the match voluntarily so that we could be led by Col. C. K. Nayudu and have the additional advantage of giving the captain's spot to a proper cricketer who could pull his weight in the team.

What I had voiced were my sincere feelings, not officially as a representative of the team but personally, as a friend. To my surprise, Vizzy misunderstood my intentions completely and thought I was fostering mutiny in the side. He flared up and said, 'The Board has appointed me as captain and I am going to remain so for all three Test matches. No power on earth can make me step down!' I apologized to him for my approach and told him that it was just a personal request and had nothing to do with any other member of the team. This was indeed true because I had not discussed the matter with anyone else, lest an impression was created that I was trying to canvass against the captain. I was prepared to succeed or fail on my own and thus took the plunge.

Although I had done my best to keep my request a guarded secret, the team had become aware of the details of the incident by that evening. A suggestion was even made by the skipper that I should be sent back to India on disciplinary grounds. The manager, Major Brittain-Jones, ruled it out immediately, stating that he was fully satisfied that my approach was entirely a personal one and had nothing to do with the other members of the squad. As a matter of fact, after the tour was over, this incident was referred to the Sir John Beaumont Committee of Enquiry, which ruled: 'Although Merchant's conduct was ill-advised, we are satisfied that the suggestion he made was made privately to the captain and that it could not be regarded in any sense as a breach of discipline.'

Two days later, a very senior member of the team called a meeting in which I was asked to take up the matter with the BCCI. I responded, 'Gentlemen, if you sign a requisition to the Board, I will be happy to sign it too. You are the senior members. I am very junior to you. I am not prepared to take up this matter with the Board on my own because my approach was a personal one and not made with a view to create any dissension in the team. I am sorry that this personal approach has been made a matter of public knowledge.' There the matter rested.

You can well understand my state of mind when there were rumours the next day that Vizzy would approach Lord Willingdon with a request that I should be sent home. Lord Willingdon had just relinquished office as the Viceroy of India and had been approached when a request was made by the Board to recall Lala Amarnath, who had similarly been sent back to India. However, Brittain-Jones was very close to Lord Willingdon and nothing materialized from these rumours.

It was in this mental state that I started the second Test at Manchester. We won the toss and elected to bat on an excellent wicket. When our score was 18, I hit a straight drive off Alf Gover. However, my opening partner, Mushtaq Ali, could not get out of the way of my shot. Thus, instead of going for a four, the ball was diverted off his pads to mid-on. Mushtaq, not knowing where the ball had gone, came running down the wicket. I shouted, 'No, no, Mushtaq, get back!' But it was too late. Arthur Fagg ran up to the wicket with the ball in hand and removed the bails before Mushtaq could make it back to the crease. He was run out for 13.

As the innings progressed, four of our batsmen got their eye in only to get out for moderate scores. Wazir Ali made 42 and Cotar Ramaswami 40, while Amar Singh added 27 and I contributed 33.

Our first innings total was only 203. Then came England's turn to bat. Wally Hammond played an innings the likes of which I have never seen. From the first ball he faced, he did as he pleased with the bowlers, hitting eight boundaries in his first 50 runs.

Hammond got to his century off only 138 balls and in just a hundred minutes. The manner in which he played Mohammed Nissar and Amar Singh—two of the world's finest bowlers of the time—drew the admiration of the very large crowd. He scored 167, Joe Hardstaff 94, Stan Worthington 87, Walter Robins 76 and Hedley Verity 60. England declared at 571 for 8 on just the second afternoon. You can imagine the rate at which they scored!

It was a three-day match, and with 135 minutes left of the second day, Mushtaq Ali and I opened the innings again. During the changeover, word had gone around that Mushtaq had been advised by the captain to run me out in the second innings because I had run him out in the first. As we walked out with practically no hope of saving the game, Mushtaq turned to me and smiled. 'Don't worry, Vijay,' he said. 'No one is going to run you out.' That put me at ease.

Then Mushtaq went on to play a gem of an innings, scoring all around the wicket with square cuts, cover drives, on-drives, pulls to leg and leg-glances on his way to a century. This was Mushtaq at his best and it was champagne cricket. At the other end, I was inspired by the flow of strokes from Mushtaq's bat and, although a slow scorer normally, I went on to make 79 runs that evening. I played second fiddle to India's most entertaining batsman and, believe me, it was an education. We ended the day having put on an unbeaten partnership of 190.

That night I went to Mushtaq's room and said, 'Mushtaq, if we make another 134 runs together tomorrow morning, we shall have beaten a record that has stood for the last twenty-four years.' Mushtaq never cared about records and didn't bother even knowing about them. He played for the love of cricket. So, I was not surprised when he asked me what record I was talking about. I told him, 'The Englishmen Jack Hobbs and Wilfred Rhodes put on 323 runs for the first wicket against Australia in the 1911–12 season and we have a chance to break it.' Mushtaq asked, 'What do you want me to do, Vijay?' I replied, 'For the first four overs, Mushtaq, just take care not to lose your wicket. After that you should be all right.' Mushtaq promised to do so.

The next day, we went out to a standing ovation from the large crowd. Mushtaq played one over sedately, but off the third ball of the next over, bowled by Robins, he jumped yards out of the crease to try and hit him over the top. The ball went straight and a little above the bowler's head. If it had been any other bowler but Robins, the stroke would have fetched Mushtaq a four. But Robins had the reputation of being the best English fielder of his time. He anticipated the stroke, jumped two feet high and stopped the ball with his right hand. As the ball came down, he caught it. Mushtaq was out to the finest catch of the match. He looked at me with an apologetic face as if to say, 'I am sorry, Vijay, I have let you down.' Mushtaq never played such an innings again.

Although I was very disappointed, I carried on because the job was still an arduous one and I knew that if I relaxed and lost my wicket, anything could happen. Thus, I continued to concentrate as I had never concentrated before. I took my own time to build up a score because the runs did not matter, but staying at the crease did. I had to be everything in my power to draw the match. I was ultimately out LBW (leg before wicket) to Hammond for 114. I was of course disappointed to get out but walked off knowing that the game was all but saved.

This innings gave me the greatest satisfaction because we had started our second innings with a deficit of 368 with eight hours still to bat. The opposition bowlers were of high quality and anyone who has played in Manchester will know that late in the afternoon the light gets very dim and it is not easy to see the ball clearly. This, they say, is due to the smoke from the chimneys of the various factories in that area.

I had never concentrated during an innings as much as I did on that occasion. I did not take the least risk that could threaten my wicket and also played an important role in curbing the ebullient Mushtaq Ali. Whenever it seemed like he was close to losing control, I would try to calm him down and get him to focus. He appreciated that. It was not only my personal innings that gave me satisfaction but also helping Mushtaq to play one of the finest innings ever seen in international cricket.

What more does one require to make a Test innings the most memorable one? It had every aspect of a drama: the mental strain, personal anguish, adverse circumstances, failure in the first innings, a big score against us, playing with our backs to the wall. It was an innings that helped my team and my country draw a match that had been written off as a loss by nearly everyone. Could any match be more memorable for me?

5

MEMORIES OF C.K. NAYUDU

K.N. Prabhu

C.K. Nayudu was a legend even in his lifetime. Just a mention of his initials would draw a crowd. Those who had seen him bat will remember him as a mighty hitter and perhaps recall that fine frenzy of sixes at the Bombay Gymkhana against an MCC side in 1926. Lucky were those who saw him in his prime—when he was a great hitter against the turn, a skilful manipulator of spin and a thoughtful, intuitive captain. He was the first Indian to be honoured by *Wisden* after a successful tour of England in 1932, during which he stirred the imagination of English followers with his own inimitable style of play. Like Ranji, Duleep and Iftikhar Ali Pataudi, he brought to the Anglo-Saxon game an exotic touch of the East.

On that 1932 tour he was often compared to Sir Donald Bradman, but Neville Cardus spotted the essential differences. He wrote, 'Nayudu is lithe and wristy and volatile; Bradman is steady and concentrated. He never suggests that elusive and poetic

41

quality which is best called sensibility. Nayudu is a very sensitive batsman; from each of his strokes you get the impression of a new-born energy, of a sudden improvisation of superb technique. Nayudu is not at all mechanical. Watching him from the ring you get a delicious suggestion in his play of fallibility. Unlike Bradman, his skill is his servant, not his master. The glorious uncertainty of cricket is not endangered by Nayudu.'

Nayudu's technique was founded on such firm ground that even when the chips were down he could play the Englishmen at their own game. The Second World War years restricted his customary appearances down south in the annual Europeans versus Indians carnival match, but the Holkars were always in the news and thus so was Nayudu. For the Holkars' glory was Nayudu's glory. He fashioned them into a champion side, breathing his daring spirit into the side. One could see his influence on every Holkar player.

Nayudu's very presence was power. Even if the years took a toll on his skill, his courage and indomitable spirit remained. There is the well-known story of the time he was hit on the mouth by a bumper but rejected medical attention with contempt, spitting out blood and broken teeth as he carried on batting. Another story tells of how he placed himself in the 'suicide position' at forward short leg with the plan of taking a hook shot on his chest so that it rebounded for an easy catch to a nearby fielder. There was no denying C.K. Nayudu's will and authority.

6

ADELAIDE, 1948

Vijay Hazare

Nostalgic memories improve their flavour with the passage of time, not unlike a certain potation, of which I must confess thorough ignorance. The Australians, however, are great connoisseurs of this beverage, and indeed it is my Australian adventures that I will relate here. Even thirty years after my tour of the land of the kangaroos, I still vividly recall the imposing Melbourne Cricket Ground, the pleasing Sydney Cricket Ground with its famous hill and, above all, the lovely Adelaide Oval. There are few grounds in the world to rival the picturesque grandeur of the one at Adelaide. Against the backdrop of Mount Gambier rises the stately cathedral that flanks the ground with an aura of benevolence as the River Torrens rushes past.

It was in these idyllic surroundings that I was privileged to play and put on some of my best performances in the august presence of some of cricket's all-time greats. Among them was Sir Robert Menzies—the Australian Prime Minister and a knowledgeable

43

student of the game—and two former Indian cricketers who were then covering the tour as journalists: K.S. Duleepsinhji and Prof. D.B. Deodhar. The latter was the doyen of Indian cricket and my captain during my playing days with Maharashtra. Also in the crowd was my cricketing guru, Clarrie Grimmett. He had coached me in India ten years ago and wanted to satisfy himself that his efforts were not wasted.

It was the fourth Test of the series, and we were 0-2 down. The opposition captain was Donald Bradman, a shrewd and ruthless leader with all his imposing batting reputation. The Australians scored 674 in their first innings. Our reply, though brave in patches, was just at 140 when half the side was sent back to the pavilion. I desperately wanted to do something worthwhile as I felt I was in form.

Luckily, I was batting with Dattu Phadkar, who was also feeling confident. Together we settled down and gradually took the edge off the attack. Ray Lindwall and Keith Miller hurled their thunderbolts at us. Bill Johnston tried his tricks and even Sid Barnes wanted to repeat his Melbourne feat of getting me and skipper Lala Amarnath out in the space of just three deliveries.

This time I stood firm and was soon receiving the applause of the crowd for my century. It was my first Test hundred and I had scored it when the side desperately needed runs. At the other end, Phadkar stood up to the pace and spin attack with the aplomb of a veteran. He fearlessly hooked the bogeymen Lindwall and Miller, and I too joined in with a few cover drives. Our sixth-wicket partnership was worth 188—at the time an Indian record—when I was out for 116. I was pleased to see young Phadkar also get his ton, but our efforts were not enough to save the follow-on, as the rest of the batting collapsed.

Within five minutes of the start of our second innings I was back at the crease once again to face the music. It was now the afternoon of the fourth day and the wicket had started showing signs of wear. Lindwall got a lot out of it and sent several of our batsmen to their doom. Miller tried to emulate him, but I managed to hook him to the fence, after which he gave up.

As in the first innings, I found my touch and was middling the ball as I would have liked. I was hoping that somebody would stay with me to bat another day. That turned out be Hemu Adhikari, at the time my Baroda teammate. Together we weathered the storm. In an innings when six of my teammates failed to score, Adhikari's fighting 50 was a commendable effort. As the evening shadows started lengthening, my own score crept towards the three-figure mark. By the end of the day's play, I had managed to complete my second century of the match. My stand with Adhikari was worth 132 and I was the last batsman to be dismissed. My contribution was 145 out of our side's total of 277.

Imagine my joy when I was told that I was the first Indian to score a century in both innings of a Test. I had not played with the aim of getting my second ton, focusing my attention on boosting the side's total. In all modesty I may add that I was not unduly weighed down by the adverse situation. I simply played the attack on its merits. Naturally, I was pleased with the rich reward that I got for my efforts.

The praise showered on me by the elite of the cricketing world was enough to turn my head. But I remembered that I owed a lot to Grimmet—who had decided that I had been worthy of his attention after all. I had graduated with honours in his eyes. Years later, whenever I recalled my knocks in that Test, the first thing that came to my mind was the happy and contented—and perhaps a little proud—look on my mentor's face.

7

PANKAJ ROY: THE ZAMINDAR WHO LOVED SPORTS

Pranab Roy

It's a privilege to write about the life and career of my legendary father, the late Pankaj Roy. He was born in 1928 to a family of zamindars. Right from his school days, he excelled at sports. Like most Bengalis, his favourite sport was football. He represented Sporting Union, a First Division team in Kolkata. He was prolific, scoring many goals in the First Division league, including against clubs such as East Bengal and Mohammedan Sporting Club. He also represented an Indian Football Association team against a team from Burma and scored a goal.

Pankaj excelled at table tennis as well and was ranked fourth in Bengal. In addition, he was a brilliant shooter and a terrific swimmer. He played cricket after the football season ended. Once, during a First Division football match against Mohammedan Sporting Club, he was tackled by an opposition defender after

Indian women's cricket team to Australia, 1991.

Photo courtesy Shubhangi Kulkarni's personal collection

Indian captain Shubhangi Kulkarni with her English counterpart
Carol Hodges during the India vs England match on
26 June 1986, Cheltenham.

Photo courtesy Shubhangi Kulkarni's personal collection

Pankaj Roy and Vinoo Mankad after
their world-record opening stand in
Madras against New Zealand,
11 January 1956.

Photo courtesy Pranab Roy

Pankaj Roy and Nari Contractor opening
the innings for India vs West Indies, 1958.

Photo courtesy Pranab Roy

Itinerary of the Indian cricket team's first tour of England, 1932.

Facsimile of the souvenir released on the occasion of the Indian team's tour of England in 1936.

Photo courtesy Boria Majumdar

(L–R): Ramakant Desai, Nari Contractor and Pankaj Roy sipping milk, England, 1959.

Photo courtesy Nari Contractor's collection

(L-R): Bishan Singh Bedi, Erapalli Prasanna and B.S. Chandrasekhar at a BCCI function in Mumbai.

Photo courtesy Aditya Bhushan

(L-R): Venkat Sundaram with Kapil Dev and Kirti Azad, New Delhi, 2021.

Photo from Venkat Sundaram's collection

(L-R, sitting): Bharat Reddy, Kapil Dev and Karsan Ghavri. (L-R, standing): Dilip Vengsarkar and Yajurvindra Singh. Mumbai, 2017.

Photo courtesy Yajurvindra Singh

scoring a goal. He fell and fractured his forearm and could not play for three months. That was when most of his close friends advised him to play cricket seriously instead of football.

Following such advice, my father started concentrating on cricket. He went to Bombay for university tournament matches and was picked for an All-India University team against the West Indies in 1948. Before that match, he played his first Ranji Trophy match and scored a century against Assam on debut. Unfortunately, despite this, he was still sent in to bat at No. 10 against the West Indies and hence could not make much of a mark. He returned disappointed. But as luck would have it, he got another chance to play against the West Indies soon after, this time for the East Zone team. Pankaj scored a century batting in the middle order.

The BCCI arranged a camp in Poona for the current Indian players and some younger ones close to selection. Pankaj played four matches during this camp and impressed Vijay Merchant with his batting. Merchant said to my father, 'Pankaj, why don't you open? You have an excellent technique, and India needs an opener as my partner because Mushtaq Ali will retire very soon. If you position yourself as a middle-order batsman, you may have to wait longer to play for India.'

My father remembered this advice. When he was made captain of the All-India University team for the match against the Marylebone Cricket Club (MCC), he asked the selectors if he could open the batting. They agreed, and he scored a brilliant 86 as an opener. That knock helped him get selected for the Indian team and he made his Test debut against England in Delhi. However, he only scored 12 runs. He was very disappointed. He went back to Calcutta, played some local cricket and scored heavily.

When he went to Bombay for the second Test match, India captain Vijay Hazare asked him what he had done during his stay in Calcutta between Tests. My father replied, 'Sir, I played four games and scored a triple century, a double century and a hundred.' Hazare said that he would only congratulate Pankaj if he scored a century in the Bombay Test. Pankaj duly scored 140.

There were lots of congratulatory telegrams and letters that arrived immediately after the match. Hazare came to him and said, 'Congratulations, young man, you played wonderfully well. I am sure you will score many more runs in the future. But my only advice is that the more you play and the more your name is recognized, the more you will have to be humble.' My father remembered these words for the rest of his years and passed on this message to his sons as well.

He scored another century in the fifth Test in Chennai. It was India's first Test victory. However, the return series in England the following summer was a disaster for him. He couldn't score any runs and came back empty-handed. This was when he realized that his eyesight had deteriorated and he needed corrective eyewear. People started saying that his career was finished because he had to wear glasses. However, the selectors were very kind to select him for the tour of the West Indies in 1953.

This time Pankaj didn't let down the selectors and was the highest run-getter on that tour. In the Kingston Test at Jamaica, he made scores of 150 and 85. My father's next overseas tour was to Pakistan and he had ordinary returns, resulting in him being dropped for a couple of Test matches. He made a comeback against New Zealand and scored a century at his home ground in Calcutta. He then put on the world-record opening partnership of 413 with Vinoo Mankad at Chepauk in Madras.

On his next tour to England in 1959, Pankaj was named as vice-captain of the team. But England was never a happy hunting ground for him and his scores were average. Following this tour, West Indies visited India. During that series, he scored a brilliant 90 to save the Bombay Test and had a few other decent knocks.

During Australia's tour of India, he scored 99 in Delhi. However, he was not selected for the tour to the West Indies in 1960–61, and his international career came to a close. He played first-class cricket till the 1967–68 season before retiring from the sport.

8

MY CRICKET MEMORIES

V.V. Kumar

From my days as a cricketer—a career that spanned almost twenty-five years—there are many anecdotes worth narrating, some of which I would like to share in this chapter.

Golf Ball in Cricket?

This may sound strange, but my experiments with a golf ball changed my thoughts on spin bowling. During my school days, the price of a cricket ball was seven rupees for a new one, and a rupee for used ones. This was considered expensive at the time. By comparison, golf balls could be bought for four annas (about a fourth of a rupee) in second-hand stores. The behaviour of the golf ball fascinated me and paved the way for my spin addiction.

When I applied leg spin to the golf ball and threw it against a wall, the ball bounced back to me as an off-break. The opposite happened if I applied off-spin to it. Later I found out that this was because of the small depressions on its surface, which resembled air pockets. Golf balls were good for street cricket as they lasted longer than cricket balls. They were also lighter, so we had to apply more spin to get them to turn.

Different Types of Pitches

In the 1950s, there were jute matting pitches for Ranji matches at certain grounds. Jute pitches are similar to turf but slower. The jute fibres are thin and long and only partly yield to pressure. I was fascinated by the phenomenal success Jasu Patel and Ghulam Ahmed had on these pitches. They were a real terror on those wickets. In 1992, Jasu Bhai revealed to me that the little resistance from the jute matting created seam movement and got the ball to deviate. In comparison, coir matting's thick knotty fibres and very low resistance made the ball bounce, turn and grip. Those pitches were more bowler-friendly.

Baptism by Fire

There was no easy entry for me into Ranji Trophy cricket. I made my debut in the 1955–56 season, playing for Madras. My first match was against the champions, Bombay—which had the likes of Polly Umrigar, P.K. Kamat, Madhav Mantri, Ramnath Kenny, Rusi Modi, Avinash Desai and others. Mantri made a hundred while Rusi and Kenny made useful contributions. I had never come across a fleet-footed batter like Kenny before this. He never allowed you to pitch ball up. I bowled about forty overs and gave away 87 runs for my 2 wickets. It was a great moment for me when Vinoo Mankad and Rusi personally congratulated me saying, 'Very good, son, keep going.'

In those days, the LBW dismissal was rare. Indian wickets were mostly batting-friendly, whether jute or turf, and if you had military-medium pacers, you could not succeed. In some games, bowlers had to bowl up to thirty overs each, and wickets were difficult to get. As a spinner, you had to get loop and drift—those pushing the ball flat and with side-spin found it difficult to be among the wickets.

Perception and Practice

I was fortunate to have had two great captains under whom I learnt a lot about spin bowling. Lala Amarnath and C.D. Gopinath were both shrewd and analysed the batsman before setting the field. I had the opportunity to bowl to the greats such as Gary Sobers, Conrad Hunte, Ted Dexter, Doug Walters, Ian Redpath, Bill Lawry, Ken Barrington and Rohan Kanhai, among others. Let me tell you that all greats have their moments of insecurity in the first few overs. If you want to get them into your web, this is the time.

You can understand their approach from their stance and whether they grip the bat with the top or bottom hand. If you get on top and dictate the proceedings, half the battle is won. In those days, it was sacrilege to play lofted strokes. In fact, Kapil Dev was once dropped for doing this in a Test match. The standard shot of the time was referred to as a 'carpet drive'.

Test Trials and Training Camps

Luck favoured me and I attended over five training camps at various locations. When Col. Hemu Adhikari was in command of the camps, there were rigid rules and regulations and exhausting field exercises. The only redeeming feature was when, in the dorms at night, Tiger (M.A.K. Pataudi), Tat (Vijay Manjrekar), Tiny

(Ramakant Desai) and Charlie (V.M. Muddiah) enlivened the dullness with their jokes. Tat was a great singer who rendered classics from *Baiju Bawra* and *Barsaat*. The medical examination was a tiresome affair—everything was tested, including our brains!

Types of Cricket Balls

There used to be two types of cricket balls: 'four piece' and 'two piece'. In four-piece balls, the leather was not stretched, and it had ridges that helped the bowlers. Two-piece balls had the leather fully stretched, and control of swing was difficult—they were predominately seam-oriented. The Duke and Kookaburra balls had submerged seams, which were more suited to soft wickets. Their leather was affected by changes in the weather. The SG balls were sturdy and hard, with the upright seam that is preferred by bowlers.

New Kinds of Bowling

Bowlers such as Shane Warne, Saqlain Mushtaq, Danish Kaneria and Harbhajan Singh were credited with discovering 'new' kinds of deliveries. However, the cricket ball is not a magic wand. The supposed 'new' types of bowling were already established deliveries, but now called names such as 'flipper' or 'slider'. A 'carrom ball' is nothing but a delivery manipulated by the fingers to make the ball turn from leg to off. Jake Iverson of Australia would bowl this delivery. He never bowled with the support of the palm. He worked wonders with only his fingers and was known as 'Wrong-Grip Jake'. The new names seem to be for marketing purposes!

No bowler can be termed great unless he can run through the opposition on a good wicket. In spin bowling, that is achieved by imparting revolutions, varying loop, using drift and flighting the ball when bowling against the breeze. Control is paramount.

Great spin-bowling duos bowl in tandem and set up the batsman. Examples of such partnerships are Tony Lock and Jim Laker, Subhash Gupte and Vinoo Mankad, and Anil Kumble and Harbhajan Singh.

In a Lighter Vein

The Sinhalese Sports Club in Colombo had a very good swimming pool. In 1958, after a nail-biting finish to a local match, the teams fraternized at the club. A few players sought permission to swim in the pool that night. The manager consented, not knowing that the pool had been drained for cleaning that evening. The swimming pool was painted blue all over, including the bottom, so it was hard to tell that there was no water. One of our players jumped in—there was a huge thud and our opening batsman was covered in bruises all over!

Another incident involved a Haryana cricketer in the early 1970s. It was at a camp for Test prospects held at Madras. Being a resident of the city, I had offered to share my room with the cricketer. One night he told me that he had an upset stomach and was vomiting. I called a doctor immediately and he was prescribed pills for three days—a total of twenty tablets. The next morning, he came to me and said that he was feeling better—he had consumed all twenty tablets that morning to get quick relief!

9

REMEMBER THE PAST

Partab Ramchand

I have noticed that many among the current generation of cricket lovers seem content to know just about contemporary players. Their knowledge of past greats is very limited. I have come to this conclusion not just through interactions with hardcore cricket enthusiasts but also from polls conducted by various publications with questions pertaining to the greatest Indian cricketers. Most of the votes for the best-ever teams and the greatest players invariably are for cricketers who played after the 1970s.

As there is minimal footage of cricket played from the 1930s to the 1960s, many younger followers of the game are ignorant of the feats performed by the likes of C.K. Nayudu, Lala Amarnath, Mohammed Nissar, Amar Singh, Vijay Merchant, Mushtaq Ali, Vinoo Mankad, Subhash Gupte, Vijay Hazare, Vijay Manjrekar, Polly Umrigar and Tiger Pataudi. In the 1960s, we were brought up on books, not video—so it was through reading that we learnt about the exploits of great cricketers of previous eras.

I remember reading avidly about Nayudu and Merchant but also about foreign players such as Victor Trumper, Jack Hobbs, Wally Hammond, Len Hutton, Bill O'Reilly and Clarrie Grimmett in books written by Neville Cardus, Ray Robinson, R.C. Robertson-Glasgow, A.A. Thomson and Berry Sarbadhikari. But today most cricket lovers prefer videos to books, and thus tend to dismiss the facts, figures and statistics associated with cricketers from a period predating video.

I think that writers and historians closely associated with the game have a role to play in educating today's cricket followers about the heroes of yore. In my books, I have often recounted the great performances, players and matches from the 1930s to the 1960s. These are the eras about which many cricket followers today are not very aware.

It's easy for cricket fans today to point out that Nayudu's Test batting average was 25 and Mushtaq Ali's 32 whereas Sachin Tendulkar and Rahul Dravid average over 50, or that the bowling strike rates of Mankad and Gupte do not compare favourably with those of Anil Kumble and Ravichandran Ashwin. However, it is never easy to play for a national team in its formative years. The dice was frequently loaded against these early cricketers and they were often fighting a losing battle against far more experienced sides who also had better players.

While retaining my admiration for today's cricketers, I have always held in high regard older cricketers who had to swim upstream because they symbolized courage in adversity. In the formative years of Indian cricket—when our national sides suffered one setback after another and had very few victories to show for their efforts—the country was fortunate to have many courageous players who defied the odds to come up with performances that attracted attention from all over the cricketing world.

It was 1971 when the Indian team first won series in West Indies and England and a certain Sunil Gavaskar announced his arrival. The establishment of a world-class spin quartet, greater solidity in the batting and vast improvement in the fielding also contributed to these successes, which could be seen as major turning points in Indian cricket. Since then, Indian cricket has gone from strength to strength and Indian players have become recognized as among the best in the world.

Indian cricketers today have not only the skill, subtlety and artistry traditionally associated with cricketers from the subcontinent but also technical excellence, ideal temperaments and the important qualities of courage and dedication. But the achievements of Tendulkar and other modern-day heroes should not in any way dim the lustre surrounding the feats of Nayudu and his contemporaries.

Two out of the four Indian cricketers who have scored a century and taken five wickets in an innings in the same match did so before the 1970s, albeit in losing causes—Mankad at Lord's in 1952 and Umrigar at Port of Spain ten years later. This despite the stars of yesteryear not having the kind of playing opportunities that today's cricketers enjoy. I have unstinting admiration for today's cricketers but still advocate that cricketers from the formative years of Indian cricket should be judged by their circumstances and not by statistics alone. They should be given their due in a world that is fast forgetting them.

LEGENDS OF THE PAST

10

NARI CONTRACTOR:
MAN OF STEEL

Navroze D. Dhondy

It was 7 March 1934, and a heavily pregnant young lady was on a train from Dohad in Gujarat to Bombay. Along the way, Piroja Jehangirji Contractor suddenly felt labour pains, and knew that the baby could be born any time, even though it was a few weeks before the due date. As luck would have it, the train's driver was Dali Wadia, a cousin of Piroja's husband. The labour pains and spasms came just before the train steamed into the town of Godhra, where the driver finished his shift.

When Wadia came to say goodbye to Piroja, she looked extremely uncomfortable. He suggested that it was best she get off the train and rest at his home. If she felt better, he would get her a seat on the next day's train. However, that very night in Godhra, Nariman Jehangirji Contractor was born.

Nari, as he is fondly called—by family, friends, teammates and adversaries—was destined to be born in Gujarat, as eventually this place of birth would be a huge factor in his getting a first opportunity to play top-level domestic cricket. Nari grew up studying at Boy's Town school in Nashik, where he captained the cricket team. He then moved to Bombay University, where he made an immediate mark in local cricket tournaments.

Yet, the wait to play for the Bombay first-class side went on. It was making him restless. After a session at the Cricket Club of India, he was approached by a gentleman by the name of Mr Cambhatta who had been watching him bat. Mr Cambhatta got straight to the point and asked: 'Nari, would you like to play for Gujarat? You can, as you were born in Godhra.' Nari did not immediately agree as he was still optimistic that he would play for Bombay. However, a few weeks later he decided to write to the gentleman, agreeing to play for Gujarat.

Soon after the move, Gujarat captain Pheroze Cambhatta had to pull out of a game due to a stiff neck. This gave Nari the opportunity to make his first-class debut. And what a start it was. He scored a century in each innings (152 and 102 not out), becoming only the second-ever cricketer—after Arthur Morris of Australia, who was also a left-handed opening batsman—to score a century in both innings on first-class debut.

He was eventually called up to the Indian team as a top-order batsman, but again made his debut in unusual circumstances. Vinoo Mankad could not reach Delhi in time for a match, leading to Nari being pencilled in at the last minute. Nari has always had a simple policy of being grateful for whatever comes his way. He knew that if Vinoo had arrived on time for that game, he might not ever have had the opportunity to make his Test debut. He applied the same philosophy on that fateful day in 1962 after being hit by a Charlie Griffith bouncer in Barbados, a blow that ended his international career. Nari did not believe in regrets.

That head injury to Nari was one of the most shocking incidents in cricket history. He came close to losing his life. Farokh Engineer recounted his experience of that moment: 'As Nari collapsed on the pitch after the ball hit him, I was one of the first few to rush to him at the crease. Speaking in Gujarati, I asked him, "*Nari, kem che* (How are you)?" The gutsy fellow that he is, Nari replied "*Badhusaru che* (All is well)." He wanted to carry on, but I saw blood trickling from his nose and ears. Being a doctor's son, I knew that this was serious.'

Over the years, I have had the pleasure of bumping into Sunil Gavaskar at various cricket events. Once, I asked him how he reacted to the news of Nari's injury. Gavaskar was only twelve in 1962. 'I was way too young to fully understand what had happened,' he recalled, 'but I knew that it was serious and life threatening. The next few days I scanned the papers to get more information on how he was recovering. Not just Indian cricket lovers, but the entire cricketing world breathed easy after he was declared to be out of danger.'

Gavaskar went on to add, 'I remember watching him bat in a Duleep Trophy match after making a comeback from his injury. During that innings, he once cupped his hands around his ears and looked straight down the pitch. It reminded me of a horse with blinkers. He then practised a straight drive.' Many years later, Nari explained to Gavaskar that the curious practice helped get his concentration back after he had played a loose shot. Gavaskar adopted the practice, sometimes doing it after reaching a century if his concentration wavered.

One piece of advice Gavaskar received from Nari was to write a journal, especially on the day he had batted well. Nari would write down every detail—how he felt after waking up that day, what he ate for breakfast, what clothes he wore going to the ground, how he held the bat—that he could remember of the day he scored runs. This stood him in good stead during periods of poor form. Gavaskar took his advice. 'Writing down all that I had done on the day I made a good score meant that I could compare it with what I was doing when I wasn't scoring runs,' he recalled with a smile. 'It gave me the belief that I would big again if I made a few adjustments. It was magical.'

Nari's younger sister Shernaz (Sherry) recounts how the family was glued to the radio when Nari was playing in England and was hit in the ribs by an express delivery from Brian Statham. It was Nari's first experience of a green top at Lord's. Despite suffering a broken rib, Nari carried on batting and went on to score 81 out of a team total of 168. That innings became a bit of folklore, and his gustiness was something for younger cricketers to emulate.

According to Behram, Nari's younger brother, Nari was more like a father to him. Success and fame hardly changed the man, who was devoted to his family. Both Sherry and Behram recall how Nari would often have cricketers from touring teams visit their home at Cusrow Baug for a meal. I met Richie Benaud at a Wisden event a few decades ago and he fondly remembered both the home-cooked food served by Nari's mum and the warmth of their close-knit family.

At twenty-six, Nari was made captain of the Indian team and became India's youngest Test captain at the time. Over some Parsi chai one afternoon in Cusrow Baug, I asked him how he learnt that he been made captain. 'It was lunchtime and I had stepped out of the office near Churchgate with some office colleagues to grab a bite, when suddenly a crowd came across to me and started shaking my hand,' he recalled. 'They were saying "Congratulations, Contractor, you are captain of India", but I had no idea. There was no letter, telegram or call from the Board, but it seems it was already on the news. So, I learnt about it from the fans!'

He also recalled the time when Pakistan came to play in India. The crowds at each Test venue had one deafening slogan in common: '*Pakistan se harna nahi hai* (We cannot lose to Pakistan)!'

When I spoke with some of Nari's teammates whom he had captained, they provided some very interesting insights. It seems Nari was the first captain to start the practice of team meetings at the end of each day's play. To create better camaraderie and team spirit, he initiated the concept of mixing up the players' rooms to prevent them from staying cocooned in their own regional coteries. This helped the players get to know each other better. There were a few management lessons business leaders of today could learn from Nari!

One evening a few years ago, Nari left home to run a little errand but tripped and fell. He hit his head against the sidewalk kerb. It was a blow to the head after over fifty years since that fateful incident in Barbados. He was rushed to the hospital and placed in the ICU. He kept everyone on tenterhooks for a few days, but then, being the fighter that he is, he came around. I happened to be in Bombay that day and visited him in the hospital. He was propped up in the hospital bed reading the newspaper.

I gave him a big smile and said, 'Nari-kaka, what is all this? Next time when you go out shopping, please wear a helmet!' He flung the newspaper at me and in his typical style swore, 'Saala, I faced balls at a hundred miles an hour without a helmet and you want me to wear one now?' That made everyone, including the nurse in the room, burst into laughter. Of course, the one to laugh loudest was Nari himself.

I remember an incident after he had just retired from cricket. As a result of his visit to our family business in Allahabad, my dad had had to pull the shutters down as a swarm of fans had followed him there. It was too difficult to control so many people wanting to shake Nari's hand and hug him.

Whenever we discuss the crazy changes the game has seen over the decades, he is always open-minded and positive, though quite scathing about technique and doggedness being sacrificed at the altar of 'instant cricket'. Yet he does sometimes wish he could have played in the Indian Premier League (IPL). He is an ardent supporter of this innovation and believes it's given the game of cricket a new lease of life.

After that near-fatal injury in 1962, Nari followed his doctor's advice religiously. As Sherry testifies, he would run many laps around the maidans to get back his strength. He would practise strokes at home by hitting a cricket ball hanging in a sock from the bedroom doorway, all to get back to playing cricket. He managed to do it in great style.

Though he never played for India again, he scored 93 in his final first-class match. Another 7 runs would have made him possibly the only cricketer in the history of the game to have scored two centuries on debut and another in his last innings. But Nari never believed in 'ifs and buts'.

For me, Nari is my uncle, but he is also my idol ever since I was a little kid growing up in Allahabad. As I grew from being a starry-eyed kid to a belligerent and argumentative cricket fan, I had some of the most wonderful and cherished moments of my life with Uncle Nari. I have learnt about humility, team management and having a never-say-die spirit from the man who embodied it best.

After nearly sixty years of having a steel plate inserted in his skull to save his life, the plate was finally removed. However, Nari Contractor remains the Man of Steel.

11

TIGER PATAUDI: PRINCE OF A SMALL STATE, KING OF A GREAT GAME

H. Natarajan

Tiger Pataudi's achievements at the international level as a batsman can be better appreciated by reflecting on how the careers of Colin Milburn, Saba Karim and Mark Boucher ended after they suffered eye injuries. When Tiger visited Karim in the hospital after the latter's eye injury, the wicketkeeper asked the former India captain: 'How long did it take you to recover from the eye injury?' To which Tiger replied, 'I never recovered.'

Despite his royal upbringing, Mansur Ali Khan Pataudi was made of steel. He never showed his feelings, whether on or off the field. Five months before his debut, he had virtually lost his right eye in a horrific car accident in Sussex, UK. Consequently, he lost perspective when it came to judging distances. 'When trying to light a cigarette, I found that I was missing the end of it by a quarter of an inch. I was also liable to pour water from a jug straight on to the table, instead of into a tumbler as I intended,' he wrote in his autobiography, *Tiger's Tale*.

It took him five years, he says, before he could come to terms with his huge handicap. He soon found that he could no longer hook and had to curb his natural inclination to drive half-volleys because he was so frequently beaten by the yorker. The flight of spin bowling became difficult to follow. He worked on finding out his limitations and then playing strictly within them.

Imran Khan once said, 'I grew up admiring two persons. One was my first cousin Javed Burki, and the other was Mansur Ali Khan of Pataudi.' Burki and Pataudi played together at Oxford University, and the former told Imran that if Pataudi had not suffered his handicap, he would have broken all the batting records. He added that the quality of strokes Pataudi could play with just one eye could not be matched by other batters with perfect vision.

Pataudi was asked to lead the President's XI against Ted Dexter's Englishmen in 1961. He found out that he was 'seeing two balls, six to seven inches apart'. But he picked the inner of the two and managed to score 35! This was his first big match after the accident and the selectors were probably impressed, despite being unaware of his predicament. He was to make his Test debut against the same Englishmen, and in his fourth innings he scored his first Test hundred.

For those who have seen, appreciated and retained the memories of a bygone era, Tiger Pataudi will remain the mastermind behind the game's greatest spin combination—that of Erapalli Prasanna, Bhagwat Chandrasekhar, Srinivas Venkataraghavan and Bishan Singh Bedi. He launched all-out attacks with the dreaded spinners much like Clive Lloyd did later with the pace quintet of Andy

Roberts, Michael Holding, Joel Garner, Colin Croft and Malcolm Marshall. Pataudi was also one of the greatest fielders of his time, comparable to Colin Bland and Jonty Rhodes.

India was still far from being a 'first-world' cricketing nation, but Tiger's body language was awe-inspiring. There was an imperious air about him, which had much to do with his royal background. He lived in a palace with 150 rooms and over a hundred servants, eight of whom were assigned to take care of his needs. His body language oozed confidence and self-belief, yet gave a subtle message to his teammates that there was nothing to feel inferior about. This attitude reflected in his attacking approach to both batting and captaincy.

Tiger captained forty of his forty-six Tests and his term as skipper lasted from 1962 to 1975—albeit interrupted. It is by far the longest such term of any Indian. That the forty-six Tests were played over thirteen years speaks for the limited amount of cricket played in that era. Yet, Pataudi's forty Tests as captain have since been bettered only by a select group of Indians: Virat Kohli (sixty-eight), M.S. Dhoni (sixty), Sourav Ganguly (forty-nine) and Sunil Gavaskar and Mohammed Azharuddin (forty-seven).

Thirteen captains had led India before Tiger and the record for the most number of games as captain had been held by Lala Amarnath with fifteen. These statistics show that Tiger was head and shoulders above others of his era in leadership skills and man-management. In fact, history will rank him alongside the likes of Richie Benaud, Imran Khan, Clive Lloyd and Mike Brearley as the top cerebral generals of cricket.

Tiger had played just three Tests when he was forced to lead India for the first time at the age of twenty-one—which made him the youngest captain in Test cricket, a record he held till 2004. The opponents were a mighty West Indies side led by Sir Frank Worrell. It was most unexpected and under very difficult circumstances. The selectors had chosen Pataudi as vice-captain on that tour in the hope of grooming him, but the career-ending blow to captain Nari Contractor's head by Charlie Griffith propelled the young man into a very uncomfortable lead role with no time for preparation. The inexperienced Pataudi was asked to lead established stars such as Polly Umrigar, Vijay Manjrekar, Chandu Borde, M.L. Jaisimha, Bapu Nadkarni, Salim Durrani and Ramakant Desai. He hardly knew any of them, having played most of his cricket in England.

Pataudi kept batting very simple. He would just pick any bat in the dressing room and go out to bat. Though he has an unbeaten double hundred in Tests, his finest innings came at Melbourne against Bobby Simpson's Australia on the 1967–68 tour. Pataudi missed the first Test of that series due to a pulled hamstring. India lost by an innings. A hamstring injury could rule a player out for up to sixteen weeks. Yet, Pataudi declared himself fit to play the second Test at Melbourne despite not having trained for a month. Graham McKenzie played havoc on a green top, reducing India to 25 for 5. But with just one good leg and one good eye, Pataudi scored 75 in the first innings and 85 in the second. Pataudi's audacious strokeplay reminded Lindsay Hassett of his legendary teammate, Sir Don Bradman.

Tiger was celebrating his eleventh birthday with his siblings when he learnt that his father had died of a heart attack while playing polo. The senior Pataudi, Iftikhar Ali Khan, was just forty-one. It's never easy to step into the shoes of a famous father—Pataudi Sr played under Douglas Jardine in the Bodyline series for England and later for India. But Tiger's life was all about grit and glory and he took every challenge that came his way to surpass the efforts of his father.

Pataudi was a thinker of the game and his views were much sought after. For a while, he was the editor of the now-defunct *Sportsworld*. It was the kind of journalism that you don't get to read today. He was known for his remarkable sense of humour. When the English cricketer Sir Gubby Allen asked Pataudi when he first thought he could play again despite his handicap, Tiger replied, 'When I saw the English bowling!' Clearly, this breed of Tiger is also an endangered species!

Tiger was also a prankster, and cricketers and cricket journalists who knew him recall hilarious anecdotes about his ability to pull someone's leg with a straight face. Sunil Gavaskar captures this facet of Tiger's personality with an anecdote he shares in his book *Sunny Days*. Tiger had invited a few players to play a match in Bhopal. Recalls Gavaskar, 'On the rest day, they had decided to go on a shikar. They had hardly entered the jungle when suddenly they were surrounded by "dacoits" who fired a few rifle shots in the air, warning them not to try anything funny.'

Gundappa Vishwanath, Erapalli Prasanna and the other members of the party were asked to step out of the jeeps and hand over their belongings. When one of the men accompanying them tried to run, he was 'shot down' by the 'dacoit' leader. 'Vishwanath and Prasanna were told that they were being held to ransom,' writes Gavaskar. 'The petrified Vishwanath, who was tied to a tree, started weeping and explaining that he was an India Test cricketer and the country needed his services.' However, his assailants had never heard of cricket and weren't in the least bit impressed.

Eventually, a 'ransom' secured their release. It was only later that they found out that the 'dacoits' were, in fact, Tiger Pataudi's servants and the whole incident was staged! 'Prasanna knew this because Tiger had told him earlier,' writes Gavaskar, 'but poor

Vishwanath to this day doesn't believe it was a make-believe hold-up and cannot help shivering in fright when reminded of it.'

India had produced many big names and royal cricketers before Pataudi, but Tiger was the first larger-than-life Indian player. It was an era before television commercials, a time when ladies were quite restrained in their show of affection for men. However, the charismatic Tiger was one of the most coveted men and eventually fell for the charms of one of most beautiful women of his times: Sharmila Tagore, an actor and a glamorous distant relative of Rabindranath Tagore.

In Ranji's biography, Alan Ross described him as 'the prince of a little state but king of a great game'. The same can be said of Tiger Pataudi.

12

AJIT WADEKAR: ELDER BROTHER, INSPIRING LEADER

Milind Rege

Many of us who played for Bombay in the late 1960s and early 1970s apprenticed under Ajit Wadekar and went on to gain laurels for the state and country. To me, Ajit was the best of the many greats who led the Bombay cricket team. His management style was unique. He appeared to be a man of few words in public, but inside the dressing room or on the field of play, he stepped in at the right time with a quiet word of encouragement that always worked as a morale booster. More importantly, Ajit gave his teammates the opportunity and space to express themselves on their own but remained available whenever they needed help.

I remember how he handled Eknath Solkar and I in an Irani Trophy match when we were teenagers bowling to the likes of Mansur Ali Khan Pataudi, Chandu Borde and Hanumant Singh. Thanks to Ajit's guidance and motivation, we snared seven wickets between the two of us in a big match against big names. In his quiet, inimitable way, Ajit turned people management into an art form.

He treated his younger teammates like his own siblings, always playing the role of an elder brother and constantly communicating with them. This gave them confidence and got the fear of failure and other insecurities out of their minds. We all respected him for his simple, uncomplicated nature. I recall a Ranji Trophy quarter-final match in which we had lost 5 wickets and were trailing by about 100 runs. I was batting with Karsan Ghavri and we were the last recognized batsmen. Ajit quietly walked up to us, put his arms on our shoulders and said, 'Fight it out and save us.' His faith in us inspired Karsan and I to pull the team out to safety.

When Ajit walked out to bat or led the team out on the ground, his walk was languid and he appeared relaxed. But appearances can be deceptive. Underneath that laidback exterior was a steely resolve to win. He was always in control of the situation, no matter how the team was placed. Bombay cricketers have a certain spirit that ensured they were never overawed by illustrious names in the opposition. Ajit personified this spirit.

One of the greatest innings he played was against Mysore in a Ranji semi-final at the Brabourne Stadium. I saw him tear apart two of the greatest spinners of our generation, Bhagwat Chandrasekhar and Erapalli Prasanna, with flamboyance and style, to help Bombay win by an innings. People who couldn't stand Ajit's success labelled him a 'lucky captain'. It was an unjustified label. Many have tried to imitate his laidback style and failed.

Those who played for India when Ajit was the manager and coach of the national team still talk about his perceptive and strategic guidance that started the second revolution of Indian cricket from the early 1990s. For my generation, we will always remember his immaculate square-cut and piercing cover drive—strokes that he played with complete nonchalance—but more than anything, we will remember him as an inspirational leader. There will never be another quite like Ajit Laxman Wadekar.

13

CHANDRA, PRAS, BEDI AND VENKAT: THE QUARTET

Partab Ramchand

For cricket fans of today's generation, the 'Fab Four' will always be Rahul Dravid, Sachin Tendulkar, Sourav Ganguly and V.V.S. Laxman. Together they were undoubtedly the most lustrous batting line-up of their time and contributed to one famous Indian triumph after another. It led to the first decade of the new millennium being the greatest period in Indian Test cricket history until that point.

But when cricket fans of an earlier generation hear the epithet 'Fab Four', they think of the famed Indian spin quartet who ruled cricket from the mid-1960s to the late 1970s and shaped notable victories at home and abroad. Bishan Singh Bedi, Erapalli Prasanna, Bhagwat Chandrasekhar and Srinivas Venkataraghavan took 853 Test wickets between them. In their own way they terrorized batsmen as much as the famed fast bowlers Andy Roberts and

Michael Holding of the West Indies or the Australians Dennis Lillee and Jeff Thomson.

Ian Chappell of Australia was one of the best players of spin bowling of his time. But he too reckoned that his cricketing education was only completed on the 1969–70 tour of India when he took on these four Indian spin bowlers at their peak. He said that while the body had to show tremendous reflexes when facing the best fast bowlers, it was the brain that had to work overtime when tackling the famed Indian spinners. They were accurate and incisive and had so many variations that the batsman was at his wit's end trying to just negotiate an over successfully.

At the time the spin 'Fab Four' played for India, there were no decent Indian fast bowlers. Thus, the spinners were often part of the new-ball attack. It was not uncommon to see Bedi start warm-up exercises in the field even as the second over of the innings was being bowled. This was because he would be bowling the next one!

The success of the spin quartet was achieved under the additional pressure of inconsistent batting by the team. Unlike in the new millennium—when India sometimes scored over 700 in an innings—the batting was largely brittle during the days of the quartet. They frequently had to defend totals below 250 and they did this successfully on many occasions. Anil Kumble touched upon this point some years ago when he said that the bowlers' task was made simpler during his career because the batsmen gave them huge totals to bowl at.

The quartet were continuing the Indian tradition of producing quality spinners, which was first seen in an earlier trio of great Indian spin bowlers of the 1950s. Vinoo Mankad, Ghulam Ahmed and Subhash Gupte were a force to be reckoned with. With minimal support from the pacers, these three spinners produced outstanding performances during a time when Indian cricket generally went from one setback to another.

Mankad, Ahmed and Gupte strove gallantly at home and abroad and even if they were not rewarded with victories during what were still the formative years of Indian cricket, they made sure that they kept a leash on even the greatest of batsmen. It is worth looking at their careers before focusing on the quartet.

Mankad was the first great Indian all-rounder, with 2,109 runs to go with 162 wickets from 44 Tests. English batting legend Len Hutton once recalled during an informal chat with reporters in Madras how Mankad had him in trouble with his accuracy and deceptiveness during the Oval Test in 1952. The left-arm spinner conceded just a single in his first 13 overs on the opening day even when master technician Hutton was at the peak of his form. Mankad's performance at Lord's seventy years ago is still remembered fondly today. It was Mankad vs England as he top-scored in both innings with 72 and 184 and sent down 73 overs to take 5 for 196—and all in a losing cause.

But Mankad had his winning roles too—like the time he took 34 wickets in the five-match series against England in 1951–52. This included a match haul of 12 for 109 at Madras as he starred in India's maiden Test triumph. He went even better with 13 for 131 against Pakistan at New Delhi later that year. Both were Indian records, and his career haul of wickets was only bettered by Prasanna many years later.

Ahmed was the first outstanding Indian off-spin bowler. He combined skill and accuracy in equal measure—which is reflected in his career figures of 68 wickets from twenty-two Tests at an average of 30. He was highly successful in England in 1952, picking up 80 wickets in first-class matches—including 15 in the four Tests for the side completely outplayed in those matches. But a particularly mesmerizing spell of his was against Australia at Calcutta in 1956, when he ripped through the strong Australian batting line-up that included Colin McDonald, Jim Burke, Peter Burge and Neil Harvey. He finished with 7 for 49 and 3 for 81—but despite his 10-wicket haul India lost the game because of batting failures.

Such failures were very typical of Indian cricket in the 1950s—and the bowler to suffer the most from them was Gupte. Even as opposing batsmen fumbled against his bag of tricks, the fielders repeatedly let him down by dropping the catches they offered. And with the batting lacking in guts, India had to endure defeat after defeat. But Gupte, the lynchpin of the attack, shone like a beacon in the darkness. His career figures—149 wickets from thirty-six Tests at 29 apiece—do scant justice to his mesmeric bowling in adverse circumstances.

Wazir Mohammed—the eldest of the five famous Mohammed brothers from Pakistan—summed it up best by saying, 'Subhash was a class act despite playing in such a poor fielding side.' The master bowler Prasanna would laugh at being bracketed with Gupte. 'I was a great admirer of Gupte,' he said in an interview once. 'There is no comparison. He was streets ahead of all of us.' But let the final word on Gupte come from none other than Garry Sobers. In an interview a few years ago, the legendary West Indian all-rounder expressed the view that 'while Shane Warne is a great bowler, the best leg-spinner I have ever seen is Subhash Gupte. He could do things with the ball I still don't believe all these years later.' There cannot be a higher tribute to Gupte's sublime art and craft.

Gupte mesmerized three great West Indians—Frank Worrell, Everton Weekes and Clyde Walcott—during the 1953 series in the Caribbean on his way to a haul of 27 wickets. Against New Zealand in 1955–56, Gupte was virtually unplayable, taking 34 wickets in five Tests. He was equally unfathomable in Pakistan the year before when he had 21 wickets. Against the West Indies at Kanpur in 1958, he became the first Indian bowler to take 9 wickets in an innings. Though time has added to the gallery of great Indian spin bowlers, Gupte remains arguably the greatest.

For all the great work done by the legendary trio of the 1950s, Indian spin reached its apotheosis with the emergence of the quartet—the genesis of which was in Madras in January 1962, when Prasanna made his Test debut against England. Two years later, Chandra played his first Test in Bombay against the same opponents. Venkat made his debut against New Zealand in Madras in February 1965, and Bedi joined the ranks against the West Indies in Calcutta on the last day of 1966.

The quartet that would provide sheer delight for the cricket connoisseur was now complete: a classical left-arm spinner, an unorthodox leg-spinner and two very different off-spinners—all of whom would give batsmen no respite. For well over a decade the quartet was Indian cricket's potent force. However, this embarrassment of riches meant that all four could not be accommodated in the same playing eleven. There was one glorious exception in Birmingham in 1967, when all four played together for the only time. In all other matches, an unfortunate game of musical chairs had to be played and one had to sit out.

Scyld Berry notes in his book *Cricketwallah*, which covered the England tour of India in 1981–82: 'Then occurred one of the strangest coincidences in cricket. A quartet of spinners who were to turn India from a second-rate cricket power into a world force emerged simultaneously in the sixties.' In 1971, when the quartet enjoyed a glorious phase—scripting series victories in West Indies and England—John Arlott paid a handsome tribute when he wrote: 'The Indian spinners are the finest slow-bowling combination, perhaps the most dangerous attack in the contemporary game.'

At home, the spin quartet shaped one victory after another. But their record abroad is outstanding too. In their time together, India won Test series in New Zealand, West Indies and England besides notching up their first victories in Australia. Almost every win was scripted by the quartet. Such was the mastery over their craft that their long reign is hailed as the deification of Indian spin bowling—a status that has never been equalled, let alone surpassed.

Even at the start of the 1978–79 season, there was still no challenger to the quartet for a place in the team. They were all getting on in years but could take comfort from the cricketing adage that spinners mature with age. All four were in the squad when the Indian team visited Pakistan after over seventeen years for a barrier-breaking tour. By then, Prasanna was thirty-eight, Venkat and Chandra were thirty-three and Bedi was thirty-two. They were still respected as bowlers with rich experience and a varied repertoire of tricks.

There was nothing to indicate that the tour would mark the break-up of the longest-serving partnership of spin bowlers the cricketing world has ever known. And yet this was precisely what happened. The placid pitches of Pakistan were perfect for batting and even the vast experience and incomparable skill of the quartet came to nothing. For the first time in the twelve years the famed spin quartet had been playing together, India could not bowl out the opposition even once in a series.

At the end of the series, Chandra had taken 8 wickets at an average of 48 while Bedi's 6 wickets came at an astronomical 75 runs apiece. Prasanna played in two Tests and took only a couple of wickets at the horrendous average of 125. Worse, the series was lost 2-0. The inquests started. Venkat did not play in any of the Tests on that tour, so it was the three others that came under the scanner.

Was their time finally up? Was the quartet finally over the hill? Perhaps the time had come to do the unthinkable and replace one of them with a young untested spinner. During the home series against the West Indies that followed the Pakistan tour, the selectors finally broke up the quartet by bringing in M.V. Narasimha Rao and Dhiraj Parsana to replace Chandra and Bedi. Prasanna was dropped without a replacement. He did not ever play again.

Venkat was now the fulcrum of the spin attack. However, neither Rao nor Parsana impressed, and the selectors fell back on Bedi and Chandra for the tour of England in 1979. But the pressure was already on the group that had now become a trio. Chandra and Bedi were unsuccessful in England and played their last Tests on that tour. That was effectively the end of the spinning 'Fab Four'.

During the transition period, Venkat played three Tests against Australia at home in 1979–80 until the phasing out was completed, with Shivlal Yadav replacing Venkat even as Dilip Doshi finally stepped into Bedi's shoes. Venkat did make a comeback in 1983 and played seven Tests that year. But by then he was well past his best and played what proved to be his last Test in September that year. Yet, even after forty years, for the old-timers who were lucky enough to see this legendary spin quartet in action, the mere mention of the 'Fab Four' makes their eyes sparkle with delight.

14

TIGER PATAUDI

Yajurvindra Singh

On 22 September 2011, I lost one of my heroes and India one of their greatest cricketers. Nawab Mansur Ali Khan of Pataudi, known as 'Tiger' to most, was no more. In January of that year, I had paid a surprise visit to Tiger's home on his seventieth birthday. I had somehow felt that I should be there. It turned out that I was the only guest who was not family. Looking back, I feel so glad to have been there to spend Tiger's last birthday with him as I considered him to be my mentor, friend, supporter and well-wisher. I arrived on the eve of the big day and received a typical Tiger comment: 'What are you doing coming here a day early? Anyway, now that you are here, fix yourself a drink.' He had opened a bottle of malt whisky and—as on numerous occasions before—had explained why the golden liquid was rare and exclusive.

During our many years of friendship, he was always there to impart knowledge, give advice and correct any mistakes I may have made. He knew my family and therefore felt that it was his duty to look after me. I can still recollect the confusion that he created when I made my Test debut in 1977. He told the press that I was his nephew, a comment which was duly published, despite many being perplexed by the idea of a nawab being related to a Hindu prince. When I jokingly confronted him later, he said with his naughty chuckle, 'Let them decipher this one.'

My first encounter with Tiger was in 1964. I was a young boy watching India take on Australia in a Test match in Bombay—a match in which Pataudi scored two scintillating half-centuries and was instrumental in India's astounding win. My grandfather had reserved the entire Patiala Pavilion at the Cricket Club of India for the Test match and the victory celebrations were held there. I was introduced to Tiger as a young aspiring cricketer. He gave me a pat on the back and ruffled my hair, adding a few words of encouragement that convinced me that cricket is the game that I should pursue. After all, the God of Indian cricket had blessed me.

The next time I met Tiger was during the 1973–74 season. I had started playing first-class cricket by then and had been invited me to play for his team as an upcoming youngster in the Pataudi Memorial tournament held in Bhopal. He welcomed me at the breakfast table to make me feel comfortable, and his presence and aura had me completely starstruck. The next exhilarating encounter between us was when we walked out to field. He came to me and asked me where I fielded. Nervously, I replied: 'Anywhere.' 'Well,' he said, 'then you must be a very good fielder, so go and field close to the bat at short-leg.' That was not the position in which I preferred to field but I reluctantly went and stood where told. I took three catches at that position that day.

Tiger was quite impressed and told me that I should make it my permanent fielding position. Any encouragement coming from him would thrill me, so I worked hard to make it my specialized fielding position thereafter. The credit for my record of seven catches in a Test match and five in an innings should go to Tiger—if it were not for him, I would have never stood at what is considered to be a 'suicidal' position. To me, it was fitting that Tiger was present at the ground when I achieved my records. That evening, I could see his eyes expressing the sentiment: 'I told you so!'

During that Pataudi Memorial match, Tiger had asked me where I normally bat. I had replied that I was a middle-order batsman, to which he said, 'Then you may as well open—and make sure you don't get out, as none of us in the middle order want to bat.' Fortunately, I managed to keep my wicket intact. On returning to the pavilion, I received a 'well done' from Tiger. I felt I had passed my first test with the cricketing legend.

We had many wonderful moments over the years. Tiger had a dry sense of humour—there was plenty of mischief in him and he had a personality that made one a jester in his court. His royal upbringing and good looks with the lean physique of an athlete gave him an aura not many could match. He was the Indian cricket captain with a glamorous wife by his side.

Despite being the fittest and fastest on the field, Pataudi was very lazy off it. He loved the good things in life and had servants to cater to all his needs. He hated flying, so he always travelled by train. These journeys with him were experiences to cherish. He had an attendant called Bahadur who ensured that we were always comfortable. If we ran out of ice, water or soda, replenishments were secured promptly when we stopped at the next station. When the nawab decided to eat, the food would be heated at the next stop by Bahadur at one of the facilities at the station—with the train waiting till he was done. He was a superstar for the masses and if the crowd got wind that he was on the train, we would be hounded.

Tiger once tried his hand at politics and lost badly. The main reason for the loss was that he refused to canvass during the election. He felt it below his dignity to go begging for votes from home to home. He was better at playing pranks. He once had some of the Indian cricketers pleading for their lives when he pranked them by having fake 'dacoits' hold them for 'ransom'. Tiger was known for his witty one-liners. There was an incident in which an immigration officer at Heathrow asked Pataudi if anyone could vouch for him in the UK only to receive the reply: 'Yes, the Queen.'

The greatness of Tiger Pataudi is better understood not from his cricket statistics but from the challenge that he overcame to perform at the highest level of the game. When he was just out of college, Pataudi was talked about as one of the most exciting young cricketers of the world. He had scored a scintillating century against Fred Trueman, the world's most dreaded fast bowler of the time. However, shortly thereafter, a car accident led to a tiny glass particle damaging the lens of his right eye.

After such a setback, most people with Tiger's wealthy background would have found solace in their palace and family fortune and abandoned the idea of becoming a professional sportsperson. But the young Nawab of Pataudi was of a different breed. His performances in England before the accident had already put him in contention for a place in the Indian side that was to play England in 1961. He was called for a trial match in which he scored a half-century despite his new disability. It made him a certainty for a Test cap.

Pataudi did not reveal the problems with his vision to the team management. Fortunately for the cricketing world, there were no serious physical fitness tests in those days. Had there been, Tiger's visual impairment would have been found out and he would have lost his place. This was because after his accident, when facing a delivery he would see not one but two balls. Years later, when I asked him how he chose the correct one, he jokingly said that the closer one would be the natural choice.

In those days, cricket was played on uncovered wickets and batters did not wear helmets. The back-foot no-ball rule allowed the bowlers to overstep the front crease and bowl from not 22 but 18 yards. Now imagine seeing *two* balls from the famous fast bowlers of the era racing towards you at over 150 kilometres per hour in these conditions. Tiger decided to cover his bad eye with his cap and go by the vision of only his good one.

Against all odds, Pataudi became one of India's best batsmen of the 1960s. He was the darling of the Indian cricketing world and his slim, graceful build and debonair looks brought thousands of spectators to grace his majesty's durbar, the cricket ground. Today, we all realize the importance of hand–eye coordination after seeing Sachin Tendulkar and Virender Sehwag bat. Pataudi's achievements were all the greater as he overcame a major disability to succeed.

We also admire Dhoni's captaincy in the modern era, but in his time, Pataudi was a shrewd captain who led India to its first overseas Test series win. In fact, he was brought back to play for the country in 1975 only for his captaincy. Apart from his batting, Pataudi was also good in the field and was considered to be one of the best fielders of his time. He made the Indian team believe that they could win. It was under his captaincy that the spin-bowling quartet of Bishan Singh Bedi, Erapalli Prasanna, Bhagwat Chandrasekhar and Srinivas Venkataraghavan, and the batting maestro Gundappa Vishwanath, all blossomed.

Tiger was an avid reader and no matter the condition in which he went to bed, he needed to read before falling asleep. His English was impeccable, and he always kept himself abreast of current affairs. He was a man of few words and only spoke when he was absolutely sure of what he was saying. This meant that challenging him on any subject of his interest was not a good idea. He loved ghazals and on many occasions he invited me to Lucknow to listen to his favourite singer, Begum Akhtar, who was a family friend. Tiger enjoyed Indian food and always said that a cook's ability could only be gauged by how he made a raan. He never ate at banquets as he felt food needed to be relished, and would make it a point to go home to eat.

Tiger Pataudi was my mentor and close friend. He was the one who helped me during my playing days and supported me in all my ventures even after I had retired. To me, he was a superstar and a true hero.

15

SALIM DURRANI:
THE PRINCE CHARMING
OF INDIAN CRICKET

Aditya Bhushan

A player with 1,202 runs at an average of 25.04 along with 75 wickets in twenty-nine Tests would at best be termed a mediocre all-rounder. But with even this record, just the mere mention of Salim Aziz Durrani is enough to bring a smile on the faces of Indian cricket fans of the 1960s and 1970s. A world obsessed with statistics and records would be confused by the hoopla around him. So, one may wonder why he was so aziz (dear) to the Indian cricketing fraternity? To understand this, one needs to look beyond numbers. Had there been a scientific way to measure the impact that a player has on the cricket field, then Salim Bhai (as he is referred to by his friends) would have sat comfortably at the top of the list.

Take for instance the Test win over the West Indies at Port of Spain in 1971, which is still regarded as one of the greatest moments in Indian cricket history. Durrani was at the forefront of that win. Port of Spain had been a happy hunting ground for Durrani as he had scored a century in his previous Test there in 1962. But this time the team needed his skills with the ball. The scorecard will state that Durrani's contribution was just taking a couple of wickets for 21 runs in the second innings. But it fails to communicate the magnitude of those wickets and the impact that it had on the eventual outcome of the Test, which India won by 7 wickets.

After India had taken a lead of 138 in the first innings, the West Indies seemed to be in control at the end of day three with the score at 150 for 1. The slide began on the fourth day with the run-out of Roy Fredericks for 80. And then Durrani came to the fore. Legend has it that the previous night Durrani had told his skipper, Ajit Wadekar, that he would get the wickets of Garry Sobers and Clive Lloyd. And that is what he did.

During my chats with Durrani, he had always downplayed his role. He said, '*Ajit bade ache captain the. Woh jaante the kya karna tha. Unhone socha ki main wicket dila sakta hoon* (Ajit was a good captain. He knew what had to be done. He thought that I could get wickets).' Elaborating further on his wickets, he explained how he had exploited the rough outside the off-stump for the two left-handers. He also credited Wadekar for the catch that he took to dismiss Lloyd. 'Though I got the wicket of Lloyd, I would like to think that it belonged to Ajit. He took the wicket with a spectacular catch,' said Durrani. Even though I had just asked him to talk about the wickets that he had taken, being the humble man that he is, Durrani didn't forget to mention that it was on that tour that India had found its future hero, Sunil Gavaskar.

Interestingly, Durrani had not bowled a single delivery in the first innings. But people who knew him were not astonished by his impact in the second innings as he had the knack of crafting brilliance out of nothing. About ten years previously, he had been instrumental in scripting back-to-back wins over England in Calcutta and Madras. At Eden Gardens in the former game, he had taken 8 wickets, and at Chepauk in the latter he had a 10-wicket haul.

If Durrani was an artist with the ball, he was a magician with the bat. He was different from most players of his generation and did not mind hitting the ball in the air, being renowned for his six-hitting ability. When the crowd yelled for sixes, he would often oblige them with a few hits over the fence. Durrani relished his game and provided supreme entertainment to the fans. So, it's not a surprise that he was the darling of the crowd. The tall and handsome Durrani also had charm and could make an emotional connection with the fans. For him, one could say that cricket was not just a game—it was an emotion.

When he was dropped in 1973 for the Tests against England, the crowd brought placards to the stadium that read: 'No Durrani, no Test!' Unfortunately, being in and out of the team was something that he had to bear with throughout his career. In fact, he was not selected for the Indian team between 1966 and 1970. He lamented this in an interview to *Sportstar* much later, saying that he could not pinpoint a reason for not being considered during that period: '*Samaj main nahi aa raha hai* (I don't understand it). I did not talk to anyone. The teams were selected, and they left.'

Nevertheless, Durrani was happy to have played a part in many Indian victories and was satisfied with his first-class career of twenty-five years. He had no regrets—and given his contributions to Indian cricket, he shouldn't have any. In his retirement, he led a quiet life in Jamnagar, Gujarat. I will never forget his hospitality when I visited his house in 2017 for an interview. Not surprisingly, I just had to ask for the home of Salim Durrani to locate his house, even in the absence of any house number or building name. He treated me not just to home-made delicacies but also stories from his playing days.

One after another, enchanting stories flew like sixes from his bat. He smoked a cigarette and narrated anecdotes with childlike enthusiasm. Watching the cigarette smoke rise in the air, I could not stop myself from visualizing him singing the famous Hindi movie song that went: '*Main zindagi ka saath nibhata chala gaya* (I just kept on going with life), *Har fiqr ko dhuen mein udata chala gaya* (Every worry, I blew it into smoke).' Incidentally, Durrani did star in a movie named *Charitra* with Parveen Babi in 1973.

At one point during my conversation with him, he took me to the dining room. There, one wall was covered with his photographs. Durrani told me in detail about each of the photos. There was a shine in his eyes as he spoke about his photo with the Duleep Trophy in 1970. Apparently, his great run in the Duleep Trophy that year had led a journalist to label it as the 'Durrani Trophy'. He laughed when he recalled that anecdote.

When I asked him about his favourite cricketer, he responded immediately with a chuckle: 'Salim Durrani!' We both burst into laughter. Then he added, 'On a serious note, I liked many cricketers, and India has produced many great cricketers. I don't believe in comparing cricketers of different eras. But Vinoo (Mankad) Bhai was special for me. Perhaps it is because I grew up watching him play in Jamnagar.'

It was Vinoo Mankad who was instrumental in shaping Durrani's early days as a cricketer. There is a story that after watching Durrani play a fine innings, the Maharaja of Udaipur had asked Mankad who the player was and if he would go to Rajasthan. So, Mankad went and asked Durrani, '*Tu ayega mere saath* (Will you come with me)?' Durrani asked him where he wanted to go, to which Mankad replied, 'Udaipur.' The rest, as they say, is history. He played Ranji Trophy for Rajasthan for twenty-two years, from 1956 to 1978. During this incredibly successful period for Durrani, he guided Rajasthan to five Ranji Trophy finals.

Of course, he also had a lot of help from his father, Aziz Durrani, who was also a cricketer. Aziz had represented India in an unofficial Test match against Australia in the 1935–36 season. He had migrated to Pakistan after Partition and is credited with being the coach of the great Hanif Mohammad. Thankfully for Indian fans, Salim Bhai stayed back in India.

Those who have not seen Durrani play can gauge the joy that he gave to the fans by the incident related by former cricketer Raju Mukherji. According to Mukherji, even fifty years after Durrani last played for India, people in Calcutta are still crazy about him. When Mukherji was working on a book on the 150th anniversary of Eden Gardens in 2014, a cricket addict said to him, 'I will buy the book only if Durrani's photo is on the cover. No one was more popular than Durrani at Eden.'

It's not just the fans. Durrani was loved by one and all in Indian cricketing circles. I understood this when one common question arose in many meetings with former cricketers: 'You met Salim Bhai?' they would ask with a deep sense of respect. They would then inquire about his well-being and fondly remember the times spent with this genius. In fact, the great off-spinner Erapalli Prasanna went to the extent of telling me that the only reason he would read my book is because he saw his friend Salim Bhai's photo in it.

Durrani's heroics on the cricket field used to entertain people in the stands and now his photo is enough to draw readers to a book. To make people happy is a unique quality that he was blessed with. Salim Durrani will forever be remembered as Indian cricket's Prince Charming!

16

SUNIL GAVASKAR: THE LITTLE GIANT

Milind Rege

Whenever we cricketers indulge in picking an all-time World XI, two Indians are always on that list—the two 'kars', Sunil Gavaskar and Sachin Tendulkar. But what makes these two names inevitable choices? Is it their grit? Determination? Talent? Courage? I guess it is all these factors put together, because Gavaskar and Tendulkar were both amply blessed with each of these qualities.

I have known Gavaskar for over seventy years. We were neighbours in a modest middle-class neighbourhood and played cricket all year round in a quadrangle where the only scoring shot was the straight drive. Anything that was hit above the ground-floor level was declared 'out'. Gavaskar hated that rule, but I guess that was the beginning of his transformation into a player who preferred ground shots to lofted ones.

Apart from his batting technique, Gavaskar's standout quality was his power of concentration. To my mind, that is the most important ability for any sportsman. He was relentless, batting for hours in tennis-ball cricket from the age of ten. In fact, on most occasions, we had to cheat to get him out. He would sulk as he hated cheating.

Gavaskar heard stories of great batsmanship from his uncle, the former Indian cricketer Madhav Mantri, who would regale us with tales about Vijay Merchant on weekends. The young Gavaskar once tried on his uncle's India cap for which he was chided. I guess he decided that day that he would adorn the India cap only when he deserved it.

At St Xavier's high school, all our cricket was played on torn matting. He represented his school at the age of twelve. In his first-ever knock, he batted at No. 10, facing players twice his size! I was No. 11 that day. Despite getting a mention in *The Times of India*—'G. Sunil not out 30'—he was disappointed at batting so low in the order and asked to bat at a higher position.

Eventually, the chairman of the city's school cricket, Khandu Rangnekar—who toured Australia with the Indian team in 1948— invited Vijay Manjrekar to watch Madhav's nephew. Manjrekar pronounced that Bombay would have a great player. Gavaskar had earned the headline: 'A prodigy has arrived in the true legacy of Bombay batsmanship.' The prophecy was to come true.

Gavaskar was never coached the way cricketers are today. He learnt the basics from his father, Manohar—who was a prominent club-level batsman—while his uncle Mantri gave him lessons in mental toughness and made him understand the value of the India cap. Others such as Vasant Amladi and Luma Kenny also played a big role in his formative years and later he received guidance from Vijay Manjrekar, Vinoo Mankad and Raj Singh Dungarpur.

Then T.S. Worthington, the Derbyshire opening batsman, was asked by the BCCI to coach a bunch of lads who were to tour the UK as the India Schools representative team. I was part of the contingent, along with Gavaskar and Surinder and Mohinder Amarnath, among others. We had a two-month camp in Hyderabad during which Worthington taught Sunil the art of opening the batting.

Once I was facing a fiery spell from Karsan Ghavri and was struggling to put bat on ball. I asked the maestro batting with me about what I should do. Gavaskar smiled and said to watch his feet when he faced Ghavri. It became easier to face Ghavri after that!

As a person, Sunil is a true friend, always supportive and helpful with no expectations in return. Once he makes a commitment, he never changes his mind. He is easy-going and always great fun at parties. On one such occasion at Ravi Shastri's residence, West Indian greats Viv Richards, Gordon Greenidge and Malcolm Marshall were present. We were all having a great time when Sunil walked in. The foreign cricketers stood and saluted, and Viv said, 'The master has arrived.' Such was the admiration for the little giant.

17

GUNDAPPA VISHWANATH:
THE PEOPLE'S CHAMPION

R. Kaushik

Some sportspersons cannot be judged by mere statistics and numbers, however impressive they might be. They are the ones who entertain and exhilarate, excite and enthral, providing joy through the expression of their craft. They leave behind memories that last a lifetime. Gundappa Vishwanath, the pint-sized batsman from Bengaluru, is such a sportsperson—one who does justice to the label of 'genius'.

Born in the steel town of Bhadravati some 250 kilometres from the Karnataka capital, 'Vishy' was inner steel couched in an affable, ever-smiling persona that won him nearly as many fans as his mesmeric batting did. If Sunil Gavaskar lent respect and identity to the Indian batting in the 1970s with his wonderful technique, immense powers of concentration and the ability to blunt the most potent of attacks, then Vishy provided the 'wow' factor, almost apologetically dismantling the best in the word with a magical twirl of his wondrous wrists.

He moved to Bangalore at a young age, where he was brought up on a steady diet of tennis-ball cricket on matting surfaces. This led to Vishy becoming a master of back-foot play almost by default. Playing with 'soft hands'—among the more prominent phrases in the current lexicon of cricket—came naturally to him, and because he was slightly built and lacking in power, he relied more on the areas behind the stumps to score runs. As a result, the square-cut became his go-to stroke. Over time, the stroke became synonymous with him, and nearly two-thirds of his 6,080 Test runs came through his trademark square-cut. However, though the square-cut is the shot Vishy is most associated with, the man himself loved the square drive as much, if not more.

Vishwanath had the knack not only of being in the right place at the right time but also of making a deep impression on the men who matter. In his case, these men were the two stalwarts of Indian cricket at the time—national captain Tiger Pataudi and his great friend and trusted lieutenant, M.L. Jaisimha.

Overlooked for the Mysore state schools' team because of his small stature—the Chairman of Selectors Dr K. Thimmappaiah infamously justified his decision by saying, 'What will I tell his parents if something happens to him?'—Vishwanath grew under the patronage of Chandra Shetty, a cricket enthusiast who was completely bowled over by the young lad's composure and skills. Shetty, who ran a cricket club in the local league, fast-tracked Vishy's career by enrolling him in Spartans Cricket Club. The young Vishwanath responded with a string of big scores that caught the attention of the state selectors.

The Indian team touring Australia in 1967–68 had several players from Mysore, and the state was already out of contention for a knockout berth in the Ranji Trophy. These circumstances allowed the selectors to try out a youngster, and Vishy was drafted in for the final game of the season against Andhra in Vijayawada. It was November 1967 and Vishy was not yet nineteen.

Pencilled in at No. 4, he shuffled to the middle at 15 for 2 inside the first hour. When he left the ground at close of play six hours later, he was unbeaten on 209. He had announced his arrival in grand style, but he was not yet finished. The next day, he took his score to 230—at the time the highest individual score on Ranji Trophy debut—before he was finally dismissed. The world was his oyster now.

Vishy has often spoken about how that knock was the first big turning point of his career. 'It catalysed a change in my thinking, attitude and mindset,' he said. 'It suggested to me that I was closer to realizing my ambition of playing for India than I was even two days before that knock and proved to me that I was not mistaken in trusting my skills and ability to score runs at every higher grade. I have several cherished memories of my performances for India, but this is the one innings that will forever remain number one in my eyes.'

The record-breaking double-hundred had made influential figures in Indian cricket aware of the presence down south of a pocket-sized dynamo with a scimitar for a willow. His stunning exploits on debut opened several doors, including a job offer from the State Bank of India—where he would play alongside several stalwarts of Indian cricket—but more importantly, it also made an impression on Pataudi.

Vishy went on to make attractive, composed runs in difficult batting conditions, first for Mysore against Indian skipper Pataudi, who was playing for Hyderabad under Jaisimha, and then alongside Pataudi for South Zone in the Duleep Trophy. Having witnessed these performances first-hand, the Indian captain was convinced that Vishwanath was the real deal. Chairman of Selectors Vijay Merchant wasn't so sure, not having seen Vishy in a match, but Pataudi put his foot down.

In November 1969—two years after his first-class debut—Vishy was selected for the second Test against Australia in Kanpur. Understandably, he was a bundle of nerves in his first-ever international match and was dismissed without scoring in the first innings. He feared that his Test career was over before it had even begun. Reassuring words from Pataudi between innings restored his confidence somewhat. Vishy responded to his captain's faith with a memorable 137 in the second innings. The little man was here to stay.

Until the ill-fated tour of Pakistan in early 1983, for over thirteen years Vishy formed the bedrock of the Indian batting alongside Gavaskar, the brothers-in-law adopting contrasting methods in their desire to drive the team forward. At the top of the order, Gavaskar was the immovable object, lending solidity and reassurance and an extraordinary sense of calm; at No. 4, Vishy was the irresistible force, an amalgam of dextrous wrists, strong forearms and nimble feet.

Pataudi's influence on Vishy's career extended beyond pressing for his selection. After he first saw Vishy bat—in a Ranji Trophy game at the Central College grounds in Bangalore—Pataudi advised the young man to work on strengthening his weak wrists by lifting buckets of water at home. Vishy initially suspected that it was another of the acknowledged practical joker's pranks; it took him some time to realize that Pataudi was being serious. He immediately put that advice into practice and saw instant results—when batting, his cuts began packing more punch and in the field, his throws thudded into the wicketkeeper's gloves with ferocity.

Buoyed by his debut hundred and secure in the knowledge that he had realized his biggest ambition of playing for his country, Vishy went about entertaining crowds the world over. His humility instantly endeared him to many, but it was when he started wielding his willow with sweeping arcs that scythed through the air and dismissed the ball from his presence that he left audiences in a trance. He wasn't always the most consistent—it took him thirteen Tests and more than three years to become the first Indian debut centurion to score a second Test ton. It was a milestone that even opposition captain Tony Greig celebrated—by effortlessly lifting the little fella and cradling him at the Brabourne Stadium in Bombay.

Vishy's career was destined to be played out under the giant shadow of Gavaskar—a relentless run-maker who eschewed risks very early into his international career once he understood that the Indian batting revolved around him, and went on to become the first in history to score 10,000 Test runs. But Gavaskar himself has said that Vishy was the best Indian batsman of his generation. After the former blunted and wore down fierce opponents, Vishy got on top of them and imposed himself, playing some of the most defining knocks by an Indian batsman of his generation—much like V.V.S. Laxman was to do more than three decades later.

It's no coincidence that India never lost a Test when Vishy made a hundred. He scored fourteen centuries in ninety-one matches—and none of them was what is uncharitably called a 'cheap' hundred. The times when his team had their backs to the wall and the opponents were scenting blood were the ones that seemed to bring the best out of him. He responded not by grafting or grinding but by taking the attack to the bowling. This approach was best exemplified by perhaps the greatest-ever innings that fell short of a hundred.

It was January 1975 and India were in all kinds of strife at 76 for 6 on a spicy deck at the M.A. Chidambaram Stadium in Madras against a West Indian attack that had Andy Roberts in all his fury. Roberts had taken four of the wickets on the first day, and was ably supported by Keith Boyce, Bernard Julien and Vanburn Holder. That was when Vishy decided it was time to show them who was boss—he unleashed a couple of whip-drives from off-stump off Roberts and two wonderful punches off the back foot against Boyce. The latter two shots hurtled past the bowler and crossed the boundary so quickly that the slip cordon was left with open-mouthed astonishment. The slip fielders were none other than Clive Lloyd, Viv Richards and Alvin Kallicharran—no mean batsmen themselves.

First with Karsan Ghavri, then alongside Bishan Bedi, Vishy steered India towards a respectable total. He was finally left stranded three runs away from his century when his good pal B.S. Chandrasekhar was caught behind off Roberts. By Vishy's own estimation, his 97 not out easily trumped a hundred, and those who were at Chepauk that afternoon simply couldn't stop talking about that knock. It was an effort that catapulted him to superstardom in Madras—where he was to later register his highest Test score of 222.

A knee injury prevented Vishwanath from fulfilling his bowling potential—his leg-spin fetched him only 15 first-class wickets, although he did have a 4-wicket haul in 50-over cricket. His sole Test victim was Jim Higgs, coincidentally himself a leg-spinner from Australia. But thankfully the bad knee didn't prevent Vishy from scoring runs all over the world against various attacks in all kinds of conditions. As much as the impressive volume of runs, it was his sinuous grace that captivated the connoisseur. With greatness sitting lightly on his slender shoulders, Vishy wowed West Indian legends Garry Sobers and Rohan Kanhai, his original hero Neil Harvey and even Don Bradman himself.

An inveterate walker who never waited for the umpire's decision when he knew he was out, Vishy came to be known as a gentleman cricketer who always showed respect for the game and the opposition. Nowhere is his popularity more evident than at the Chinnaswamy Stadium in Karnataka's capital city, where life comes to a standstill when he comes calling and where he is treated like royalty by veterans and kids alike. Yet, he remains a humble champion who fills rooms with his diminutive yet towering presence.

Vishy only led India in two Tests—against Pakistan in Calcutta and in the Jubilee Test against England in Bombay. Neither was without incident. In the first, opposition captain Asif Iqbal picked up the coin after the toss without allowing his counterpart to have a look at which way it had landed—only to tell a stunned Vishy that it was the Indian skipper who had won the toss. In the second Test, with England completely on the back foot, Vishy recalled Bob Taylor after he and most of the Indian team believed that the wicketkeeper had been erroneously given out. Taylor and Ian Botham turned the Test on its head and spearheaded a famous fightback that drove England to victory. Yet, Vishy maintains even today that he doesn't regret his decision to withdraw the appeal against Taylor. 'To win that way wouldn't have been satisfying,' he says. 'That's not how I wanted to play cricket.'

Vishwanath was integral to the Karnataka team that won its first Ranji Trophy title in 1974. It was a time when national team players were able and willing to represent their states and clubs. Vishy drew crowds by the thousands to first-class and club

matches in Bangalore and his battles in the Ranji Trophy with
S. Venkataraghavan and Bishan Bedi—half of the famed spin
quartet—are the stuff of legend. The other two of the quartet—
Erapalli Prasanna and B.S. Chandrasekhar—played for Vishy's
team, which meant that any great battles with them were restricted
to the nets.

For a purist who had no taste of limited-overs cricket at the
international level during the first few years of his career, Vishy
found it hard to take that format seriously. However, he did play
in the first two ODI World Cups in England. Unsurprisingly,
his highest ODI score of 75 came in completely bowler-friendly
conditions. At the 1979 World Cup, the West Indian pace battery
of Michael Holding, Andy Roberts, Joel Garner, Colin Croft and
Collis King were breathing fire upon India in Birmingham. Vishy
battled for over two hours, all the while relishing the challenge of
testing himself against the best even as his mates crumbled around
him. The next-highest contribution in India's 190 all-out was
16—from the 'extras' column. While there was disappointment at
not taking the team to a more sizeable tally, Vishy took pride in
having taken on the might of the Caribbean pacemen.

An ordinary tour of Pakistan in 1983 saw Vishy dropped for
the subsequent tour of the West Indies. He never again received a
call-up to the national side. By then, he had played eighty-seven
Tests without missing any, which was a tribute to his fitness in an
era in which it wasn't given the importance it gets today. Vishy
continued to play domestic cricket for five more seasons, both in
the hope that he might nudge the selectors with a mountain of
runs and to guide the surfeit of youngsters who had broken into the
Karnataka Ranji team. While he succeeded in his second objective,
the primary aim remained unfulfilled.

After retirement, Vishy donned several cricketing hats. He served as manager of the national team, as a national selector—and then as chairman of the senior selection panel, as an International Cricket Council (ICC) match referee, as an administrator and as the head of the Karnataka Cricket Academy. By this time, he had been bitten by the golf bug. At every opportunity, he would hit golf courses in Bangalore and beyond, enjoying smacking a stationary ball as much as he did the ones hurled at him at more than 140 kilometres per hour.

Vishy has also dabbled in Kannada commentary on television, where his natural and quick wit have endeared him to audiences and where he continues to hold his own even among much younger commentators. In his early days, Vishy's fascination for newspapers was driven by the desire to see his name in print for his exploits in the local leagues. He quickly progressed from a passing mention to a screaming headline and to this day, he confesses to a gentle thrill when his name appears in the papers.

Vishwanath always has time, patience and a broad smile for anyone who stops him for a selfie—which has replaced the autograph as the memento of choice for today's generation. For all the jaw-dropping shots he played, Vishy will be loved more as the people's champion—an approachable and relatable hero who often doesn't seems to acknowledge his own greatness. He may no longer delight with the willow, but he continues to charm and entertain his vast legion of supporters.

18

AFTER THE KISS

Abbas Ali Baig

Having taken a shower after the fifth day's play of the third Test in Mumbai, content that India had saved the match against Australia, I relaxed happily with the thought that I had left the kissing saga on 6 January 1960 well behind on the field. But to my great bewilderment, this was not to be. A gentle knock on the door led to my finding a respectable-looking elderly gentleman standing outside, along with a few pretty young ladies. I knew him as a senior Board official; maybe at one time he was a member of the selection committee.

Before I could ask him in for a cup of tea, he said that he had a request to make. The lovely young ladies with him were from respectable families and were watching the match from one of the guest boxes—and they would be very happy if I would allow each of them individually to do what the naughty girl had so boldly done on the field, that too in front of some 50,000 spectators.

And this would be done quietly in my room with no prying eyes distracting from the action.

This put me in a bit of dilemma, but considering the seniority of the gentleman making the request and the fact that the ladies were quite eye-catching and seemed eager to get on with the job, I agreed. One after another, the ladies and I 'went through the process'. The gentleman, having set the ball rolling, had beaten a dignified retreat. He was to remain a well-wisher and friend all through the rest of my career.

The reason I am recounting this incident is not to brag about the fact that some young ladies found me worthy of their affection, but to point out that even in those days—when restraint and strict discipline were given great importance—there were people in responsible positions who were sensitive to the wishes of the followers of the game and were broad-minded and bold enough to help them in whichever small way they could. In this case, young followers of the game had had their innocent and harmless wishes fulfilled.

It is another matter that years later I ran into one of those young ladies, who was by then the wife of a longtime friend. Neither of us was embarrassed about our past encounter. Cricket certainly teaches us to live in the now, learning from the multiple ifs and buts that life habitually thrusts upon us and cheerfully marching on, imbibing only the positives to compile a well-earned century.

19

MY THEATRE OF DREAMS

Dilip Vengsarkar (in conversation with Aditya Bhushan)

Sometimes in life, the start doesn't show what is to come. My relationship with Lord's is an example of this. When I got out for a duck in my first outing at Lord's, I never thought that this was would be the beginning of a beautiful alliance. It was 1979 and we were bowled out for just 96 in the first innings at the mecca of cricket. Thus, I was understandably nervous when stepping out to bat in the second essay.

Batting in England tests one's skills and the match situation with our backs against the wall only made it tougher. By grace of God and my own determination, I was able to forge a partnership with Vishy (Gundappa Vishwanath) and save the game for India. In the process, both Vishy and I scored centuries. I was satisfied that we had weathered the storm, seen out the English bowlers and avoided a defeat.

Three years passed before my next match at this prestigious venue, but from a cricket perspective, there didn't seem much of

110

a change—we found ourselves in a similarly dire situation. After England scored 433 in their first innings, our innings folded at 128. My own contribution was a meagre 2 runs. So, yet again, there was tremendous pressure when I walked in to bat in the second innings.

I got good support from Yashpal (Sharma), but in the end it wasn't enough. Though I was able to score my second century at Lord's, we lost the Test. I was disappointed. For me, the satisfaction comes not just from scoring a hundred but also from the impact that my knock makes in the game. My first two centuries at Lord's had not led to an Indian victory and I wanted to change that script.

The opportunity to rewrite history arrived in 1986. Our morale was quite high after we had won the 1985 Benson & Hedges World Championship of Cricket in Australia. But this was a different format and in a different country. History was also against us. In India's previous ten encounters at Lord's, we had never emerged victorious.

Like on the previous tour in 1982, it was early summer in England—a time when the ball seams quite a bit. Thankfully, many of us had played in England earlier, so we knew how to get acclimatized to these conditions quickly. Kapil Dev won the toss and invited England to bat first. Riding on (Graham) Gooch's century, the home side made 294. In response, we lost (Kris) Srikkanth early.

When I walked in to bat, the score was 31. I had some useful partnerships with Sunil (Gavaskar), Jimmy (Mohinder Amarnath) and Azhar (Mohammed Azharuddin). I must say that Azhar had come out as a hugely talented player and had lots of shots in his repertoire. Unfortunately for us, after Azhar's wicket there was a slide. We found ourselves eight down with 264 on the board. Debutant Kiran More hung around for a bit and we added a useful 39-run partnership for the ninth wicket.

When last man Maninder (Singh) came out, I was still 5 runs short of my century. But more than the century, the priority for me was to score as many runs as possible and get a sizeable lead to gain that psychological advantage. Luckily, Maninder gave me good company, much to the dismay of the English bowlers. We got a lead of 47 runs, and I also reached my third century in as many matches at Lord's.

When England came into bat in the second innings, Kapil was in full flow and reduced them to 35 for 3. Maninder also chipped in with wickets and the home side were bowled out for 180. This meant that we had to chase 134. After few hiccups, we eventually chased down the target with 5 wickets in hand.

The headquarters of cricket had been conquered and we were over the moon. I remember that Colin Cowdrey and the Maharaja of Baroda were in our dressing room to congratulate us. We went to the balcony and the people downstairs were dancing, shouting our names. It was a great sight and a wonderful atmosphere.

Lord's has a rich tradition and the atmosphere is absolutely electrifying. But this victory had made it even better. Like any other cricketer, it was my dream to score a century at Lord's. Although I have enjoyed all the matches I have played here, the one in the summer of 1986 was special. The elusive victory had been won and I was a satisfied man. Lord's has indeed been my 'Theatre of Dreams'!

20

KARSAN GHAVRI: THE COMEBACK KING

Clayton Murzello

Karsan Ghavri was known as a Bombay cricketer because that was the team for which he played the most first-class matches, but his career started off with Saurashtra. Bombay had asked him to play for them after he impressed Ajit Wadekar in some Ranji Trophy league matches against them. Moving to Bombay meant that he had to have a job—Polly Umrigar helped by arranging for the Associated Cement Companies (ACC) to employ him. But there were still challenges as he hailed from a small town. It took some convincing for Ghavri's family, especially his grandfather, in Rajkot to allow him to move to Bombay.

At first, he stayed with a family in Bombay. Despite their hospitality, he felt uncomfortable. The family then asked him if he would be more at home in the office of their estate in Dadar West. That suited him much better, even if it meant sleeping on a large desk and then converting the area from a 'bedroom' into office space each morning before the caretaker walked in. One day, the caretaker arrived earlier than usual and found Ghavri still 'in bed'. The kind man found him a place to rent in Matunga West. Ghavri moved and was still living there even after making his India debut.

On days when there were no matches, he had to report to the ACC office. Ghavri would kill time sitting at Chowpatty Beach before eventually heading to work. He had an outrageous dress sense, which didn't miss the attention of an ACC bigwig while in a lift at their Churchgate office. His bright yellow shirts were soon replaced by proper office wear after a visit to a clothing shop in Flora Fountain.

Apart from inter-office cricket, Ghavri played club cricket for Parsi Cyclists. Luncheon intervals during home Kanga League matches were spent at a Churchgate restaurant that served biryani and beer. Post-lunch dropped catches by the Parsi Cyclists team were often attributed to the excesses during the break. Ghavri made his Bombay debut in the 1973–74 season. Clashing with his former team, Saurashtra, was inevitable. And when he did, he claimed 2 for 27 and 5 for 36 in an innings victory for Sunil Gavaskar's team at the Brabourne Stadium.

The following season saw Ghavri selected for the national team for the third Test against the West Indies in Calcutta. India had lost the opening two Tests in Bangalore and New Delhi, and the opening bowlers in those matches, Abid Ali and Eknath Solkar, were replaced by Ghavri and Madan Lal. Ghavri could only get a solitary wicket in the first innings and it was not one of the big West Indian batters.

In India's second innings, Ghavri was unbeaten on 5 at stumps on the third day. The selectors gave Ghavri advice on how to bat the next day. His captain, M.A.K. Pataudi, watched them silently.

As soon as the 'wise men' had left, Pataudi pulled Ghavri aside and told him not to bother about what advice had been given to him and just play his natural game. The next day, with India still needing runs in the second innings, Ghavri hit a precious 27 before Andy Roberts castled him.

In the next Test at Madras, Ghavri got the best view of Gundappa Viswanath's courageous, grand and epic 97 not out. 'Vishy's bravado against the West Indian quicks was unbelievable,' Ghavri recalls. 'It must go down as one of the greatest innings in Test cricket.' Ghavri managed only 12 in India's total of 190, but in the second innings, he helped himself to 35. Though his sole victim of the Test was the dangerous opener Roy Fredericks, Ghavri had plenty to smile about because he was part of a rare Indian victory—one which brought them level in the series after being 2-0 down.

The Wankhede Stadium's inaugural Test was to be the decider. India had never been close to winning a Test series against the West Indies at home and this one was going to be tough. The men from the Caribbean were skippered by a man on a mission—Clive Lloyd led from the front with an unbeaten 242 in the first innings. Ghavri claimed his best figures of the series (4 for 140), dismissing Gordon Greenidge (32), Alvin Kallicharran (98), Vanburn Holder (5) and Deryck Murray (91). He got Lloyd in the second innings for 37 before India collapsed 201 runs short of the target. There were several batsmen who were either great or on their way to greatness in that West Indies side. But for Ghavri, Kallicharran stood out. 'Kalli used to come in and nudge a few around,' he recalls, 'and before you knew it, he'd have scored 40 or 50.'

Ghavri, although part of the inaugural ODI World Cup in England, was not picked for the 1975–76 tour of the West Indies.

He made his Test comeback against the touring New Zealand team the following season. Switching to left-arm spin against England, he bagged his first 5-wicket haul in the 1976–77 Bombay Test against Tony Greig's team despite questions about his action. 'The fact that Ghavri, with left-arm spin, purveyed with an action that caused eyebrows to be raised, took five wickets, and Prasanna, Bedi and Chandra only one between them, shows how India's famous had an abortive last day,' wrote John Woodcock in the *Cricketer International*. Two years later, Ghavri's action would come into focus again during a tour game against Leicestershire on the 1979 tour of England. His 5 for 23 helped skittle out the county side for 81. Dicky Rutnagur reported in *Sportsweek* magazine that Ghavri struck four batsmen in various parts of the body and the players who had toured India in 1976–77 raised a storm about his action.

Ghavri's career-best innings figures of 7 for 34 was in a Ranji quarter-final against Haryana in 1976–77. The opposition included a young Kapil Dev, who would go on to form a new-ball partnership with Ghavri for the national team that never once allowed an opposition's opening pair to put on a century partnership. The Ranji final that season was against Bishan Singh Bedi's Delhi at the Kotla. It was a memorable game for Ghavri with both bat and ball.

Bombay were five down for 145 when Ghavri was asked to get stuck into the wily Bedi. He later revealed that skipper Gavaskar had offered him his bat to combat the formidable Sardar of Spin. Ghavri responded by scoring 61 with 7 fours and 2 sixes. Bombay ended up with 317 and Delhi fell short by 26 to concede the first-innings lead. In Bombay's second innings, no batsman could surpass Ghavri's unbeaten 70.

Delhi was set a target of 251 but Ghavri sent back Chetan Chauhan with what Gavaskar called a 'nasty lifter' in *Sportsweek* later, before dishing out a 'killer' bouncer to Venkat Sundaram with the next ball. The hosts succumbed to a 129-run loss. At the trophy ceremony, Gavaskar let Ghavri hold the silverware. Later, he wrote: 'When I handed over the Ranji Trophy to Karsan Ghavri, it was just my way of saying "thank you" to this strong young man who magnificently responded to everything I asked for.'

Ghavri didn't have much of a say on the 1977–78 tour of Australia until the series-deciding fifth Test at Adelaide, in which he claimed 7 wickets with pace and spin. India had again levelled a series after losing the first two Tests, but like in 1974–75 against the West Indies, India lost the final Test. However, they came close to pulling off a chase of 493, having been 415 for 6 before Ghavri was dismissed for 23.

A disappointing tour of Pakistan in late 1978 was followed by a fruitful home series against Kallicharran's West Indians. With 27 scalps in six Tests, Ghavri was a happy man again and deserved the plaudits. He enjoyed bowling on the pace-friendly Chepauk pitch in a match that India won by 3 wickets. Jamaican Herbert Chang was out hit-wicket in that game, Ghavri's delivery hitting him on the head off a top edge before he lost balance and landed on the stumps.

The following season, Ghavri enjoyed successes against the touring Australian and Pakistani teams. In the sixth Test against the Australians at Bombay, Ghavri smashed 86 after coming in at No. 9 to boost India's first innings total to 458 for 8 declared, which helped India achieve its first-ever series victory over Australia. Ghavri went wicketless in the first innings of the third Test against Pakistan, but then sent back Majid Khan, Mudassar Nazar, Wasim Raja and Imran Khan in the second innings as they unsuccessfully chased 322 for victory at the Wankhede Stadium.

Along with the Melbourne Test of 1981, this performance against Pakistan ranks among Ghavri's finest moments of his career. 'Yes, getting those wickets in Bombay and dismissing Greg Chappell in both innings at Melbourne were both great, but what is important is that the team won,' claims Ghavri. 'We hadn't beaten Pakistan in a Test since 1952 and it was incredible to beat them in Bombay. The Melbourne victory was the first time India had squared a series Down Under and it was nothing short of amazing.'

Ghavri became India's first fast bowler to claim 100 Test wickets. However, after that Melbourne Test in which he had dismissed the illustrious Greg Chappell twice, he was dropped after playing only one more match. If one asks Ghavri about why he was overlooked after the Tests against New Zealand in 1981, he replies with the promise: 'I'll reveal that in my book.' After he was no longer selected for the national team, Ghavri focused on making an impression in first-class cricket.

After figuring in Bombay's innings victory over Bengal in the 1981–82 Ranji Trophy quarter-final, Ghavri was not in the playing XI for the semi-finals against Karnataka in Bangalore. The media was told that Ghavri wasn't fit, which enraged the bowler. He decided to leave Bombay and played the rest of his first-class career back home with Saurashtra till his retirement at the end of the 1984–85 season. Ghavri's association with Bombay cricket didn't end, though. He still played the Times Shield for Nirlon until that star-studded team was disbanded. Ghavri also had success as manager of Ravi Shastri's 1993–94 Bombay team that won the Ranji Trophy.

He won yet another Ranji title in 2019–20 as coach of Saurashtra just before cricket and life got disrupted by COVID-19.

When cricket was back to normalcy, Ghavri spoke out in the media about how Saurashtra shouldn't miss out on the Irani Cup game, even though there was a new Ranji Trophy champion in Madhya Pradesh. The BCCI found merit in Ghavri's suggestion of having a combined Ranji champions team to take on Rest of India and decided to organize a Saurashtra vs Rest of India match in 2022–23.

There's a quality Ghavri has that often goes unnoticed—he always wants to give credit where it's due. For years now he has been urging authorities at the Mumbai Cricket Association to make a correction in the records section of the Kanga League fixtures books handed out to cricketers annually. 'K. Ghavri' features as a hat-trick taker when it should be Dhanji Ghavri, Karsan's brother, who bagged three Dadar Union SC wickets in three balls while representing Sunder Cricket Club in the 'A' division of Bombay's best-loved tournament in 1977. It's particularly important for Karsan as Dhanji is deceased.

Karsan Ghavri's heart has always been in the right place. His teammates, captains and even opposition players would vouch for that.

21

KAPIL DEV: PLAYING IT STRAIGHT

Yajurvindra Singh

Kapil Dev Nikhanj has been appropriately referred to as the 'Haryana Hurricane'. A cricketer par excellence, his achievements on the field led to two distinct and significant legacies in Indian cricket. The first was the belief that an Indian could be one of the best pace bowlers in the world. The other was the realization that Indian cricketers had the mental and physical strength to compete at the highest level. A carefree attitude in combination with genius cricketing skills made Kapil one of the all-time greats of the game. However, the path he took towards his success makes one admire him more.

My times playing with and against Kapil Dev have been unforgettable. We first played against each other in a Duleep Trophy final in 1977. I had just become an Indian Test cricketer, while Kapil was a young North Zone fast bowler yet to make his

120

mark. A few months later, Raj Singh Dungarpur—a cricketer and cricket connoisseur who later became president of the BCCI—was taking a cricket team to Kenya. The team was led by Tiger Pataudi and among the travelling squad were Sunil Gavaskar, Gundappa Vishwanath, Dilip Vengsarkar, Aunshuman Gaekwad, Eknath Solkar, Brijesh Patel, Parthasarathy Sharma, Syed Kirmani, Suru Nayak and myself. A couple of days before our departure, Raj Singh asked me to look after a young cricketer who would be on the tour. His name was Kapil Dev.

Although we had played against each other recently, I had very little recollection of him. Kapil Dev was not in the initial squad, but he had gone to Raj Singh's residence in Bombay and insisted on being included. He refused to take no for an answer and apparently waited the whole day outside Raj Singh's door. Finally, he was included as an additional player after the Kenyan officials agreed to the change. Kapil had had no passport at the time, but a man who could be so adamant and persistent probably had no trouble getting one before departure. I met Kapil at the airport and upon getting acquainted with him, I was honestly very upset that I was given the responsibility to look after a rookie.

In Nairobi, Kapil had to stay with a Gujarati family and was disgruntled with the vegetarian food and the lack of fresh milk. He was worried about his performance without eating meat and drinking milk only from a carton. The first team we played against was an East Africa side who were determined to beat us to show the cricketing world that they were no longer an 'also-ran' team. They scored 219 batting first. With the batting arsenal that our side boasted, we thought that just our openers, Gavaskar and Vengsarkar, could probably take us past their total. The uncertainties of cricket had something else in store. Many of us got out after making quickfire 20s and 30s, and we found ourselves in a precarious position when we were 9 wickets down and still 3 runs short of East Africa's total. Our No. 11 was none other than Kapil Dev.

Being Kapil's mentor, I was summoned by Pataudi to find out whether Kapil could bat and if so, could he play straight and hold his end up? With just three deliveries left in the over and their off-spinner bowling—and with Kirmani at the other end—we felt that we could still redeem the situation and take the lead. I asked Kapil about his batting credentials, but the way he was padded up and his ungainly walk to the wicket did not inspire much confidence in any of us. Raj Singh was reprimanded by Pataudi in no friendly terms about picking a player who looked more at ease in a village than on a cricket ground.

I was sent out to the field with Kapil to discuss the strategy with Kirmani. We both turned to Kapil and said that he should play straight: 'Seedha khelna,' we told him. However, the very first ball that Kapil faced was sent soaring over the bowler's head and past the sightscreen into the car park beyond. Kapil went on to make 53 while Kirmani remained on 8.

Watching Kapil bat, Pataudi and the rest of us were awestruck. We all realized that the superstar pace-bowling all-rounder that India was in search of had been unearthed. The crowd began to cheer the lad from Haryana, and he mesmerized the opposition as well. Raj Singh was overjoyed and I basked in Kapil's success. After the match, I mentioned to Kapil that I had told him quite specifically to play with a straight bat. His reply was that he did play 'seedha'—however, the ball ended up nearly ninety metres further than I had imagined!

Later that year, Kapil made his India debut against Pakistan. India finally had a player who could bowl fast and threaten

Pakistan with bouncers and, when batting, smash their bowlers into the stand. Kapil soon became the superstar of Indian cricket and his carefree attitude towards the game made him the darling of the crowd.

I was his roommate during two fitness camps, one in Bangalore and the other in Madras. He was a voracious eater. On one occasion, I delayed having the lunch I had ordered and found out that it had been completely devoured! A sleepy Kapil told me that he had eaten my lunch too and had not even left the soup for me. Food for him was very important and kali dal was his favourite.

In the Delhi Test against the West Indies in 1978, Kapil was on the verge of his first Test century, remaining 92 not out at stumps. I was then the twelfth man and Gavaskar, knowing my relationship with Kapil, asked me to tell him to relax and play sensibly, as he might not get another chance to get a Test century. I did convey this message to Kapil, but on resumption of play the next day, he hit the first ball he faced—from Norbert Philips, the West Indian fast bowler—through the covers for four.

This was followed by two swats of the bat and on both occasions the ball fortunately missed his bat and the wicket. The fourth ball was overpitched and went flying into the square-leg stand for six. It was the original 'helicopter shot'. A toothy smile towards the pavilion with his bat held high conveyed a message to all of us, one that had been so beautifully sung by Frank Sinatra: 'I did it my way.'

Kapil may have been talented but he was also very hard-working. The greatest gift he possessed was his 'bindaas' attitude towards life. The first Test match he ever watched was the one he played in and so famous names did not bother him. Kapil had no nerves; he had confidence in himself and his ability to perform.

One marvelled at the way he approached the game of cricket. There were no uncertainties in the way he played.

Kapil was not fluent in English in his early days. He struggled to put the right words together and his teammates revelled mischievously in his mistakes. I still remember the time when he was interviewed by the BBC in 1979. We were all apprehensive about how Kapil would face the camera, especially as the interview was in English. He came through with flying colours. He was articulate and to the point, making us wonder how many would have been able to cope so well in a language unfamiliar to them just two years into their international career.

Kapil was rightly chosen by *Wisden* as the Indian Cricketer of the Century. He was a truly gritty, passionate, determined and never-say-die player who made every Indian cricket fan proud. His achievements are now milestones that every aspiring Indian cricketer aims to reach. He is India's greatest all-rounder who put Indian cricket on the world map. Throughout his career, as he had so simply put it to me in Nairobi: '*Seedha hi to khela* (I played it straight)!'

22

AN INTERVIEW WITH CHANDU BORDE

Srikant Kate

What did you learn by watching Vijay Hazare from the non-striker's end while he scored a double hundred at the age of fifty?

The match in question was the Ranji Trophy final against Services. It was played at the Moti Bagh ground in Baroda. The Services team was led by Colonel Hemu Adhikari, who had also played for Baroda. Thus, he knew Vijay Hazare very well. Adhikari was an army man, so he had a strategy ready before the match. Military people always have their plans ready.

Services was a good team, and they had a plan for how they would get Hazare out. The colonel had told Surendra Nath—who was a fast bowler playing for the national team—that when Hazare came to bat, the first ball to him should be a bouncer outside off-stump. We were two down with very few runs on the board and

Hazare was the No. 4 batsman. When he arrived at the crease, Nath bowled at the exact spot his captain had asked him to. Hazare tried to hook it but mistimed his shot. The ball went to mid-on… but the catch was dropped. There was pin-drop silence on the ground for a few moments. Then Adhikari went up to the player who had dropped the catch and said, 'Don't worry! You will take his catch again after he scores 200.' The other fielders were stunned when he said that, but that's exactly what happened.

I used to practise with Hazare in the nets every day, but it was our first time batting together in such a difficult situation. After that first ball, he controlled every delivery he faced and they all hit the middle of his bat. Watching Hazare, I started trying to play like him. I didn't even realize it, but watching him helped me bat better—and the way he batted after that was amazing to witness. Every bouncer Nath bowled after that went to the boundary. Even at that age, Hazare's concentration and footwork were immaculate. Our partnership flourished and the runs we scored together helped us win the trophy. I remember that when Hazare was finally dismissed, even the opposition applauded in acknowledgement of his innings.

Was there any sledging at that time?

No, not at all. The colonel was a fighter but also a gentleman. Sledging was never there, never! On the contrary, there was appreciation from others.

How important do you think that partnership was for you?

One dropped catch cost the opposition 200 runs, but I would say that it helped me build my career too. After batting with Hazare in that innings, my career prospects took off. For that, I am grateful to him. Watching good cricketers always helps you a lot but only if you have the urge to learn.

What about your performances in England? Why couldn't you perform well against England?

I have been asked this question several times. I think it is because in India, we mostly play in conditions where the ball doesn't swing much. But in England, it swings quite a bit—and we were not used to it. I have scored an 80 against England in Bombay when the ball wasn't swinging, but somehow I couldn't get my strokes going in their country.

I have played league cricket in England but not county cricket and the difference in standards between the two is huge. However, playing as a professional in English league cricket, you have a lot of responsibility—not only to perform on the field but also to guide the local players.

Can you tell us the story about your 100 in the first innings and 96 in the second against the West Indies?

It was the 1958–59 season and my debut series for India. At the time the West Indies were the strongest cricket team in the world. They had many quality fast bowlers who would bowl from 18 yards, as the front-foot no-ball rule had not yet come into force. It was a big challenge to face them without helmets or elbow guards and only thin thigh pads. During the first two or three matches against them, we got absolutely nowhere. In Bombay, I played three or four balls but couldn't even understand when the ball left the bowler's hand and was soon dismissed.

Though we were not used to that kind of pace, we were not scared of them. The fear was more outside than inside the ground.

Outside, the crowd builds up the pressure but when we enter the ground, we only focus on performing. But Wes Hall was a very clever bowler. The very first ball of the match, he bowled a bouncer. Pankaj Roy didn't know where the ball would land after it bounced. It flew over the wicketkeeper for 4. The crowd went silent and Pankaj looked shocked. They got us out very easily.

The fourth Test was played at Madras. I hadn't performed in the first two matches and had been dropped for the third Test. There was a question mark over my place in the side. Unfortunately, I again got out for a low score. I felt that my career was over. I went back to my hotel room feeling dejected. My elder brother also happened to be in Madras that day for some office work. When he saw my face, he suggested that we pray together. In the second innings, I scored a half-century. That was a turning point and after that knock I was more confident against the West Indian fast bowlers.

The next match was in Delhi. I knew what I had to do. I changed my batting grip by moving my right hand lower and left hand higher. It became a bit like Hazare's grip, and I found that I could control my shots nicely. Another thing that helped me was a session with Kamal Bhandarkar, who was the cricket coach at Wadia College in Pune. He came to the ground with a bucket of water and some tennis balls. Once everyone else had left, he bowled at me on a concrete patch with wet tennis balls from a very short distance and showed me how to dodge them. That lesson helped me understand how to cleanly leave the bouncers the West Indian quicks were very fond of.

Though both were small adjustments for me at that time, they helped me score a century in the first innings in Delhi. I played with a lot of confidence and without any fear. However, Polly Umrigar and Vijay Manjrekar were hit by their fast bowlers. Both fractured a hand. We were eight down in the second innings and I was on 96 when Manjrekar came out to bat even with a fractured hand because he wanted to help me get a hundred. I think that was such a wonderful gesture and I was inspired by his bravery.

Seeing this, the West Indians brought on Roy Gilchrist. His bouncers were also very deceptive and were hard to leave. They put in three or four slips, a gully and a third man. Gilchrist came charging and bowled a bouncer, which I tried to hook. Unfortunately, I knocked over the bails and was out hit-wicket. I was so close to being the first Indian to get a hundred in each innings of a Test. Since then, I have told myself that not many people remember those who scored a hundred in both innings, but people will always remember me because I was so close but missed it. I am very satisfied even without that achievement.

Can you tell us about your role as a coach and chairman of the BCCI selection committee?

The most important quality of a coach that I learned from Bhandarkar was to never discourage any player and always motivate them to play better. I used to be strict, but I always motivated them. I gave a lot of importance to technique. My experience as a cricketer helped me identify errors in batting technique. I have guided the likes of Ravi Shastri and Maninder Singh and coaching them was very interesting for me.

It is important to talk to more experienced cricketers whenever things go wrong with your game. Once, in a Ranji Trophy game, I was bowling against Mushtaq Ali. He hit sixes off the first two balls I bowled at him. I was shocked. In those days, it was customary for both teams to sit together at dinner and share thoughts. I sat next to Mushtaq and asked him what was wrong with my bowling. He replied, 'Your head is down at the time of release. Look at the batsman when you bowl.' After that, I learned to look at the batsman before releasing my delivery. This was a great lesson from a senior player. These things might seem insignificant but can change your entire career. I have tried to give similar advice when coaching.

When I was on the selection committee, I used to look for players who could contribute more to the team. When we selected the team for the 1983 World Cup, we gave chances to many all-rounders. Seven of the squad were all-rounders because we knew they could contribute with batting, bowling and fielding. You need the specialists but if they fail, they don't add anything else to the team. All-rounders can contribute with their second suit even if they fail in their first. We also used to see the fitness levels of the players. I remember the occasions when we had to take tough selection calls based on fitness.

When I was manager of the national team, Sunil Gavaskar was captain. It was the 1984–85 season and we were deciding on the final XI for the third Test of the home series against England. Gavaskar told me that both Chandrakant Pandit and Mohammed Azharuddin were looking good, but as the match was in Calcutta, he thought the more experienced Pandit should play. He said, 'Sir, you know the crowd here is very knowledgeable but at the same time they pass such comments that it could affect an inexperienced player.' But I told him that Azharuddin could contribute more. He was batting well and was a brilliant fielder too. Azhar made his debut in that match and went on to score a hundred.

The right kind of selection always helps the team. But when a player I selected did not succeed, I used to feel very bad and wonder where I went wrong. But fortunately, as a committee we mainly gave chances to good players who contributed a lot to Indian cricket. I am proud of the selection committee I chaired and of the players we selected.

WINDS OF CHANGE

23

1971

Yajurvindra Singh

In early 1971, India beat the mighty West Indies in a Test series in their own backyard for the first time. The victory brought joy to cricket followers in India. Ajit Wadekar and his band of cricketers were the new national heroes. Vijay Merchant, who was chairman of the BCCI at the time, was elated that his changes had brought about a winning result. This success led to early decisions on the composition of the Indian team to tour England later that year. The final selection for that tour saw M.L. Jaisimha, Rusi Jeejeebhoy and Salim Durrani being dropped and replaced by Abbas Ali Baig, Syed Kirmani and B.S. Chandrasekhar.

Fortunately for India, the BCCI abolished their own rule that players who did not play Indian domestic cricket would not be selected—this allowed Farokh Engineer to be included in the side. Although Engineer had playing commitments with Lancashire, an arrangement with his county allowed him to be available for the Test matches. Apart from his keeping and his knowledge of the English conditions, Engineer was a player who brought in aggression. His inclusion meant that India had three wicketkeepers in the touring party.

The inclusion of Chandrasekhar was expected as India's plan was to focus their attack on spin. India took only one genuinely quick bowler to England in Devraj Govindraj, which was an indication of their game plan. Bishan Bedi, Erapalli Prasanna and S. Venkataraghavan combined with Chandra—as Chandrasekhar is popularly known—to become the dreaded Indian spin quartet. Chandra's right arm was affected by polio, which meant that his control of his wrist was never consistent. Therefore, at times, he was himself not sure where his delivery would land and how it would turn. This unpredictability made it very difficult for the batsmen to read him.

Chandra was very upset and perturbed at being dropped from the side that toured the West Indies. He had done extremely well in several of the previous series and was therefore peeved at the perceived injustice. However, like all great cricketers, he staked his claim for a comeback through some good performances in domestic cricket. Merchant, however, was not entirely convinced about selecting him. He made it a point to mention this during his speech before the team's departure, stating that Chandra's inclusion was a risk. He said that it was a gamble that he had taken and that he hoped it would be fruitful. Chandra was hurt when he heard this but perhaps it was just the catalyst needed to spark the performances that would follow in the series.

Baig was brought in for his experience as he had played a lot of cricket in England. In 1959, he had made a stupendous hundred on debut for India against England at Old Trafford, Manchester. Another significant change was Hemu Adhikari being brought in as manager-cum-coach. A former India Test captain, Adhikari was also a lieutenant colonel in the Indian army and known for his strict management style. Wadekar was instrumental in bringing Adhikari on board as he felt the team needed his military-style discipline on and off the field. His stern, no-nonsense approach could help team focus on their goals.

England were regarded as the number one Test team in the world at the time. Captained by the shrewd Ray Illingworth, the England team had John Snow leading the attack and Geoffrey Boycott, Brian Luckhurst, John Jameson, John Edrich, Alan Knott and Keith Fletcher as proven batsmen. The English players were considered to be true professionals who were known to never give an inch to their opponents.

India had never beaten them and had lost fifteen of the nineteen Tests they had played in England until then. But after beating the West Indies, the 1971 Indian side were confident that they had the skills and the arsenal to do well in England. The English side, however, was also on a high—they were unbeaten in their last twenty-six Tests and had just won the Ashes in Australia. Beating a side with such pedigree seemed a difficult prospect even for a confident Indian side.

The practice sessions before the touring party left for England had a lot of focus on player fitness. The seriousness of that tour for Indian cricket can be gauged by the events prior to departure: the BCCI delayed the team's departure by two days after an astrologer who had predicted the win in the West Indies declared that the originally scheduled day was not auspicious. BCCI Secretary M.V. Chandgadkar promised the players that if they won the series, he would ensure that they received a red-carpet welcome at the airport and then at the Brabourne Stadium in Bombay.

The Indian team landed in England in the third week of June on a rainy day. However, their arrival brought about a change in the weather and the normally cold, rainy and unpredictable climate became hot and sunny, much to the Indians' delight. The team practised at the Oval in London for the first few days. The good weather ensured that they completed all the scheduled practice matches against the county teams.

India had a good start to the tour by beating Middlesex at Lord's in their first tour game. The Indian spinners helped bowl out a strong Middlesex side for 131 in the second innings. In the batting department, Gundappa Vishwanath showed his touch and class, as did India's two workmanlike all-rounders, Eknath Solkar and Abid Ali. A win at Lord's was just the right tonic to get the Indian side into a positive frame of mind. Unfortunately, this was short-lived as they lost their next match against Essex in Colchester. The Indians were undone by some good bowling from Keith Boyce and a well-compiled century by Test batsman Fletcher.

The tourists then played against D.H. Robins' XI in Eastbourne followed by a match against Kent in Canterbury. Both these matches were drawn but the stylish Vishwanath made his mark by scoring two scintillating centuries. The next four county games against Leicestershire, Warwickshire, Glamorgan and Hampshire all led to wins for the Indian side. The weather was outstanding and not a day was lost to rain. Superb centuries by Sunil Gavaskar and Wadekar against Leicester, and Dilip Sardesai against Warwickshire, were supported by 90s by Vishwanath and Abid Ali. India were still looking for an opening partner for Gavaskar and found one in the last match against Hampshire when Ashok Mankad made a fighting hundred.

Vishwanath finished with three centuries and three 50s in the tour matches and Gavaskar, Wadekar, Solkar, Abid Ali, Sardesai and Engineer all seemed to be in good batting form. In the bowling department, the spinners were mesmerizing the county batsmen. Chandra took 11 wickets at Leicestershire and Venkataraghavan's 9 for 93 against Hampshire was another standout performance. Bedi and Prasanna were also making significant contributions. Thus, the Indian batsmen were all getting runs and, combined with the success of the spinners and brilliant close-in fielding, the framework of India's strategy was taking shape perfectly.

India played eight tour games, winning five, drawing two and losing just one. The four-match winning streak had filled them with confidence that hadn't been seen before. It had been perfect preparation for the first Test, which was to begin on 22 July at Lord's. During their match against Middlesex at the legendary Lord's Old Ground, Vishwanath saw the famous honours boards that had the names of those who had scored a century or taken five wickets at what is considered to be the 'Mecca of Cricket'. He wanted to have his name inscribed on it. Meanwhile, skipper Wadekar's hope was to be the first Indian captain to win at Lord's.

The atmosphere on the first morning of a Test at Lord's is always truly amazing. The members of the MCC were present in their gaudy orange-striped ties. Illingworth was leading England for the first time against India. Like his Indian counterpart Wadekar, he was a great tactician. They were both calm and composed leaders who were respected by their team. Illingworth won the toss and decided to bat.

The powerful England top order was soon in tatters at 71 for 5 with the Indian spinners creating havoc. Bedi and Chandra captured 2 wickets each after Abid Ali had made the first breakthrough by getting the prized wicket of Boycott. The England captain then combined with an aggressive Knott to bring about something of a recovery. However, many felt that Illingworth was plumb LBW to a Chandra delivery long before he was eventually dismissed. In those days, there were no neutral umpires and every country seemed to have a home advantage when it came to close umpiring decisions. This made wins away from home a bigger achievement than they perhaps are now.

The Indian spinners unfortunately faltered tactically after eventually dismissing both Knott and Illingworth with the score at 183 for 7. This allowed tailender Snow to get his highest ever score of 73. England finished with a respectable total of 304. In response, India started very badly and soon lost openers Gavaskar and Mankad. A fruitful partnership then blossomed between Wadekar and Sardesai. The Indian skipper stamped his authority against Snow, the bowler who had terrified the Australian batsmen during the Ashes series Down Under. Snow unleashed four bouncers in an over to rattle Wadekar, but with grace and class Wadekar hooked each of them to the boundary. He scored a masterly 85 before being dismissed. Looking back, Wadekar rued missing the opportunity to score a century at Lord's after having come so close. He said later that as he approached the three-figure mark he became a bit careful and tentative and thereby lost his momentum.

Half-centuries by Vishwanath and Solkar and a handy contribution from Engineer took India past England's total. The final total of 313 meant a lead of just 9 runs but the bigger impact was on the minds of the English players, who seemed rattled at having conceded a lead. England's second innings folded up for just 191 with Venkataraghavan, Bedi and Chandra accounting for eight dismissals between them. This left India with a target of 183 to win with four hours left to play.

India started positively with the intention of chasing down the total. With Gavaskar and Engineer playing confidently, the prospect of reaching it seemed eminently possible. A terrible incident marred the chase. While taking a single, Gavaskar was barged into by the powerful Snow and went sprawling, losing his bat in the process. Snow then tossed his bat at him. Frustration was behind this deplorable behaviour, as the aggressive fast bowler couldn't find a way to stop Gavaskar and Engineer from steering India to a win. Snow had to resort to unsportsmanlike conduct in his desperation to break up the partnership.

Putting the incident behind them, India continued to chase the target. However, a rain interruption meant that India had to accelerate the scoring rate and lost a couple of vital wickets in trying. It then became prudent for India to play for the draw, and they eventually ended 38 runs short with 2 wickets remaining. It was a draw that both teams would accept as a reasonable result, but India had demonstrated that they had the firepower to beat their hosts. England then took stern action against Snow, and he was dropped for the next Test. Gavaskar and the Indian camp did not take the matter further but understood from Snow's actions that the supposedly formidable English side had some major internal problems. India felt that these cracks could be exploited during crunch situations.

The tourists then played Minor Counties at Lakenham, followed by a match against Surrey at the Oval in London. Both games were drawn, but the Indian players kept their form intact. The second Test was at Old Trafford in Manchester. In the past, India had had both wonderful as well as disastrous performances there. On this occasion, they thought they had better insights into the conditions as it was the home ground of Lancashire, and thereby Farokh Engineer. However, England sprung a surprise and the wicket at Manchester was prepared as a green top.

Looking at the centre from the pavilion, the Indian team could barely distinguish between the wicket and the outfield. England had realized that the Indian batsmen were not very comfortable in such conditions and that their spinners would find it difficult to get any purchase from the grassy wicket. The rainy and cold conditions in the north of England provided the host side the perfect weather to implement their plans.

Illingworth again won the toss and England chose to bat. The conditions suited the swing bowling of Abid Ali, who created panic among the hosts by taking the first four wickets. England were tottering at 41 for 4 before Luckhurst and Knott put on 75 together. But even at 187 for 7 England were in a dire situation. Illingworth was once again the beneficiary of a close bat-pad decision against Chandra. He went on to make a well-compiled century and put on a big partnership with Peter Lever, the fast bowler who had replaced Snow for this match. Once again, the English tail flourished, with Lever scoring an unbeaten 88. England finished with a healthy total of 386.

The juicy green wicket was a dream for the England fast bowlers. Lever and John Price took full advantage of the conditions. Gavaskar kept one end up by scoring a technically brilliant half-century, which he still rates as one of his best innings in Test cricket as the wicket was lively and Price's pace on that track was one of the fastest he had faced. Another half-century from the reliable Solkar took India to a total of 212. With a first-innings lead of 174, England then took the initiative with a brilliant century by

Luckhurst and 59 by Edrich. England declared at the stroke of tea on the fourth day, setting India a target of 420 to win.

At the end of the day's play, India were in trouble at 65 for 3. Mankad and Wadekar had both been bowled by Price and Richard Hutton had claimed Gavaskar's important wicket. Sardesai and Vishwanath were the not-out batsmen and the match seemed to be heading for an English win as India had to survive the last day with only 7 wickets remaining. However, rain came to the Indian team's rescue and no play was possible the following day. India got away with a draw.

Rain followed them to the tour match against Yorkshire at Leeds and that match too ended in a draw. That left them with one match—against Nottinghamshire—to find the right combination for the third and final Test. Ashok Mankad had been struggling as an opener, but a pleasing half-century in the second innings against Nottinghamshire sealed his place in the final XI for the deciding Test. The other selection dilemma facing India was whether to play Prasanna, who was their best off-spinner, instead of Chandra, whose leg-spin was often wayward.

Chandra resolved this himself by claiming all six wickets to fall in Nottinghamshire's second innings. They were chasing a target of 245 and ended at 115 for 6, with the match being drawn. That spell was enough for the team management to back Chandra. Venkataraghavan was contributing not only as a bowler but also with useful knocks and terrific close-in catching, which meant that Prasanna had to keep sitting out.

The final Test of the three-match series was at the historic Oval ground in London. India had gone into the second Test feeling that they should have won the previous one, but now it was England that had thoughts of what might have been after India's lucky escape in the second match. Injuries to Lever and Norman Gifford led to them being replaced by Derek Underwood and the returning Snow, back after having served his suspension. Both these bowlers had experience of spearheading the attack.

The first day was nice and sunny. Illingworth once again won the toss and elected to bat for the third time in three matches. Fortunately for India, the wicket looked dry and slow. It was because of the hot and mostly sunny summer England was experiencing that year. England started disastrously, with Luckhurst dismissed early by Solkar. The Indian bowling was then subjected to some powerful stroke-play by John Jameson, who incidentally had been born in India but on that day decided to take the Indian spinners to task. He straight-drove Bedi for two wonderful sixes into the pavilion. His partnership with Edrich took England's score to 111 before Edrich was caught by Engineer off Bedi for 40.

Edrich's dismissal was followed by a mini collapse, England losing 4 wickets for 32 runs as Fletcher, Jameson—dismissed for 82—and Basil D'Oliveira followed each other to the pavilion in quick order. After the skipper had been dismissed, the dangerous Knott came into his own with the score at 175 for 6. A record-breaking partnership for the seventh wicket followed as Knott put on 103 runs with Richard Hutton in just sixty-six minutes. The wicketkeeper made a stroke-filled 90 and Hutton—his driving through the covers reminiscent of his illustrious father, Sir Len Hutton—made 81. England were eventually bowled out for 355, which was a very respectable score, considering their position earlier in the day.

The entire second day's play was lost to rain, and English newspapers began reporting that the only two possible results were a draw or an English win. Reading this upset some of the

Indian players and made them more determined to win. The third day's play started fifteen minutes late due to the wet conditions. Soon after resumption, India lost both openers with only 21 on the board. Sardesai and Wadekar then put together a fighting partnership of 93. However, Illingworth was bowling very well and at one stage did not concede a run for 23 balls. Eventually, the English skipper brought about a collapse by bowling Sardesai for 54. He added the scalps of Vishwanath for a duck and his opposite number for 48, sending India reeling to 125 for 5 and seemingly towards a low total.

Solkar and Engineer had other ideas. The wet conditions of the morning had made the outfield slow, but the pair scored their runs through deft placements and nudges, adding an invaluable 97 together. The Indian wicketkeeper was normally an attacking player, but he restrained his instincts to score 59 without a single boundary. Solkar made 44 himself, but unfortunately for India they were both dismissed before the end of the day's play. India's score stood at 234 for 7 after three days of play.

Following an intervening rest day, play resumed for the fourth day. Useful lower-order knocks from Abid Ali and Venkataraghavan took India to a total of 284, but England were still in the driver's seat with a 71-run lead. Their plan was to get some quick runs and put India back in on a worn last-day wicket. Wadekar decided to bring on his spinners early and attack the English batsmen. However, Luckhurst and Jameson looked positive and confident until a stroke of luck came India's way. A powerful straight drive by Luckhurst grazed Chandra's hand on his follow through and hit the stumps at the non-striker's end. Jameson was out of his crease and was run out in a rather unfortunate manner.

Edrich came to the crease and faced up to Chandra. It was the penultimate ball before lunch and Chandra decided to bowl a googly. He had taken the first two steps of his run-up when Sardesai suddenly shouted: 'Mill Reef!' This was code for a faster delivery, named after a prize racehorse. Chandra was a trifle confused but decided to take Sardesai's suggestion and unleashed the quicker one. The ball was perfectly delivered. The stumps were shattered before Edrich could even bring his bat down. In came Fletcher to face the last ball before lunch. This time, Chandra produced a perfect googly with just enough bounce and Fletcher was caught brilliantly by Solkar at forward short-leg. England went into lunch at a shaky 23 for 3.

Batting after lunch, D'Oliveira did not seem in the best of form and looked very unsettled. Having already been dropped twice off Chandra, he finally holed out to deep mid-on off Venkataraghavan. Chandra was bowling a magnificent spell on a slow wicket, getting tricky bounce and turn. Venkataraghavan was bowling steadily and accurately from the other end. At the crease were Illingworth and Knott, players who had been instrumental in taking the game away from India in the first two Tests.

But India had come with a plan—devised by Venkataraghavan and Solkar—to get Knott out. The English wicketkeeper loved to turn off-spin around the corner. Venkataraghavan deliberately left that area vacant to tempt him to play that shot and then bowled the precise line and length that would allow Knott to play his favoured stroke. Solkar was at forward short-leg, aware of what to expect. As Knott shaped to play the shot, Solkar rapidly moved towards the vacant leg-slip area. The ball took the edge of Knott's bat and pad but would land where there was no fielder—or so he thought. Instead, he saw the agile and acrobatic Solkar dive forwards at full stretch and catch the ball inches off the ground. This catch is still considered as one of the best in the history of Indian cricket. It was priceless in the context of that match.

The next to depart was Illingworth, who hit a slow googly from Chandra straight back to the bowler to leave England tottering at 65 for 6. Opening bat Luckhurst was still standing through it all and was the only recognized top-order batsman left. However, India once again proved that their close-in fielding was the best in the world at the time when Venkataraghavan caught a low one-handed blinder in the slips off a fast leg-break from Chandra to dismiss Luckhurst. Apparently, during the drink breaks Solkar had been singing hits by Chandra's favourite singer, Mukesh, to cheer on their leggie, who was in the middle of the spell of his life. The music seemed to do the trick as Chandra immediately dismissed Snow for a first-baller.

By the time England had disintegrated for a total of 101, Chandra had figures of 6 for 38. Wadekar mentioned later that Chandra's spell was the best bowling performance that he had ever seen from an Indian bowler. The Indian spinner's magic blew the lid off English cricket. Former English batsman Ken Barrington had written in an article before the match that England had to be wary of Chandrasekhar as he could be troublesome for the English batsmen on the Oval wicket. As it turned out, his warning should have been heeded.

To secure their first-ever win in England, India needed 173 runs in eight hours. However, England were not a team to go quietly, and again had India's openers back in the hut early. Wadekar and Sardesai managed to bat through to the end of the day and India were well-placed at 76 for 2 with one day left to play. Although the players were excited at the prospect of the win, not a word was discussed that night about the rest of the chase.

The fifth and final day was 24 August, and happened to be an auspicious day in India. The festival of Ganesh Chaturthi was being celebrated and it was a national holiday. Lord Ganesh is considered to be the remover of obstacles to success—just the blessing needed by an Indian team trying to make history. Indian fans in London came in huge numbers to support their team. Of the over 10,000 people present that day, most were of South Asian origin. Before the start of the day's play, Illingworth joked with his team that it seemed like England were the away side.

The beginning was not ideal for India. They lost their skipper to a run-out without any addition to the total. Sardesai and Vishwanath then put on 48 together to calm nerves in the Indian camp. However, Underwood then struck two mighty blows by dismissing Sardesai—caught brilliantly by Knott for 40—and then Solkar in quick succession. India were 134 for 5, but only 40 runs from the target. Vishwanath and Engineer took no risks and India had crawled to 146 when lunch was called.

The Indian supporters were smelling victory. Some of them arranged for an elephant from the nearby Chessington Zoo and paraded it around the ground during the lunch break! It seemed that Ganesh Chaturthi had come to the Oval. The Indian team perhaps felt that the presence of the elephant was a good omen, because Engineer appeared after lunch and smashed three balls to the fence. This sudden burst of aggression tilted the balance towards India. When they were just one hit away from victory, Vishwanath played a cross-batted shot that was totally out of character. He was caught behind off Luckhurst for 33, bringing an overexcited Abid Ali to the crease.

Before he took strike, Abid was instructed by Engineer to take no risks and get the runs through singles. But the all-rounder wanted to end it in style and ran down the wicket to the first ball he faced. He missed the ball entirely and was yards out of his crease—but somehow Knott messed up a simple stumping. Engineer was livid at his partner's antics. However, with the very next ball, Abid cut Luckhurst to the point boundary for the winning runs. The Indian supporters stormed the ground and both batsmen were lifted on the shoulders of the fans and carried back to the pavilion.

No Indian player had moved from his seat in those final few moments, and every Indian cricket follower back home had remained glued to the radio commentary. The tension and nervous energy transformed into an eruption of joy when the winning runs were hit. However, there was an exception. Apparently, Wadekar had been sleeping through it all in the dressing room. When Barrington woke him up to tell him that India had won, the Indian captain replied in his lazy manner: 'I always knew we would win.'

There had been no greater moment for Indian cricket at the time. They had finally beat England away from home after thirty-nine years of being a Test-playing nation. Wadekar and Chandra appeared at the famous Oval balcony and waved to the crowd. The fans below knew that India had achieved the kind of success that they would be proud of for years to come.

Congratulatory messages came in from India even as the team had a small celebration at a local Indian restaurant. They still had to play four more county games on the tour and thus couldn't go overboard with their celebrations. Engineer was scheduled to play the famous Roses match between Lancashire and Yorkshire the very next day, so he had to leave the celebrations and drive down to Manchester with some tandoori chicken and kebabs from the party packed for later.

The next three matches for the Indian side were against Sussex, Somerset and Worcestershire, and all the games were drawn. The tour finished in just the right fashion with a win against T.N. Pearce's XI in Scarborough. It was a fitting end to a magnificently successful tour. On the return journey, the team's plane was diverted to Delhi as Prime Minister Indira Gandhi wanted to personally felicitate the team for their achievements. She did it with pomp and show.

However, the grandest of welcomes was in Bombay, where the promised red carpet was laid out at the airport. The team was driven to the Brabourne Stadium in an open-top motorcade with thousands of fans cheering them on. When they finally arrived at the stadium, the players found it packed to the rafters for the felicitations that would follow. They knew then that the tour of England in 1971 will always be remembered as one of the most significant chapters in the story of Indian cricket.

24

LOOKING BACK

Michael Dalvi

In present-day India, the word 'cricket' conjures up fabulous images of huge stadia full of hysterical hordes of fanatical fans there to watch their idols—the players whose lives both on and off the field are keenly followed by these devout followers. Some would say it is just a game. However, its mass appeal has transcended into an exalted stratosphere that makes it so much more than that—religion, fixation, pride or even mania!

The halcyon days of cricket saw white flannels, upturned collars with silken cravats knotted jauntily around sun-reddened necks and subtle, sophisticated senses of humour. The five-day game was then reduced to one-day matches of 50 overs and the advent of T20 further truncated the game. It brought in field restrictions, wides down the leg-side and coloured uniforms, with even umpires jauntily dressed. The cricket ball has changed colour from red to white to pink—who knows what colour will be next!

Even TV broadcasts have changed so much since my first Ranji season in 1966. I remember watching highlights on Doordarshan in my college common room. It was such a disappointment to see miniscule black figures darting around the twenty-four-inch black-and-white screen! Now we have cheerleaders at games high-stepping like the glamorous dancers of the Folies Bergére or the Moulin Rouge. I wonder what the great superstars of yore would have thought of the modern game. Perhaps they would be wondering whether to turn to the leg or the off-side in their graves.

There's no denying that the game has evolved into a big-money enterprise and extravaganza. There are now excellent facilities for players and spectators alike, which are in stark contrast to the extremely spartan infrastructure we were expected to put up with during my playing days. In the 1960s, we would travel by train in the most economical class with strictly budgeted meals. We received around ten rupees per day as a match fee!

In fact, my monthly pension from the BCCI today is more than I earned in my entire first-class career spanning eighteen years! I did receive a generous one-time payment from the BCCI some years ago. It had been accompanied by a satisfying citation: 'For services rendered to Indian cricket.' Those six words made all the toil, sweat and tears over the years worthwhile. I shall always be grateful for that recognition and consider myself blessed.

My father was a distinguished cricketer and a student of the game. He was very successful at cricket and hockey at university, but he was first a soldier and then a sportsman. He would see cricket as an exercise as much in cerebral application as in physical exertion. He was deeply involved in Services cricket and was chairman of the Services Sports Control Board.

I grew up with the game, following him and the Services team around the country as the unofficial bagman. I knew the players' equipment well, with one of my crucial jobs (albeit unpaid) being the application of 'Blanco' on pads and boots. It was a kind of a white powdery paste that was mixed with water and applied to canvas surfaces to whiten them. It was widely used in those days. My childhood memories are of sports fields, competitiveness and camaraderie. For me, cricket was a passion from the cradle.

I then went to boarding school and was fortunate to have a guru there in Romilly Lisle Holdsworth, known to us as 'Holdy'. He was my tutor at the Doon School and was a man to emulate. He was a 'Triple Blue' at Oxford University for boxing, soccer and cricket. While serving as the principal of Islamia College in Peshawar, he played in the inaugural Ranji Trophy for North West Frontier Province and scored a ton on debut. Holdy and my father groomed my career with care and diligence. By dint of sheer hard work, application and perseverance, I managed to achieve a reasonable school cricket career.

Thereafter, I moved to Delhi to study at St Stephen's College and took on the challenge of university cricket. Holdy from school was replaced by the equally focused Bose Sahib at college. Both were hard taskmasters—the only difference was that Holdy's pipe was replaced by Bose's filter-less cigarette. I never missed a practice in my three years at college and was eventually selected for the Delhi state team.

The state team captain was the distinguished, erudite and accomplished Akash Lal, who was a fount of encouragement for me. He called me to share a beer at the Roshanara Club ground after a satisfying knock against the law faculty side. Without much ado, Lal told me: 'You'll bat at No. 3 whether you score zeroes or hundreds.' I couldn't believe my ears. Was the captain of Delhi telling me this? I had to pinch myself!

Inter-college cricket was the tensest of all. The final in my last year was against Hindu College—an encounter fought closely to the finish. We started on a Monday and ended on a Saturday afternoon, with Stephen's eventually securing a narrow victory. Both sides scored nearly 1,000 runs each over their two innings!

After college, I got a job with a textile company based in Madras. I played for the Madras Cricket Club and then Tamil Nadu state for the decade I resided there. Those were great years. My colleagues went out of their way to put me at ease. As a North Indian in a completely alien environment, I could have been severely inconvenienced in so many ways, but not for a day did I feel out of place.

Madras was a great place to play the game—cricket was well-organized and highly competitive at all levels. My induction was facilitated greatly by my first captain—the stern, no-nonsense Prabhakar Rao. I gave him the nickname 'Skip', which he was to bear throughout his life. Another source of help was P.K. Belliappa, known as 'Belli'. He was a charming and gregarious friend and colleague. I remember that V.V. Kumar in the state team never failed to amaze me with what he could do with a cricket ball.

Highlights of the season there were the Gopalan Trophy matches played against Ceylon (as Sri Lanka was known then). This was before they achieved Test status. These matches were played in blistering heat, very unlike our cricket in the winter in North India. It was satisfying to get two tons against Ceylon as they were a very competitive side.

I switched jobs to a tea company in Calcutta. There, I played for Calcutta Cricket and Football Club, Kalighat Club and the Bengal state side. It was here that I was bitten by the golf bug and called it a day, retiring from all but club cricket. Calcutta was—and still is—a wonderful, cosmopolitan and sporty city. While I lived there, I also played five-a-side hockey, football, 'double-wicket' cricket and even cycle polo.

Looking back on my career—the matches, venues, opponents and teammates—I cannot help but indulge in nostalgic reminiscing. Whilst recollecting the runs scored and opportunities missed, it's natural to turn to the most memorable occasions. Three tons are particularly treasured and coincidentally they all came against foreign teams—my knocks of 108 and 179 against Ceylon and 112 against the West Indies.

I now wait for Old Father Time to flip the bails, call 'Stumps' and usher me back to the pavilion. I don't wish to sound morbid or maudlin but that's the truism of the progression of life. The journey has been so worth it. I end with a special tribute to the wonderful camaraderie and bonhomie the game has provided me, from teammates and opponents alike.

25

THEN AND NOW

Aunshuman Gaekwad

The era of W.G. Grace and Ranjitsinhji was one in which people played cricket more for enjoyment than for money. The game revolved around a few cricketers who became famous and were seen as entertainers by the fans. There wasn't much media exposure in those days, so the publicity came through word of mouth. But a strong foundation for the sport was laid and even today cricket still builds on it.

When my father travelled to England for a Test series, the journey took fifteen days by ship. Cricket gear was mostly minimal and there were no payments involved except for daily allowances. In fact, even in the 1950s Indian cricket was going through financial turmoil. The BCCI couldn't afford to pay guarantee money to the England and Wales Cricket Board (ECB) for a tour in 1959. Fatehsinh Rao Gaekwad, the Maharaja of Baroda, paid the fee from his personal account. If he hadn't done so, the tour would have been cancelled. Back then, Test series were played once in five years and the players would have missed a great opportunity.

The transition to financial stability took time. In the 1970s, the situation had improved a bit, but it was only in the late 1980s that the first sponsorships were secured by the likes of I.S. Bindra and Jagmohan Dalmiya. Other BCCI presidents such as M.A. Chidambaram, Raj Singh Dungarpur, A.C. Muthaiya and Anurag Thakur were all great administrators and helped the BCCI grow to become the world's richest cricket board. It is the only such organization in the world that takes care of former first-class cricketers by paying pensions and offering medical insurance.

Unfortunately, comparisons have always been made between players of different eras, but all of them were great in their own right. Anyone making such comparisons obviously does not understand cricket. The conditions, pitches, equipment—and even the rules of the game—were different. For example, there was no front-foot rule for no-balls, so tall fast bowlers could extend their front foot as much as they liked—they probably bowled from 18 yards instead of the presently legal 22 yards. Let me tell you that in those days the bowlers felt quicker than today's bowlers. Yet, the batsmen had to face them on uncovered pitches with no helmets or thigh guards and only flimsy gloves and pads.

The golden era of Indian cricket started in the 1970s, when the team had the likes of Sunil Gavaskar, Gundappa Vishwanath, Mohinder Amarnath, Dilip Vengsarkar, Syed Kirmani, Bishan Bedi, Erapalli Prasanna, B.S. Chandrasekhar and S. Venkataraghavan. By then, the there were many rule changes that favoured the batsmen more. The pitches started getting covered and more predictable, there was a restriction on the number of bouncers allowed in an over and the front-foot no-ball rule had been introduced. The umpires were given greater powers.

There was always a sense of worry in the minds of Indian selectors about what would happen after the likes of Gavaskar and Vishwanath retired. Well, in cricket, no one is indispensable. They were ably replaced by the next generation of great batsmen, including Sachin Tendulkar, Rahul Dravid, V.V.S. Laxman and Sourav Ganguly. There was no void felt at all as they took over the mantle smoothly.

By this time there was tremendous change in technology used in cricket. The game started to become more scientific and coaches used the help of high-end gadgets to improve the players' skills. It was very unlike the days when I was the coach of the Indian team. I remember having to record match videos on VHS cassettes and use them to point out where players could improve.

In those days, the support staff consisted only of a manager, a 'physio'—who was basically a doctor—and the coach. On tours, apart from coaching I had to take care of tickets, passports, transport, baggage, hotels and more. I was always left wishing that one day had forty-eight hours! How I wished I could have support staff like they have today. I would have been able to concentrate better on my primary job of coaching.

Nowadays, the players' fitness regimens, workloads and diets are all carefully controlled. It is necessary because they are playing and travelling almost 250 days a year. Despite the image of today's cricketers living luxurious lives, it comes at the cost of time with their families as well as their privacy. They are under surveillance all the time with their smallest deeds exposed in the media. I think that during my playing days we enjoyed life better as cricketers even though there was no big money. I see the present cricketers as living in 'golden cages'.

The BCCI has a robust domestic match calendar and conducts more than 2,500 matches every year in different age groups. This helps to continually provide fresh talent at all levels and eventually improve the bench strength of the Indian national team. I don't think the Indian selectors ever had such a luxury of options. Indian cricket is truly basking in the sun and will remain successful for years to come.

26

DAWN OF A NEW ERA

R. Mohan

The morning of 25 June 1983 dawned clear. There was very little of the nippy feel of a typical London morning. I left the King's Hotel on Queensway early and treated myself to a taxi ride to avoid the long walk from the Underground station to St. John's Wood. It was a big day—the World Cup final, with underdogs India taking on the mighty West Indies. My taxi driver was a talkative Jamaican who was convinced that the West Indies would win and that he would be partying with his friends that evening.

It promised to be a hot summer's day by the time I joined the chirpy conversations in the old press box. The assembled company included the venerable John Woodcock, perhaps the most senior of the lot, who was convinced that it would be a short day in which the inevitable would happen. I should have been more optimistic as I had a little blue ticket in my wallet backing India to win at odds of 66/1—it was from the betting firm Ladbrokes' tent, which I had visited during India's first game of the tournament.

The Indian team had already responded to those tabloids that had backed the home side to get into the final by knocking out the hosts in the semi-finals. With a couple of days in hand before the final, there was an air of relaxation about the Indian camp, who were already pleased to have made it this far. The BCCI had just declared that each player would be awarded Rs 25,000 for their performance. Even now, that seems a trifling sum compared to the scale of their achievements in a World Cup in which no one had rated their chances.

The feeling that this could be a short game was reinforced when India lost the toss and had to bat first. In England, conditions invariably favour the bowlers in the morning. At that time of the day, there is always a bit of damp under the pitch that leads to pronounced seam movement in addition to swing. The Indian openers were yet to provide a great start in the tournament as Sunil Gavaskar was not in the best of form. In fact, he had been left out for a couple of games. However, in deference to his status in the team, his absence was put down to a fitness issue.

The West Indies had the finest pace-bowling unit at the World Cup: Joel Garner, Andy Roberts, Michael Holding and Malcolm Marshall. The ball was zipping past at chest height from a good length and Gavaskar was dismissed early again. Kris Srikkanth, fidgety as ever, was having difficulty in getting to terms with the conditions. He told his batting partner Mohinder Amarnath that he was going to 'lagao' (hit out) as he didn't think he could hang around like this for long, and then unleashed a kneeling square drive. This was followed by some daring as well as some outlandish strokes that derived more from a predetermined resolve to get going than any great sense of conviction. But that was how Srikkanth had played for most of his career.

As Srikkanth was showing his teammates the value of standing up to the quicks regardless of how tough the conditions are, at the other end was one of the world's gutsiest batsmen against pace bowling. Amarnath was the unofficial vice-captain and Kapil Dev's most trusted lieutenant. During the World Cup campaign, he had demanded accountability from the team and it was he who had insisted on leaving out Gavaskar due to his poor form.

However, the only two games that India lost in that World Cup were the ones which Gavaskar sat out. It is possible that they missed his wise presence on the field and his excellent catching. In the days when the game was not followed with the kind of intensity as it is now, team politics played out quietly and mostly away from the public gaze. The playing XI was tactfully decided by the manager, P.R. Man Singh, so there was no ill will among the teammates.

India was eventually bowled out for 183, a score that to most was woefully inadequate. However, when the West Indies began their innings, we were treated to the spectacular sight of Gordon Greenidge shouldering arms and being bowled by a banana inswinger from Balwinder Sandhu. A few months later, I asked Sandhu why he thought the West Indian opener had shouldered arms. Had the ball had swung late? Sandhu revealed, 'I had tried to bowl an outswinger, so seeing my grip that batsman thought that the ball would leave him. I was surprised myself to see the ball swing back in and that too so much.'

However, one strike could not lead to the birth of great hope, because the next batsman in was none other than Viv Richards. He began batting so elegantly that it seemed the match wouldn't last till the scheduled tea interval. Richards was treating the bowlers with contempt and Srikkanth and Roger Binny, fielding on the off-side, were regularly fetching the ball from the boundary ropes. Brave then of Madan Lal to convince his captain to give him another over in his first spell. The event that changed the course of the match was to follow.

Madan Lal was of military-medium pace, but he put everything into a delivery that surprised Richards with extra bounce. However, the batsman had just put away the same supposedly innocuous bowler imperiously past extra cover for 4, so he went for an overconfident pull. He was into the shot too early, and the ball took the top edge of the bat. Kapil's loping strides from square leg towards the mishit seemed to take an eternity. There was, however, such certainty in the movement of the natural athlete that there was no doubt that he would pull it off. This was to prove to be one of the most memorable catches in the history of Indian cricket.

The birth of belief in the Indian camp began with the departure of Richards. They knew that West Indian captain Clive Lloyd had pulled his hamstring earlier in the game and plotted to get him by making him stretch to drive. The ploy was that if Lloyd couldn't get fully forward to a delivery, he might mistime a shot or miss one altogether. The plan worked perfectly when he hit a cover drive straight to his opposing number. There was now jubilation among the Indian players as they knew that they were on top and had created a huge opportunity to win.

With Lloyd's wicket, India had reduced the West Indies to 66 for 5 and were at the lesser batsmen in the order. Kapil began going so hard at the tail that Gavaskar, the wise old fox in the slips, had to come over and calm him down. His presence was crucial in maintaining an emotional order in the field, as the task was yet to be completed. When the ball starts swinging in the English air, it can play tricks on the batsman's mind. The men from the

Caribbean did not like it when the ball was wobbling in the air and demanding late adjustments. But that is exactly what Amarnath was making it do with his medium pace.

As India made breakthroughs and lower-order batsmen walked in, batting skills declined in proportion and the ball seemed to be hanging in the air and beating every intended stroke or defensive prod. The end was in sight, or so I thought. Woodcock thought otherwise. 'Don't be so sure,' he said even as I began typing out a victory report. However, Amarnath soon had last man Holding plumb in front.

Even as the umpire's finger was going up, the bowler was already racing down the track to pluck a stump. Curiously, he missed grabbing a souvenir as he ran down the slope—but I did not know this until Binny told me twenty-five years later! The crowd charged into the ground as well. It was a merry and mad moment. The West Indian hopes of achieving a hattrick of World Cup wins had been extinguished by the underdogs.

After the awards ceremony, I was pleasantly surprised to run into Kapil Dev. I could not believe that the captain who had just lifted the World Cup was available for a quiet chat with a journalist so soon after such a momentous victory. His exact words on how he felt about it all would be beeped out if one were to broadcast them on television. But that was Kapil for you—spontaneous and to the point. The enormity of the achievement had probably not sunk in yet for him.

The Westmoreland Hotel at the corner of St John's Wood Road was a riot with partying Indian fans going strong through the night. Back in India, the fans had been watching the final live on Doordarshan. 'India turn the cricket world upside down!' screamed the headlines of the London newspapers the next day. And how!

They had pulled off a win despite setting the lowest-ever target in a World Cup final.

There was the small matter of collecting my bet winnings. The manager at the Ladbrokes shop took an eternity on the telephone with his superiors before I was finally allowed to cash my ticket. More than the money—a tidy sum though it was in those days—it was the thrill of winning that was memorable for me. I took in the generosity of the local papers in their tributes to the Indian team's spirit before flying back home to record for posterity a truly historic achievement.

27

DESERT CLASSICS

Rituraj Borkakoty

When Abdul Rahman Bukhatir arrived in Pakistan for his school education in the 1960s, the young boy from the United Arab Emirates (UAE) had no idea that he was going to fall in love. It was not love at first sight with a fresh-faced schoolgirl in a foreign land. Rather, it was the sound of the bat hitting the red cricket ball in the Karachi dustbowls that would play in his head like a sweet melody.

Bukhatir could not get cricket off his mind. He was completely mesmerized by the classical batsmanship of Hanif Mohammad, the game's original little master. Hanif became his first cricket idol as Bukhatir began playing for his school team in Pakistan. After he returned to his native country, his love for the game became an obsession—one that eventually led to the introduction of cricket in that desert region.

After making a name for himself as a young entrepreneur in the UAE, Bukhatir established the Sharjah Cricket Stadium, bringing international cricket to the Arab world. The stadium was built in just four months' time, and became the ground where India won the inaugural Asia Cup in 1984—less than a year after 'Kapil's Devils' had turned the cricketing world upside down at Lord's to win the nation's first World Cup.

At the time, much of the Indian hinterland couldn't yet access television broadcasts. Their only way of connecting with the game was through the vivid commentary on the radio. But the meteoric rise of Sharjah as the venue for an annual cricket spectacle with the added glamour of movie stars in the VIP stands led to Doordarshan, India's national television broadcaster, increasing its reach to the far-flung corners of the country.

Cricket in the middle of a desert began to draw the biggest teams and the biggest stars, including the icons of the legendary West Indies team. But it was the matches between India and Pakistan that would resonate loudest in the subcontinent. Ali Anwar Jafri, a former university-level Pakistani cricketer, had moved to the UAE in the 1970s and found himself in charge of ticket sales for international matches at the Sharjah stadium. He saw the first signs of the India–Pakistan cricket magic at Sharjah in 1981.

'The first match in Sharjah was an exhibition game played in April 1981 between a Gavaskar XI and a Miandad XI,' he recalls. 'All the big India and Pakistan stars of that time played that match. It was a huge success. I remember people gatecrashed as we had only temporary stands at the time.' That exhibition match had been arranged by Bukhatir as a tribute to his hero, Hanif Mohammad, for inspiring him to bring about a cricket revolution in the UAE.

But Bukhatir had started working on growing the game at the grassroots level at least six years before that high-profile exhibition match. Aided by some of his Emirati friends and Shyam Bhatia, a Dubai-based Indian businessman, he started club cricket in the UAE. 'They started organizing local matches in 1975 and that's how the Bukhatir League started,' Jafri says. 'It's still the most popular local cricket tournament in the UAE. The club owners even brought over first-class cricketers from India and Pakistan to play in the league and that helped develop the sport in the UAE.'

The success of those local matches—as well as a few exhibition matches between international stars and local players in the late 1970s—eventually made Bukhatir dream big. It was a dream come true for the cricket romantic when full-strength teams from India and Pakistan agreed to play that 1981 exhibition game. Jafri says that few people are aware that Bukhatir's idea for the Cricketer Benefit Fund Series (CBFS), which became a huge success in the international matches at Sharjah, first came in that exhibition match between Gavaskar XI and Miandad XI.

'That was in a way the beginning of CBFS, which eventually saw many ex-cricketers from the subcontinent receive generous funds from the Sharjah tournaments,' Jafri reveals. 'That 1981 exhibition match was mainly for the benefit of Hanif Mohammad, but it was not just he who benefitted. Proceedings were also shared with Asif Iqbal, and if I remember right, even Madhav Mantri, Sunil Gavaskar's uncle. It was a great cause. But none of us expected to see such a big crowd on the match day. It was packed to the rafters!'

Dilip Vengsarkar has fond memories of that exhibition match, which was played on a matting wicket with people watching the action from temporary stands. 'We had just come back from the Australian tour before going to Sharjah to play this match,' recalls Vengsarkar. 'It was the first time we met Abdul Rahman

Bukhatir. The response was tremendous, and thousands of Indians and Pakistanis came to watch the match. The atmosphere was amazing—we could not believe all this was happening in the middle of a desert!'

Vengsarkar went on to play nineteen one-day internationals in Sharjah. Few could have predicted then that an exhibition game on a nondescript ground would lead to some of the most unforgettable battles in the history of one-day international cricket. Many of those memorable matches featured the Indian team.

Low-Scoring Epic

The opening game of the 1985 Rothmans Four-Nations Cup was the first India–Pakistan classic witnessed by Sharjah. India had arrived for the tournament in Sharjah on the back of an unbeaten run in Australia that culminated in victory at the World Championships of Cricket. However, on a difficult track, India found Imran Khan too hot to handle. Khan took 6 for 14 as India were bowled out for just 125 in 42.4 overs.

What followed next was the stuff of legend as an incredible Indian fightback reduced Pakistan to 87 all out. Vengsarkar recalls that Indian spinners Ravi Shastri (2 for 17) and Laxman Sivaramakrishnan (2 for 16) were unplayable on a turning track. Kapil Dev (3 for 17) also struck crucial blows.

Among the lucky ones to witness that engrossing battle between the two great rivals in Sharjah was Tariq Butt, a former Pakistani political activist who played three first-class games before becoming the most respected umpire in UAE domestic cricket. 'Pakistan were comfortably placed at around 40 for 2 in reply,' Butt recalls. 'But the Indian spinners sparked an amazing collapse. Indian captain Kapil Dev was very clever with his bowling changes and Gavaskar took four catches. I still remember almost every detail of that match.'

Miandad's Masterpiece

Of the seventy-two matches that India played in Sharjah, the 1986 Austral-Asia Cup final is the one that remains etched in most memories. India had gone into that final with a fabulous head-to-head record against Pakistan, and it seemed they were on track to maintain the stranglehold when Kris Srikkanth (75), Gavaskar (52) and Vengsarkar (50) helped them post 245 for 7, a very big total in one-day cricket at the time.

The total seemed even bigger when Pakistan lost 4 wickets for 110 in their chase. Against a steep asking rate, not even the most ardent backer would have given them a chance of upsetting the formidable Indians. But Javed Miandad refused to give up. In the company of lower-order batters, he took Pakistan to a position from where they needed 4 to win off the final ball with 1 wicket in hand.

Chetan Sharma's attempted yorker was converted into a full toss by the genius of Miandad and the ball sailed over the mid-wicket boundary, sparking delirium among the Pakistani fans. Miandad finished with a masterful unbeaten 116 off 114 balls. 'Before that game, nobody knew that this of kind of cricket can be played,' Miandad said of his own innings. 'I had never seen anybody play like that before.' It was an innings that changed how teams approached large chases.

Desert Storm

It was in 1998 that Indian cricket made its most abiding memory of the Sharjah Cricket Stadium. And there was just one man behind it: Sachin Tendulkar. The genius of Tendulkar was fully expressed during the trilateral Coca-Cola Cup tournament held at the desert venue that year.

India faced a do-or-die situation in a league game against Australia. If Mohammed Azharuddin's team couldn't beat the Aussies, they had to at least maintain a better net run rate than New Zealand—the third team in the tournament—to qualify for the final. But the odds that were already heavily stacked against them only grew longer after Australia posted 284 for 7, thanks to Michael Bevan's 101 not out and 81 from Mark Waugh.

In their reply, India were in all sorts of trouble after crawling to 143 for 4 in 31 overs. They needed 142 runs off 114 balls for victory with Tendulkar still in the middle. However, the boundaries had dried up for India. It was then that a sandstorm engulfed the stadium, creating a further obstacle in India's path to the final.

'The storm was still gathering pace and I think the match was stopped for almost half an hour,' recalls Tariq Butt, who was one of the tournament officials. 'Tendulkar looked worried because he thought he could still drag his team over the line. He asked me how long these storms last, banking on my local knowledge. But little did we know that we were going to witness another storm that day—a cricket storm from Tendulkar!'

When play resumed, India had a revised target of 276 from 46 overs, which meant India needed 133 runs off 90 balls to win. Tendulkar resumed batting, partnered by V.V.S. Laxman, who had yet to find his feet in international cricket. The Little Master suddenly launched a blistering attack on the Aussie pacers, sending the fans in the stands as well as millions of television viewers into a state of frenzy.

Though Tendulkar batted like a man possessed, India eventually fell short by 26 runs. However, his stunning hundred—142 off 131 balls with 9 fours and 5 sixes—ensured India had bettered New Zealand's run rate and secured a berth in the final, which would be a rematch against Australia. Just forty-eight hours after what they now call Sachin's Desert Storm, Tendulkar celebrated his twenty-fifth birthday by playing another majestic knock (134 off 131 balls) in the final to defeat Australia.

Among Shyam Bhatia's various business interests is Dubai's famous cricket museum. The likes of Viv Richards, Imran Khan, Kapil Dev and Shane Warne have visited this attraction. 'When Warne visited my museum,' recalls Bhatia, 'I asked him something he had probably been asked repeatedly: which batsman he found it toughest to bowl to. You should have seen the respect in his eyes when he confirmed that it was none other than Sachin Tendulkar!'

Like Miandad a generation before him, Tendulkar left an indelible mark in the cricket psyche of the desert nation. There are many like Shyam Bhatia, Tariq Butt and Ali Anwar Jafri in the UAE who gush over those old Sharjah classics. And they have only one man to thank for building a cricket stage in the middle of a desert: Abdul Rahman Bukhatir. 'I feel a sense of accomplishment,' said Bukhatir recently. 'To me, it was always about cricket and its promotion.'

Sharjah is no longer the exclusive host of international matches in the UAE, as two newer state-of-the-art stadiums in Dubai and Abu Dhabi get the lion's share of match allotments. But for Jafri, there is no doubt that it was Sharjah that was the gamechanger. 'You know, cricket became even bigger in India and Pakistan after the Sharjah tournaments,' he gushes. 'The popularity of cricket in the subcontinent owes a lot to Sharjah!'

28

WOMEN'S CRICKET IN INDIA
Shubhangi Kulkarni

I t's hard to believe that women's cricket in India has been around
for fifty years. It feels like I started playing the game just a few
years ago as some of the memories are still so vivid. Women's
cricket was officially established in India when the energetic
secretary of the Women's Cricket Association of India (WCAI),
M.K. Sharma, registered the association in Lucknow in 1973. I
was one of the pioneers of the women's game in India and since
then, it has been a thrilling journey for me.

It has been my life's greatest honour to have played cricket for
India and a privilege to have been part of the women's game since
its inception in the country, to have captained the Indian team
and to have served as an administrator in later years. To further
my involvement with the game, I later decided to pursue a career
in marketing cricket products, which has kept me connected to
the sport.

I began playing when I was still in school and remember going to the ground with my mother to attend a summer camp. During those days, girls didn't play cricket and it was considered to be a men's game. I was fortunate to have parents who allowed me to pursue my interests and supported me when I decided to play cricket. The first time I went to the ground, I recall playing on a cement wicket with a lot of wild grass outside the net. There was hardly any room to do anything other than batting and bowling. Later, when we played matches, we played on matting wickets with bumpy outfields that, if they existed today, would require fielders to wear helmets! Those were the days when we played without any protective gear except for pads and gloves.

Following the initial summer training camp, our association organized friendly matches with another team in Nainital. We took the train to Nainital in the unreserved compartment, which seemed manageable at the start. However, as the train made stops at various stations and more and more people got on, we found ourselves cramped inside the compartment with barely any room to move. I recall having to jump out of the train's windows to buy food and tea and manoeuvring over other passengers to go to the washroom. Despite the cramped conditions, we had a great time entertaining ourselves on the journey by singing, teasing each other and generally having fun amongst ourselves and with fellow passengers.

In Nainital, the entire team was housed in a dormitory that had communal bathrooms and makeshift changing rooms. This was a new experience for me, but I soon found that it was the standard arrangement for most of the tournaments we played in during our WCAI days. We became so accustomed to these facilities that we would be shocked if we were ever provided with more than one room for the team to stay in!

Even on international tours, we sometimes stayed with host families. On our first tour, which was to New Zealand, our accommodation was arranged with different families—some were Indian expatriates and others were New Zealand citizens. Some of our players who could speak only Indian languages stayed with Indian families while I, being able to speak English, stayed with a local family. But it was not just any family. During that trip, I had the honour of staying at the home of the legendary Sir Richard Hadlee. His then-wife, Karen, who played for the New Zealand women's team, had offered to host two of the Indian touring party.

Sir Richard was soft-spoken and kind to us. I will never forget how he helped us with our luggage and made tea for us while Karen was away at work. In those days, we weren't used to men assisting with household chores in India, so this was amusing to us. He chatted with us about cricket and seemed proud that his wife also played for their country.

Despite the obstacles, the joy of the game and the privilege of playing for the team trumped every hardship and challenge that was thrown at us. The journey, howsoever long and arduous, was the destination. It was our passion for the game that helped us surmount all odds. Wins were things to write home about and losses were what made us stronger, both as individuals and as a unit. The challenges we went through together helped us create bonds and friendships that have endured over time.

The sport also helped us develop leadership qualities and teamwork. One such instance was around 1978, when the Indian women's team had only played international cricket for three years. We were told that the Indian women's team was invited to the

West Indies to play Test matches. However, WCAI was going through a change in management at the time, and due to a lack of funds, had decided not to send a team overseas. The invitation was refused.

At this, the players—including Shantha Rangaswamy (association president), Behroze Edulji (vice-president), Susan Itticheria (treasurer), Sudha Shah (member), Diana Edulji (member) and I (secretary), among others—came together and formed the 'India Club'. The club included most of the Indian players. We contacted the West Indian officials and accepted their invitation to tour their country, all the while collecting funds for our airfare, kit, clothing and allowances. We arranged not only for the return journey to the West Indies but also managed to schedule some matches in England, as our flight had a stopover in London.

In London, we stayed in the youth hostels as they were the most economical option. At the time, our government policy allowed us very little foreign exchange and food was expensive in the UK. Therefore, we carried as much food from India as possible. Another challenge was communicating with the foreign cricket boards, as in those days there were hardly any telephones in India! Communication was mainly through airmail, and the details were finalized nearly a year prior to the actual tour. Our planning was so thorough that I don't recall any hiccups or oversights.

In those days, obtaining a visa for Western countries was a challenging process and applicants underwent rigorous interviews and questioning before getting their visa applications approved. To ensure that everyone was prepared, we had mock interviews a day before our visa appointments! This level of preparation showed the effort we put into organizing the tour. I was around nineteen or twenty years old at the time and this experience gave me immense confidence, which benefitted me later in business and in cricket administration endeavours. Even after this tour was over, I often had to deal with times where I had to raise funds for our association and coordinate events to keep the sport alive in my state.

This experience was invaluable for me later when I served as the secretary of WCAI from 2003 to 2006. Those years were some of the most memorable of my career as an administrator and it was during this time that I came up with a plan for the future of women's cricket in India. I realized that it was challenging to secure funds or sponsors for women's cricket—or any other women's sports, for that matter—in a country where men's sport was king. This led me to believe that the best way forward for women's cricket would be for it to come under the umbrella of the BCCI.

As luck would have it, in 2005, the International Women's Cricket Council (IWCC) and the ICC decided to merge. This led to the mandate that each country's cricket board would be responsible for administering both men's and women's cricket. This meant that the BCCI would have to take women's cricket under its wing. The Indian board launched its women's cricket programme in 2006, marking a turning point for the sport in India. The BCCI included women's cricket in its schedule and arranged for the women's team to participate in international competitions. Women players were given access to better facilities. Ever since, there's been no looking back and no spending sleepless nights due to a lack of funds for the administrators of women's cricket!

I was fortunate to be there as a player and administrator in WCAI, to be the lead negotiator for the merger of women's cricket into the BCCI and to be involved with the launch of the women's game in India as part of the Board. Over the past fifteen years, numerous advancements have been made for women cricketers in India under the BCCI umbrella, including securing salaries equal to that of male players. Women players now also have access to the National Cricket Academy.

The most recent development is the Women's Premier League. This will elevate the sport to new heights and will have a transformative impact on women's cricket in India. It is indeed so satisfying to finally witness good days for women's cricket!

29

FITNESS EVOLUTION

Ramji Srinivasan

Cricket is part of our daily lives in India, with people across age groups following the game closely and passionately. The sport has seen huge changes in the last few decades, from rules and formats to the profiles of the players and their techniques. There have also been changes in the areas of strength conditioning and fitness. We shall look at the shifts in these fields in Indian cricket.

An argument among pundits centres on the question: does fitness precede skill in cricket? The answer to this question is yet to be determined by the various stakeholders of the game. The fitness culture in Indian cricket began in the 1980s, when players such as Kapil Dev, Sunil Gavaskar, Mohinder Amarnath and Madan Lal started to allocate extra time on the field for a fitness regimen that was separate from their cricket practice. At the time, Bishan Bedi was the coach of the Indian team and he insisted on the players following rigorous fitness protocols.

In those days, fitness work mainly consisted of a pre-game warm-up of a couple of laps around the ground, followed by stretches. Even the extra fitness work the players such as Gavaskar began cannot be compared to the intense regimens cricketers now follow. Having an athlete's physique was not a focal point of cricket then. Instead, analytical mindsets and cricketing skills were given more importance. Thus, practice focused more on skills, tactics and mental preparedness. Players mostly worked on endurance rather than specific strength and conditioning for the game.

The Australian fast bowler Dennis Lillee is one of the first cricketers who brought sports science to the game when he hired a physio and used biomechanics to help him heal the stress fracture in his lower back. This was in the early 1970s, and it led to an evolution in sports science for managing the fitness of fast bowlers. Physios, strength and conditioning specialists, and nutritionists became more involved in the sport. Australia was far ahead of their time in bringing sports science to cricket.

In the 1990s, the BCCI hired doctors and physios to manage injuries and act as fitness coaches, as they felt that the Indian players would require a serious fitness regimen to be able to match cricketers from other countries. It was the appointment of Andrew Leipus as physio and trainer that brought in professional systems to Indian cricket's fitness regimens. One of the pioneers in the field of sports medicine in India is Dr Anant Joshi, who worked with the BCCI on injury management. Then came the fitness trainer Adrian le Roux, an exceptional professional who established protocols for the players to improve their fitness and enjoy doing so.

I was the first Indian strength and conditioning coach of our national cricket team. It was a huge responsibility to continue the players' professional approach towards fitness. I worked with them on setting up processes for fitness scheduling according to each individual's skill and dietary patterns. This led to the creation of a weekly log, which turned out to be a good system that stayed in place even when I was succeeded in the role by other professionals.

Another reason for the huge shift in Indian cricket's approach to fitness in the 1990s was the establishment of the MRF Pace Foundation, which brought processes and protocols into practice. Despite being initially reticent, cricketers started to embark on fitness journeys. It started with players such as Azharuddin, Robin Singh and Ajay Jadeja, who were keen to bring in a culture of fitness to the team by demonstrating great athleticism on the field.

M.S. Dhoni led the way in the 2000s, followed by the leading stars of that generation. Then came Virat Kohli and Suresh Raina, who took fitness very seriously and raised it to the next level in the 2010s. In recent years, the advent of T20 cricket has brought about a huge paradigm shift in the mindsets and physical needs of the players when it comes to fitness. The intensity of the matches now requires greater speed and agility, and players need that extra edge to perform.

Cricketers have realized the importance of being fit both physically and mentally, and also of looking good in front of the camera in the age of social media. The huge monetary rewards in the sport now also serve as a motivating factor for players to keep themselves fit and injury-free through the season. Cricket has evolved and the time when the game was played in a relaxed manner seems like a distant past. The current generation of players is like fish in water when it comes to fitness work. They are happy to see the benefits that come when fitness, diet and other protocols are followed and are aware of their importance.

There is still a long way to go before Indian cricket becomes the best in the field of strength and conditioning. To achieve that, the fitness protocols need to be smart and adaptable. Nevertheless, we are on our way there and there is always place for new ideas that suit our players. We must continue with a thorough professional approach and have the right people in the right places with accountability to ensure that we produce the fittest cricketers in the world.

30

AT A CROSSROADS

Venkat Sundaram

Sir Neville Cardus, the doyen of cricket journalists, had observed that cricket reflects the times in which it's played. He stated that if one analysed the evolution of cricket over the decades, one would see that the game mirrors the development of society. This opinion could be subject to debate, but looking at international cricket through this prism, you may well agree with his viewpoint.

Cricket has evolved from being the exclusive preserve of white men to being dominated by a former British colony. Today, India is the main promoter, sponsor and supporter of cricket worldwide. This change is also reflected when one examines the social context, with the Indian economy now the fastest-growing in the world and its population on the way to becoming the world's largest. Cricket has united India, and the national team is adored. However, it took decades for the sport to be elevated to this status.

Sachin Tendulkar recently turned fifty, and the landmark was warmly celebrated across the country. Many of his best innings were replayed on TV and social media. While talking about the development of the game since his debut in 1989 until his retirement in 2013, Sachin mentioned that Indian cricket has changed significantly since the early part of this century. He said that the grounds and wickets have improved considerably and that fielders are no longer afraid to dive to stop the ball as they used to be when he had started playing. It is special to see a player of Sachin Tendulkar's eminence talk about this aspect of the game. But it is not surprising, as I have personally had the opportunity to discuss preparation of pitches and related infrastructure with Sachin and several other Indian captains.

The pitches improved because the BCCI invested in qualitatively improving the playing conditions. The Grounds and Wickets Committee of the BCCI is the board's apex committee that works with curators, ground staff, maintenance professionals, umpires and match referees. It even has interactions with the ICC regarding preparation of pitches. As I have held the post of chairman of this committee twice, I have experienced first-hand the nuances of staging national and international matches at over a hundred venues across India. With this experience, I can say that the period from 2002 to 2004 and again from 2010 to 2012 saw significant changes in Indian cricket.

In my first stint at the helm of the committee, I insisted that we should slowly change the structure, maintenance and upkeep of our iconic venues. The five major Test centres were chosen for the first stage of implementing this strategy. At the time, these venues were Delhi (Kotla), Mumbai (Wankhede), Kolkata (Eden Gardens), Chennai (Chepauk) and Kanpur (Green Park). We brought in irrigation using modern automatic sprinkler systems, introduced special hybrid grass, improved drainage and restructured the outfields by using sand.

This was a major task, but it took much persuasion before the BCCI agreed to import modern maintenance machinery. Training was provided to curators and ground staff and mechanics hired for the maintenance of the machines. A new air of optimism crept in. Seeing the benefits of modernization, other venues started clamouring for similar attention from the BCCI. A revolution had started.

When I started my second term as chairman in 2010, I decided that we needed to start a curator's certification course in India. At the time, no country had such a course. The curators and ground staff were trained in modern methods of maintaining moisture in the pitch and of rolling and mowing it.

We also drew up a concrete plan for improving the pace and bounce of Indian pitches for domestic cricket competitions, while retaining the 'home advantage' for international fixtures. As a result of this decision, Indian pitches that were usually bereft of grass cover now had a generous sprinkling of green. Neutral venues were mandated for domestic matches with curators and match referees also made neutral at all venues. Slowly, Indian pitches changed from being spin-friendly to having pace and swing.

A very significant development initiated by a private enterprise was the establishment of the MRF Pace Academy in Chennai. This contributed to the development of young, fit and pacy Indian fast bowlers who went on to hit the headlines. This not only benefitted the Indian bowling strength but also strengthened the batting, as with greater exposure, our batters lost their fear of fast bowling and green tracks. India started winning not only at home but also overseas. A new era had surely begun.

'Indian Cricket is at a crossroads' is an oft-repeated lament down the years. We are all used to it. When, to keep pace with modern demands, the BCCI started the IPL, the sceptics and cynics were convinced that this would destroy the traditional longer versions of the game. 'It will kill cricket,' was their loud criticism. Yet, crowds swelled at cricket matches all over India as the jamboree caught the imagination of the public. T20 cricket became a sensation, and in the process the BCCI emerged as the richest organization in world cricket.

Cricket has changed from its early days when it was just a pastime. It is now a new paradigm of professional excellence.

THE MODERN AGE

31

SACHIN TENDULKAR: THE GOD OF BIG THINGS

H. Natarajan

The nineteenth-century German philosopher Arthur Schopenhauer had said: 'Talent hits a target no one else can hit; genius hits a target no one else can see.' Schopenhauer's words came to my mind when I watched an interview in which tennis great Andre Agassi explains how he could differentiate fellow legend Boris Becker's various booming serves by reading the German's lip movements. After losing his first three matches against Becker, Agassi lost only once in their next eleven matches after having cracked the mystery.

Becker had a Howitzer serve that was difficult for all his opponents to return. But the genius of Agassi saw something that no other player on the ATP circuit could. 'The hardest part was not letting Boris know that I had figured him out,' Agassi recalled. Becker was stunned when Agassi revealed his formula for success to the German after his retirement. Becker said, 'I used to go home and tell my wife, "It's like he reads my mind." Little did I know he was reading my lips!'

This is pure genius that cannot be taught by any coach in the world. Closer to home, such genius can be seen in our very own Sachin Tendulkar. During his fascinating duel with Chris Cairns in a Test match at Mohali, his 'out-of-the-box' thinking helped him outsmart Cairns in helpful conditions for the bowler. 'The ball was reverse-swinging and Cairns was beating us two or three times in an over,' Tendulkar recalled. 'We were sort of clueless because we couldn't see the shiny side of the ball.'

Tendulkar had an idea and told his batting partner, Rahul Dravid, that the non-striker should watch the bowler closely as he is closer to the ball. At the time Cairns grips the ball, whichever side is shiny, the non-striker should hold the bat in that hand. 'If he was going to bowl an out-swinger, the bat would be in my left hand at the non-striker's end,' said Tendulkar. 'If he was going to bowl an in-swinger, the bat would in my right hand. So that's the only time in my career when the batsman on strike was not watching the bowler but the non-striker's bat!'

Suddenly, Dravid unleashed a couple of cover drives for boundaries followed by on-drives piercing mid-wicket and mid-on. Cairns was bewildered and suspected something wrong. He looked at Tendulkar and asked, 'What do you know about this?' But Cairns didn't realize that Tendulkar had also warned Dravid that if he wasn't sure what was coming, he was going to hold the bat in the middle! 'In short,' summarized Tendulkar, 'It was about being a step ahead of the opposition.'

Balwinder Singh Sandhu, the 1983 World Cup hero who later coached the Bombay Ranji team, told me something equally fascinating about the genius of Tendulkar. 'I was once standing behind the nets watching Sandeep Dahad yards away at the top of his run-up, preparing to bowl,' Sandhu recalled. 'Sachin not only spotted the shine on the ball from that distance but could also accurately tell whether Dahad's delivery would come in or leave him. Sachin's computer-like memory stored every little detail about a bowler: the run-up, pace, rhythm, whether he delivered from close to the stumps or not—and he could spot changes in these patterns that revealed the bowler's intentions. It is inputs like these that gave him the time to play his shots that other batsmen didn't have.'

Tendulkar was addicted to cricket. He was twelve or thirteen when he led the Bombay Under-15 team to Ahmedabad. The boys went off to sleep after getting there at around 4.30 a.m. At 6 a.m., officials learnt that Sachin was missing. The team manager and coach went searching for him and finally found him on the terrace practising! He was bouncing the ball off the wall with his left hand and then quickly gripping his bat with both hands to practise his shots. Sleep was not important; practice was. And such was his concentration that he failed to notice the presence of the two officials. This incident was narrated to me by columnist Makarand Waingankar.

Even in sleep Tendulkar is known to not stop thinking about cricket. Salil Ankola—who was one of the debutants on the 1989–90 tour of Pakistan along with Tendulkar—told me of an incident during the Sialkot Test on that tour. 'At around 11 p.m. I heard a commotion outside my room,' he recalled. 'I came out to find Sachin being led into his room by Maninder Singh and Raman Lamba. Sachin was walking outside his room in his sleep, asking for the man from Malik Sports who was supposed to have delivered his bats but hadn't. Of course, he didn't remember the incident the next day and thought we were pulling his leg. It showed his obsession for cricket even in his sleep.'

My very first impression of Tendulkar was that of a hungry tiger released from a cage. He was just fourteen and already in the Bombay Ranji team. He was kept in the reserves to get a feel of the big-match environment. The close-of-play nets was the moment he had waited for all day. Raju Kulkarni, then arguably the quickest bowler in the country, pitched one short; the ball rose disconcertingly and came in at Sachin like a guided missile. The response was not to duck or sway but to get inside the line and flick it off the face with disdain. Fire was countered with fire.

During an interview with Tom Alter before the 1988–89 Indian tour of the West Indies—which preceded the tour of Pakistan in which Tendulkar would make his debut—a very young Sachin countered the critics who felt that he was too young to face the dreaded West Indian pace attack in the Caribbean. He told Alter that he wasn't scared of facing the pace barrage of Malcolm Marshall, Curtly Ambrose, Courtney Walsh and Ian Bishop. 'I like playing fast bowlers,' he said with quiet confidence and self-assurance.

On the tour of Pakistan that followed, the writer Suresh Menon overheard Imran Khan telling someone that he was uncomfortable at the thought of bowling to a schoolboy. Suresh told Sachin what he had heard. Tendulkar replied, 'Please tell Mr Imran Khan that I don't need any charity.' Imran's words were probably in sixteen-year-old Tendulkar's mind when he refused to leave the field after being struck on the face by a Waqar Younis delivery in the final Test of that tour at Sialkot.

A match-saving unbeaten 119 in England at age seventeen and 148 in Australia while still in his teens underlined Tendulkar's rare precocity, the kind Test cricket had not seen before. The back-to-back ODI hundreds against Australia in Sharjah—what are famously known as the 'Desert Storms'—while still only twenty-five were extraordinary works of art. A few years later, the Aussies felt that they found a chink in the master's armour and could get him caught when he played the cover drive. But Tendulkar thwarted the Aussies by curbing his natural instincts and not playing a single cover drive in the 2003 Sydney Test. Tendulkar went on to score 241 in the first innings of the Test, hitting thirty-three boundaries but not one cover drive! Only a genius could conceive such a counter-attack and execute it to perfection.

Jaw-dropping innings like these made Tendulkar attain a godlike status not just among fans but also among his teammates. Even iconic, hardened opponents hero-worshipped Tendulkar. Writer Dwarkanath Sanzgiri recalled an incident in the Indian dressing room after India had beaten Australia in the final of the Coca-Cola Cup at Sharjah in 1998. Sachin had scored 134 off 131 balls in that match and had been named Man of the Match as well as Player of the Series. Shane Warne had gone to the celebrating Indian players in their dressing room, taken off his shirt and asked Sachin to autograph it. Recalls Sanzgiri, 'Behind Warne were six other Australian players standing in a queue waiting for their shirts to be autographed as well!' These were hardened pros, not fanboys!

Tendulkar played cricket at all levels with equal seriousness and often took responsibility to lead the charge. Milind Rege, the former Bombay Ranji team captain and later selector, revealed how Tendulkar took the onus upon himself to deliver results in adverse circumstances. 'It's a moment that's etched in my memory,' recalls Rege. 'It was a sizzling Sachin drive that left Robin Singh just standing on the cover fence. That boundary was the culmination of an act of defiance by one man, which took Mumbai past Tamil Nadu's 485 in the 1999–2000 Ranji Trophy semi-finals. Sachin had to do it all, and he did it in style.' Though Sameer Dighe was officially the captain, says Rege, it was Tendulkar's decision to play five fast bowlers in April and it was also he who chose to field first. Mumbai were reduced to 449 for 8, but 41 runs were added for the last 2 wickets—with Tendulkar scoring them all. He remained not out on 233.

Writer Aldous Huxley had said, 'The secret of genius is to carry the spirit of childhood into old age.' Having seen Tendulkar from his Sharadashram school days till his retirement from Test cricket, I can say without fear of being contradicted that the maestro exemplified Huxley's quote more than any other player in cricket history.

32

KUMBLE

Suresh Menon

The ritual began on a Sunday afternoon in February 1999 at Delhi's Feroze Shah Kotla stadium. On a sports field, no one looks down upon superstition. Anything to attract luck or to keep it is seen as part of teamwork. There is no record of a sportsman saying, 'I am a science graduate, I don't believe in superstition.' The engineering graduate Anil Kumble was happy to let Sachin Tendulkar carry his sweater and cap to the umpire at the start of every over if it would somehow hasten the end of the Pakistan innings. After all, it had led to a wicket earlier.

Pakistan's chances of making 420 to win on the fourth day of the second Test were not high. But India had lost the previous Test in Chennai by just 12 runs and the team was hurting. The Pakistani openers, Saeed Anwar and Shahid Afridi, batted as if they thought there was a chance to reach the target. Kumble had bowled six wicketless overs from the Football Stand end before skipper Mohammed Azharuddin switched him to the Pavilion end after lunch. The thought uppermost in Kumble's mind was: It has to be me.

On the opening day of the match, Kumble had arrived at Kotla feeling good. This was the first series against the old enemy in a decade, and excitement was high. He went on to take 4 wickets in the first innings. One wicket will interrupt the flow, Anil kept telling himself as he bowled in the second innings. Eventually, he bowled a fast and straight delivery to Afridi who edged it and was caught behind. The score was 101 when that first wicket fell. The next ball, Ijaz Ahmed was leg before to one that pushed him onto the back foot.

Anwar, whose record against India is impressive, was threatening a counter-attack. Kumble initially bowled to him from round the wicket, attempting to hit the footmarks of the pacers. Anwar remained ominously comfortable but could only watch from the other end as Kumble bowled Inzamam-ul-Haq and then trapped Yousuf Youhana leg before, before Moin Khan was caught by Sourav Ganguly. Kumble now went over the wicket to the left-handed Anwar. A slow leg-break did the trick. Anwar was caught at short leg and Pakistan were 128 for 6.

In 44 deliveries, Kumble had taken 6 wickets for 15 runs. 'That was the moment,' Kumble said, when asked at what point he thought he might take all 10 wickets. Only one bowler in history had claimed 10 in an innings before. Jim Laker's 10 for 53 against Australia in 1956 is one of the famous figures in cricket, like Don Bradman's batting average of 99.94—a record unlikely to be broken.

Pakistan were reduced to 198 for 9, with Kumble having taken all the wickets to have fallen. Javagal Srinath started to bowl wide in an attempt to not take a wicket as last pair Wasim Akram and

Waqar Younis battled in a hopeless cause. Someone once asked Laker if his teammate Tony Lock—the left-arm spinner bowling from the other end the day he took all 10 wickets—eased up towards the end when the 10-wicket haul became a real possibility. Laker's reply is memorable: 'Eased up? Locky?' he sneered. 'At one stage Lock was appealing for leg-before with the ball hitting the batsman on the chest.' Srinath, Kumble's colleague from Karnataka, was too much the gentleman to adopt that approach.

The next over, Akram was caught by V.V.S. Laxman and Kumble had all 10. In the excitement, Kumble forgot about the ball. That was unusual. 'Right from the start of my career, I preserved the match balls when I got to significant landmarks,' he said. 'Every 5-wicket haul, the ball with which I took my 435th wicket to surpass Kapil Dev's record and the ones with which I took my 500th and 600th wickets.'

Laxman remembered throwing the ball in the air after taking the catch and then nothing else. He had been caught up in the excitement. The team physio went back on the field to look for the ball, which should have landed somewhere between fine leg and mid-wicket. But neither he nor the masseur, who went to look too, could find it. It was nearly an hour since the match had finished and Kumble was beginning to despair when Venkatesh Prasad told him that he had the ball. 'I picked it up as a souvenir from deep square leg,' he said, adding—just in case Kumble thought this had been a selfless act—that he intended to keep it.

The leg-spinner offered a trade: the stump he had picked up in return for the ball. No dice, said Prasad, who was enjoying Kumble's predicament. However, the pacer—who had played so much cricket with Kumble since their early years—eventually handed the ball over to Kumble. 'Someday I must give him that stump,' Kumble said later.

Kumble loved it when experts underestimated him. India's former captain Tiger Pataudi had said that Kumble was at best a 'restrictive' bowler. Years later, Kumble was delivering the Pataudi Memorial Lecture and said, 'After 619 wickets, it's my misfortune that I cannot confront him. Had I done so, he would have had a great laugh.' After flying down to South Africa to assess him ahead of England's tour of India in 1992–93, England coach Keith Fletcher told his team that they had nothing to fear from Kumble. The leg-spinner went on to take 21 wickets in the three-Test series as England were beaten 3-0.

The description 'leg-spinner' is not accurate as Kumble bowled at a greater pace than traditional leggies. He was not easy to classify. As Scyld Berry wrote in Wisden: 'He is a brisk top-spin bowler making the ball turn a little both ways.' For a while, describing Kumble's bowling became a national pastime; comparisons were made with Bhagwat Chandrasekhar, who told Kumble that even as he grew increasingly successful, coaches would have contradictory advice for him. 'You must have the strength to ignore such advice,' he said. Chandrasekhar had studied at the same college as Kumble and they grew up in the same neighbourhood. Kumble, of course, was nearly twenty-five years younger. He recalled that Chandrasekhar had initially asked him to lengthen his run-up.

Kumble is India's most successful bowler in two formats of the game, with 619 wickets in Tests and 337 in ODIs. But his impact went beyond the figures. He was a tough competitor who fought without compromising on integrity, which he saw as equally important to the number of wickets he took. As captain, Kumble handled the so-called 'Monkeygate' controversy in Australia with a kind of dignity that made all Indian cricket fans proud.

Kumble emerging from the pavilion in Antigua with his face bandaged but still ready to bowl is one of cricket's most inspiring moments. He sent down 14 consecutive overs and dismissed Brian Lara despite bowling with a broken jaw. He was due to fly back to Bangalore the following day for surgery. Before he left, Kumble said, 'At least I can now go home with the belief that I tried my best.' Viv Richards later said that it was one of the bravest things he had seen on the field of play.

Kumble had played forty-one Tests fewer than Kapil Dev when he went past Kapil's Indian record of 434 wickets. He bowled India to more victories than the legendary spin quartet of the 1970s, yet was condemned to being defined by negatives. The pundits said that he did not spin the ball, that he did not have the classic leg-spinner's loop, that he did not bowl slowly enough to get the ball to bite. Kumble was described by what he did not do rather than by what he did.

However, in the combined 231 Tests that the fabulous spin quartet of Erapalli Prasanna, Bishan Bedi, Bhagwat Chandrasekhar and Srinivas Venkataraghavan played, they claimed 853 wickets. Had Kumble played that many Tests he would have finished with 1,083 wickets, as he took 4.69 wickets per Test—a ratio higher than any of that quartet. Another way of looking at Kumble's figures is from the perspective of balls per wicket. Kumble took a wicket every 65.5 deliveries, just ahead of Chandrasekhar. By comparison, spin greats Richie Benaud and Derek Underwood needed 77 and 74 deliveries, respectively, to take a wicket.

Kumble is among the finest to have played the game. He reduced bowling to its basics, like an artist who simplifies but still retains the meaning of his work. When the ball is spinning across the face of the bat, it only needs to deviate a couple of inches to miss the middle and take the edge. As befits an engineering student, Kumble was comfortable with angles and understood that the difference between a good delivery and a bad one is only a matter of inches. The amount of bounce he was able to generate often surprised batsmen. Above all, he was able to create doubts in the batsman's mind.

Kumble was also an accomplished captain and later served as the president of the Karnataka Cricket Association, and then as the national team coach. He also had a stint as chairman of the ICC and served the game he loved with passion and dignity. There is something about sportsmen from Karnataka, the best of whom are polite and modest despite being supremely gifted—they are old-fashioned gentlemen who respect what they do. Examples are Prakash Padukone, Gundappa Vishwanath, Chandrasekhar, Rahul Dravid and, of course, Kumble.

Anil Kumble remains the same unaffected soul who began his international career at age nineteen, slightly surprised at being elevated to the highest level so early but accepting it as his due. The steely determination was there even then and has remained with him throughout.

33

MATCHWINNERS

R. Kaushik

Some players can change the course of a match all on their own with flair, panache and style, entertaining audiences while still ensuring that they take their team to victory. From Gundappa Vishwanath to Sachin Tendulkar and B.S. Chandrasekhar to Jasprit Bumrah, India has produced players who draw you to the edge of your seat, unable to keep your eyes off the action. Here's a look at some of the iconic cricketers who have contributed immeasurably to elevating the stocks of Indian cricket to where they are today.

Vinoo Mankad

It's a shame that an all-rounder who had so many memorable performances over a first-class career spanning twenty-six years is mainly remembered for one passage of play: stopping in his bowling run-up to run out Bill Brown at the non-striker's end during India's tour of Australia in 1947–48. Vinoo Mankad's name became forever associated with this form of dismissal.

However, what should be remembered are his achievements at a time when Indian cricket struggled for respect and recognition at the global stage. Mankad stood tall despite his team's lack of success, regularly producing stirring deeds as a daring right-handed opener and a crafty left-arm spinner. Blessed with wonderful hand–eye coordination, Mankad the batsman was ahead of his times. The straight bat wasn't necessarily his favoured ally; he was willing to discard the coaching manual if it came in the way of scoring runs. A delectable cover drive was his calling card, though he was unafraid to turn to cross-bat shots if that meant he could keep the score moving.

Unlike his batting, Mankad's left-arm spin was more conventional, with his stock ball turning away from the right-hand batsman. However, he had a mean quicker one that came in with the arm and befuddled many a batter. It was with his bowling that Mankad played a key role in India's maiden Test win—he took twelve wickets in that match against England in Madras in 1952.

B.S. Chandrasekhar

Loose-limbed, mild-mannered and fun-loving, B.S. Chandrasekhar—popularly known as 'Chandra'—lost none of his politeness on the cricket field. But once he had the ball in his hands, he would grow fangs. His whiplash action and speed through the air made him unplayable once he had found his rhythm.

Chandra had been afflicted by polio when he was young. However, he made light of his disability to quickly climb the rungs of grade cricket. He was fortunate that junior-level selectors did not consider his unorthodox action as a disadvantage. Instead, they encouraged him to follow his instincts, and he soon made his international debut. On that stage, Chandra had a captain in Tiger Pataudi who was willing to back him to the hilt. Pataudi was convinced that even though he was spoilt for choice when it came to quality spinners—such as Bishan Bedi and Erapalli Prasanna—Chandra was the ace in his pack. Chandra seldom disappointed his captain.

Chandra has said that he was only concerned about the positions of four fielders—slip, forward short-leg, leg-slip and a man by the square-leg umpire. By his contention, if he bowled well, these four would suffice; if he didn't, it didn't really matter to him where the other fielders were! Chandra was one of the rare Indian spinners who has had as much success overseas as at home. His 12-wicket haul at Melbourne in 1977–78 was one of his standout performances in an away series.

However, six years prior to that, Chandra had bowled India to a sensational Test series win in England. He had been overlooked for the tour of the West Indies that had preceded the England tour, and only reinstated to the team as a 'gamble', according to then Chairman of Selectors Vijay Merchant. Chandra channelized his angst to produce a telling 6-wicket burst in the final Test at the Oval to script a historic maiden success for India in England.

Gundappa Vishwanath

Initially considered too short to warrant selection to school-level teams, Gundappa Vishwanath overcame his doubters to capture the imagination of many who watched him bat—including the national team captain, M.A.K. Pataudi. Vishwanath—or 'Vishy', as he is universally known—made his India debut in 1969 and embarked on a career that had many memorable moments.

Vishy's signature stroke was born out of necessity; too slight of build to generate enough power, he chose to use the pace of the bowlers instead to garner most of his runs through his favourite square-cut. India didn't lose any of the fourteen Tests in which Vishy made a hundred, though his most celebrated knock was not a century.

Against an inspired West Indian attack led by Andy Roberts on a bouncy track at Chepauk in 1975, he played one of the all-time great innings and finished unbeaten on 97. To the man himself, that 97 was more satisfying than some of his hundreds. Vishwanath played ninety-one Tests in a career that won him legions of admirers. Of all the batsmen who played for India, few were eulogized more for the joy they provided over the runs they scored.

Kapil Dev

Until the late 1980s, Kapil Dev was the fastest Indian bowler by a distance. Prior to his dramatic debut against Pakistan in 1978, bowling fast didn't appeal to Indian youngsters brought up on mesmeric spin bowling. Single-handedly, Kapil altered the psyche of the aspiring Indian cricketer, triggering a revolution that now sees the country boasting an enviable arsenal of world-class pace bowlers.

Kapil was more than just a supremely skilled bowler. He was equally adept at all three disciplines of the game, and his ability with the bat meant that he could have even played as a specialist batsman. His uncomplicated approach to batting was best illustrated at Lord's in 1990 when India needed 24 runs to avoid the follow-on and Kapil had only last man Narendra Hirwani for company. He struck the last four balls of Eddie Hemmings' over for sixes to prevent the follow-on before Hirwani was dismissed off the first ball of the next over.

However, Kapil is most remembered for his feats during India's triumphant World Cup campaign in 1983. He scored an epochal 175 not out against Zimbabwe at Tunbridge Wells, inspiring India to the final. In that decider, his crucial catch running backwards from mid-wicket to dismiss a marauding Viv Richards epitomized his lithe athleticism and untameable spirit.

Sachin Tendulkar

Sachin Tendulkar was a free spirit, a pocket-sized bundle of raw aggression with a maturity well beyond his years. It was the authority with which he imposed himself on seasoned bowlers across the world that put him in a league of his own. He was the bedrock of the Indian batting for the entirety of his international career, which lasted twenty-four years. During that time, he managed the unprecedented feat of scoring a hundred international centuries.

Tendulkar was not yet nineteen when he made two hundreds on the 1991–92 tour of Australia. His 114 in Perth was particularly memorable for the ease with which he handled the pace and bounce generated by Australia's quick bowlers. The punches through the covers off the back foot during that innings suggested that he was a batting superstar in the making.

To maintain his performances for over two decades even as the nation followed his every move required great reserves of mental strength. Tendulkar used the cricket ground as his sanctuary and the pitch as his ally and temple. In a symbolic gesture, he strode out to the centre at the Wankhede Stadium and offered his prayers to the pitch at the end of his career.

Virender Sehwag

Virender Sehwag was a Tendulkar fan and made a conscious attempt in the early part of his career to copy the Little Master's batting style. In fact, when Sehwag made his Test debut at Bloemfontein in 2001 and shared an exhilarating fifth-wicket partnership of 220 with his hero, so similar were strokes played by the two small-statured men that it was difficult to differentiate between them.

However, it didn't take long for Sehwag to establish his own brand of aggressive cricket. Captain Sourav Ganguly and coach John Wright knew that they had to find a place for a batsman like Sehwag in the Test XI. As there was no vacancy in the middle order, they pushed him up to open the batting on the tour of England in 2002. It turned out to be a masterstroke and Indian cricket was never the same again.

Resisting the temptation to play the percentages, Sehwag backed his seemingly high-risk approach and redefined the art of opening the batting in the longer format. Sehwag saw opportunities galore to stack up runs quickly against the new ball. Contrary to popular perception, there was a method to his madness. Sehwag might not have thrilled the purists with his minimal foot movement when playing shots, but the fans couldn't have enough of him. The damage he inflicted at the top of the order meant that by the time the likes of Rahul Dravid, Tendulkar and V.V.S. Laxman came out to bat, the opposition was already on the back foot mentally.

It is said that when Laxman made 281 against Australia at Kolkata in 2001—at the time the highest individual score in Tests by an Indian cricketer—Sehwag told him, 'You have missed out on a triple—now watch as I become the first Indian to score 300.' Fulfilling his own prophecy, Sehwag became India's first triple-centurion in 2004, and followed it up with another 300 four years later.

Jasprit Bumrah

Former New Zealand captain John Wright became India's first overseas coach in 2000 and struck up a fine rapport with Ganguly as India finally began to believe that they could compete away from home. But of all the stellar contributions Wright has made to Indian cricket, discovering Jasprit Bumrah must rank at the top of the list.

It was as a talent scout with the Mumbai Indians IPL franchise that Wright found the unpolished gem in the anonymity of lower-grade cricket. When bowling, Bumrah had an awkward walk-up, followed by a short burst of acceleration and a unique delivery style with a braced left knee. Such an action should not have caught the eye of an avowed conservative like Wright. But he saw something in Bumrah that others might have missed.

It didn't take long for Bumrah to make the cricket world sit up and take notice. He took the white-ball route to international cricket in 2016 and eventually made his Test debut in South Africa in 2018. He had soon established himself as skipper Virat Kohli's go-to man in the longer version too, becoming the spearhead of a pace unit that orchestrated successive series wins in Australia in 2018–19 and 2020–21.

Bumrah is a hard worker and a good listener with a willingness to learn. Combined with a sharp cricket brain and natural ability, these traits make him a winner. He has evolved into a versatile paceman and the suspicions that the novelty of his action would wear off remain unfounded. However, the fears that his action could place undue stress on his body are gradually proving true. Yet, he is far from done yet. Jasprit Bumrah may not have the most wickets or the best average, but for sheer impact, India will be hard-pressed to find another pacer of his quality.

34

MAHENDRA SINGH DHONI: THE MAVERICK CAPTAIN

S. Kannan

At a time when there is constant chatter about too much cricket being played, leading to player fatigue, one man is still showing incredible longevity. It is Mahendra Singh Dhoni, or 'MSD' as many refer to him. Still young at forty-one, he has been the face of change in white-ball cricket in India. It seems like yesterday when a young man with long locks, an unorthodox batting stance and grip and unconventional wicketkeeping skills took world cricket by storm. From day one, MSD has been different.

His unique brand of cricket—be it as a batsman, wicketkeeper or captain—did ruffle a few feathers. But sport likes mavericks because normal is boring and predictable. MSD has kept his habit of springing surprises and has always backed the people he believes in. He has been a daredevil in the true sense and Indian cricket should be grateful he is still playing, albeit only in the IPL.

Many books have been written on MSD, most of which are unauthorized biographies. Writing a biography in the digital age is so easy. You just need to throw in stats, photos and a few quotes. But statistics alone would not paint the full MSD picture because at best they can offer a perspective in terms of numbers and records. MSD goes beyond numbers, holding his sparkling value over years of ups and downs.

MSD was a magician with the Midas touch as captain. However, there are some who say he was boring as Test captain. The main criticism was that he was too defensive. It is easier to pick apart a superstar in the age of social media. Yet, even in the new era, MSD still has a strong presence. MSD was captain when India won the T20 World Cup in 2007, a tournament in which few had thought the Indian team a chance.

In fact, most of the senior players had skipped the event in South Africa altogether, giving MSD the opportunity to lead. Only when India beat Pakistan in the final did it sink in that we had won a big trophy. It was 24 September 2007, and I was in Khan Market in New Delhi, sipping beer and watching MSD and his young team celebrate with an unexpected ICC trophy. There were many heroes that emerged from that tournament, including Gautam Gambhir and current India captain Rohit Sharma, along with the brilliant bowlers R.P. Singh, Irfan Pathan and Joginder Singh. For those who love old scorecards, this one against Pakistan will remain special.

Though one must credit the skipper of the side for this win, MSD was humble as ever, to the point of being meek. He never did things for his own gratification and has always been a leader who helped others along. However, even after the 2007 win, people might have laughed at the suggestion that MSD was soon going to become the captain of Team India in all formats of the game.

It is only when we look back to reflect do we understand what MSD achieved as captain in his first major challenge. He backed players instinctively and brought the best out of his team, flummoxing rivals by being unconventional and daring. That became a template of sorts for MSD. Perhaps it was that swagger of a billionaire and instincts of an inveterate Las Vegas gambler that saw MSD win more and more.

His irreverent approach rattled the old timers but he believed what he was doing was right. Captaincy is both an art and a science. Some captains are born leaders and some grow into the role through experience. MSD took to captaincy like a fish to water. But to say that MSD never faced flak would be akin to saying a heavyweight boxer never received blows on his face.

At each stage of his career, MSD made smooth changes as if he always knew when and how to do the right thing. But it is wrong to say that he was a lucky captain. He was more than a captain—he was a mentor and a guide, a leader who gave chances to youngsters and backed them to perform. The list of players who owe their success to MSD is long. Some may not want to acknowledge his role, but others are eternally grateful.

However, MSD never demanded reverence from these young players. For MSD, handling an Indian side with legendary players such as Sachin Tendulkar came easily and naturally. Perhaps it was a willingness to also be a soldier and not just a field marshal that allowed MSD to bring the best out of the veteran players.

On 2 April 2011, India won the ODI World Cup at the Wankhede Stadium under MSD. The captain himself hit the winning runs, as memorably immortalized by commentator Ravi Shastri: 'Dhoniiiii finishes off in style! A magnificent strike into the crowd and India lift the World Cup after twenty-eight years!

The party's started in the dressing room. And it's an Indian captain who's been absolutely magnificent on the night of the final!' MSD never cried with the trophy or hugged and kissed it. He let Tendulkar do all the posing for photos and rejoicing. MSD had great chemistry with coach Gary Kirsten, a duo that will continue to be talked about until India win their next ICC title.

MSD handled success and failure with the same straight face. His fitness levels were amazing and despite having slowed down, he still holds the reins at Chennai Super Kings (CSK) in the IPL. It shows how he is still loved by the franchise and that he is still fit enough to perform for them. MSD was his own man and as instinctively as he played his cricket, he knew when it was time give up captaincy. He did so unexpectedly in Australia after having mentored Virat Kohli as his successor.

Today, people compare stats and say that Kohli was a better Test captain, but greatness cannot be defined by statistics alone. Kapil Dev instilled a winning spirit in Indian cricket during India's victorious World Cup campaign in 1983. MSD has done something similar, but on numerous occasions. Incidentally, the man from Jharkhand started off as a clerk in the Indian Railways. Today, he is an honorary officer in the Indian army and he takes the title seriously.

What can one say of MSD in his avatar as the enigmatic leader of a Madrasi team? For those who do not know the love affair between MSD and Chennai fans, he is referred to as 'Thalaiva', which means 'king'. MSD and CSK are made for each other and neither wins nor losses have defined his greatness. In a tournament where switching franchises after a few seasons is the norm, MSD has remained a one-franchise man. He has the backing of N. Srinivasan, a powerful figure in Indian cricket. During his time at CSK, MSD made champions out of younger players such as Suresh Raina and Ravindra Jadeja.

Behind the stumps, MSD is still quick. His wicketkeeping skills and fast run-outs have not diminished even though his six-hitting abilities and helicopter shots may have. His running between wickets is still smart and he still connects with the youth, the millennials and the elderly alike. Uncles in veshtis (dhotis) and maamis in nine-yard podavais (sarees) can be seen cheering him on. This rare connection spanning generations makes MSD special even today.

35

VIRAT KOHLI: THE HERO OF NEW-AGE CRICKET

Vijay Lokapally

Each era of Indian cricket has produced a hero to capture the nation's imagination, from Mansur Ali Khan Pataudi and Sunil Gavaskar to Kapil Dev and Sachin Tendulkar. The present-day hero is Virat Kohli—an enigma for the opposition and a talisman for his team, one who carries with aplomb the enormous responsibility of motivating a generation of players.

Kohli was introduced to cricket when he tagged along with his brother to an academy near his home. The coach there was Rajkumar Sharma, who had no particular claims to fame at the time. Yet, when Kohli came under his tutelage, his world changed. Sharma noticed that the young Virat was comfortable playing and competing with older boys, which convinced him of the lad's innate drive and ability. Sharma knew that he had been given the opportunity to work with a diamond in the rough.

Delhi cricket is known to ignore talent. Apart from Kohli, even the likes of Virender Sehwag and Rishabh Pant were initially ignored by the Delhi selectors when picking the junior teams. However, when they amassed runs in the local cricket circuit, the embarrassed selectors had no choice but to pick them.

Senior players in Delhi began frequenting the tournaments where Kohli played and sparkled as an aggressive batsman. There was a streak of brilliance in his play and he was making rapid progress. Critics began to say that he was destined for greater things. Chetan Chauhan recognized Kohli as a 'precocious talent'.

Fortunately for Kohli, in the Delhi team he was playing with seniors such as Sehwag and Shikhar Dhawan, who encouraged and advised the prodigy. The same side had another future star in its ranks—the growth of Ishant Sharma coincided with Kohli's progress. It was just a matter of time before Kohli made his first-class debut.

In a match against Karnataka, Kohli showed some of the determination he would become famous for. Batting with Puneet Bisht, the pair ended the day as the not-out batsmen as Delhi fought to avoid a follow-on. Kohli returned home to learn that his father had passed away. Yet, he returned the next day to continue his innings because of his team's precarious situation. The Delhi dressing room was shocked to see Kohli pad up even though his father's body lay at home. Kohli and Bisht saw Delhi past the follow-on mark. Kohli earned the respect of the opponents and his teammates with that tremendous knock, which showcased his tenacity and discipline. A hero was born that day at the Kotla.

During Kohli's initial years in international cricket, he came across as a player who was in conflict with his approach to the game. He was naturally aggressive and always keen to establish early supremacy over the opposition. A busy man at the crease, Kohli found new ways to make runs. In the process, he also found new ways to get out. Critics did not appreciate his style and often slammed him for getting out to casual shots.

The 2014 tour of England was a shattering experience for Kohli. Despite having already scored six Test centuries in his career by the time he went on that tour, he struggled to adapt to the conditions and couldn't even go past 40 in 10 innings. Knives came out and the doubters began to ask if Kohli was overrated. Was he merely a flat-track bully?

Thus, Kohli had a lot to prove when India toured Australia in 2014–15. The bounce that bowlers extract on Australian pitches compels the batsmen to adapt and adopt different strokes. Kohli did not have much experience playing the rising ball until that tour to Australia, which proved defining for his career.

It was a challenging phase for Indian cricket. The incumbent captain, M.S. Dhoni, had retired from Test cricket suddenly and captaincy had been thrust upon Kohli midway through the tour. The task was humungous as Kohli was saddled with a team in the process of transition. Living up to the high expectations and repaying the faith shown in him, he took his first steps towards becoming a great leader by scoring a century in each innings on Test captaincy debut.

Captaincy brought the best out of Kohli. It also made him realize that he was a role model in world cricket, bracketed with the likes of Kane Williamson and Joe Root as the batsmen for younger players to look up to. Kohli did not disappoint, even though at times it did impact his game. It seemed he was again at conflict with his natural desire to dominate, wondering if he should change his approach and eschew risks as he now held a position of responsibility. He struggled for a while but did not succumb to the inner demons that may have lured him into a false assessment of the situation.

At the time, Test cricket was in danger of dying out as the younger generations felt more connected to T20 cricket. The traditional form of the game sorely needed a champion, and Kohli emerged as the statesman that world cricket needed. He took it upon himself to become the advertisement for Test cricket by playing and captaining aggressively and always looking to win instead of playing out safe draws. He reminded younger players of the importance of playing the longer format of the game and advised them not to ignore the domestic first-class competition.

Being captain meant that Kohli was under relentless scrutiny. He was the poster boy of Indian cricket and the official broadcaster even dedicated a camera to focus only on Kohli. The camera panned on his face and reactions at every incident on the field. No movement of his went unnoticed. Kohli knew that apart from leading India to wins, he had to moderate his behaviour and maintain his batting form to keep his fans happy and critics quiet. 'It is not easy,' he admitted once. 'I have to be at my best at all times and it is not humanly possible. I am bound to fail like others, but I try to ensure that I stay consistent as a player and captain.'

One of Kohli's major contributions to Indian cricket is the introduction of high fitness standards. He was obsessed with being a supreme athlete and made sacrifices to achieve the best fitness levels possible. He changed his food habits and became a vegan. His passion for fitness rubbed off on his teammates. They followed his example and soon there was a new culture of fitness in the Indian dressing room.

Indian cricketers were looking far more athletic on the field, and it had the desired impact in matches. Kohli was happy to see his team adopting his philosophies. 'I will not ask my players to do things which I can't,' declared Kohli even as the BCCI introduced new norms of fitness at the National Cricket Academy.

Kohli knew from an early stage that he would have to evolve and make himself almost indispensable if he wanted a long career. He did not give a chance to the selectors to look at him any differently. The tons of runs he scored acted as a cushion for an inevitable bad phase. When it hit, experts were quick to point out to his weakness against the moving ball, allowing for his off-stump defence to be exploited by seamers. Sunil Gavaskar noted that a flaw in Kohli's game was his tendency to play shots early, causing him to reach out for deliveries wide of the off-stump and edge to the slips. It had become a pattern for Kohli's dismissals.

As captain, Kohli would spend time with teammates working on correcting their weaknesses. Perhaps as a result he didn't give his own technique as much attention and certain flaws had crept into his game. It puzzled Kohli as he did not find any issues with his bat-swing nor his footwork. The more he thought about it, the more he failed. He was uncharacteristically getting out even to poor deliveries.

As his game deteriorated, even his fans started questioning his performances. His Test century against Bangladesh in Kolkata in 2019 was not enough to silence his critics. Finally, Kohli decided to reinvent himself by stepping down as captain to dedicate more time to improve his own game. Soon, he was back to his best.

One Kohli knock that won't be forgotten was in the game against Pakistan in the 2022 T20 World Cup in Australia. On Diwali eve at a packed Melbourne Cricket Ground, Kohli produced one of the greatest knocks in the history of the game. In a high-pressure match against India's arch-rivals, he single-handedly powered his team to victory from a hopeless situation. Fans knew that the Kohli we had long celebrated was back. This was the born-again Virat Kohli, setting new benchmarks.

World cricket was enriched by the contributions of Indian heroes such as Pataudi, Gavaskar and Tendulkar. Virat Kohli then stepped up when Indian cricket needed a new hero, and his status among the legends of the game is secure.

DOMESTIC STALWARTS

36

A BEAUTIFUL JOURNEY
Saad bin Jung

Living the life I do, with daily challenges including elephants smashing borewells, leopards abducting my pets and wild boar digging up my prized fruit trees, all I think of is the present. My cricketing past has become just a memory four decades old. So, when my old batting partner Venkat Sundaram asked me to do a piece on cricket, I was reluctant. Not because I don't love or miss the game, but just that our playing days are from a bygone era that is never going to come back.

Yet, his request made the memories come flooding in again. How can one forget the trudge to the stadium at the break of dawn, bat handle peeping out of the open kit bag? Once there, we were ordered to sprint up and down the steps of the stadium. It made no sense to me. When sometimes an overenthusiastic coach would ask us to go for a long run on the roads, I would wait for everyone to pass and then take a rickshaw the rest of the way.

At nets, I would be the first to pad up as I was an opening batsman. But I would do it only while complaining that practice should be out in the middle and not in the nets as they disturb our peripheral vision. I insisted that by batting in these claustrophobic rectangles we were spoiling our technique, and pointed out that bowlers who were getting smashed in matches were kings in the nets. But no matter how much I grumbled, no one ever paid me any heed.

Once, during nets with the Hyderabad team, our captain showed up in immaculately pressed tracksuit bottoms. Our burly coach started to thunder and screamed at the captain for not being in whites. He was asked to leave. Now, the captain was my best friend, and I decided to stage a walkout. The team followed, although some were rather reluctant to show dissent. Nonetheless, at that moment we stood united and asked for an apology from the coach. The apology never came. Instead, we were all dropped for the next game. I was nineteen, full of beans and with raging testosterone levels. This attitude of not respecting authority was not well received by the powers that be. But I played for the love of the game and that's just how I wanted to play my cricket.

Once, I was called by a former Test off-spinner before a match. His warning was dire: 'This will the last match of your life if you are not serious. Make full use of it or else you are finished.' But when batting, well-set at 20, I attempted a few ludicrous shots. One was a hoist over square leg to a ball that was on the middle stump, another was a late cut to a googly that would have taken out middle. Even now I cannot fathom why I played those shots, but it made me realize that cricket to me would always be a sport meant to be played for enjoyment. Play within your limitations, I was always told. But how would I know my limitations unless I go out there and try each shot?

Cricket had taught me a lesson also applicable to life: risks are meant to be taken; some would work out well and others would not.

Navigare necesse est, vivere non est necesse!

(To sail the seas is a necessity, to live is not)

This quote is attributed to Pompey, but I first heard it in the film *Out of Africa* and adopted it as my motto in both life and cricket. It was necessary to enjoy playing the sport but not necessary to always win. However, I fear this attitude to the sport was solely because cricket was more a lifestyle than a sport for my family.

You see, my connection with cricket is rather old. The story begins when Nawab Iftikhar Ali Khan Pataudi returned to India after having disagreed with Douglas Jardine during the 'Bodyline' series. Pataudi felt that the spirit of cricket was being abused and he wanted to play no further part in Jardine's tactics. Thus, despite a century in the first Test, he was dropped after the next match and sat out the rest of the series.

It was the 1930s, and Indian royalty was met with both deference and contempt the world over. The British were the colonial powers, but the local royals had stepped in to fund and manage cricket in India. The English were happy to step back and monitor these developments with a feeling of satisfaction. Thus, if Pataudi wanted to play cricket in India, he would need the blessings of both the BCCI and the local ruler of the state team he would play for.

Once in India, he took the personal train of Hamidullah Khan, the nawab of the beautiful lake city of Bhopal, to visit the ruler at his residence, Qasr-i-Sultani. By no stretch of imagination can it be said that the men liked each other at first sight. The opposite was true when Pataudi saw his host's daughter. He fell head over heels in love with Princess Saijida Sultan and a flaming love affair ensued, much to the chagrin of the ruler of Bhopal.

When the cricketer proposed to the princess, she accepted in the blink of an eye. But the proposal did not get very far with her father. Pataudi was not a person who gave up easily, so he tried to woo his prospective father-in-law with a hunting trip. But the reply to his invitation was a short and curt 'No'. Bhopal wanted nothing to do with the miniscule state of Pataudi.

Despite the rejection, Pataudi had a stuffed tiger placed in his sugarcane fields—where never before had a tiger been seen. The palace staff were ordered to set up a ring around the dummy animal. While a guard acted as if he was about to spear the tiger, Pataudi's younger brother made a show of pulling him back. The scene was completed by Pataudi himself, who aimed his rifle at the 'beast'.

Photographs were taken of the scene and the best one framed in silver. Embossed with the Pataudi logo, the framed photograph was sent by personal courier to Hamidullah Khan with ten kilogrammes of the sohan halwa made only in Pataudi. In response, the ruler of Bhopal banned Pataudi from crossing his state boundaries. Despite this, Pataudi continued his courtship of the princess, arranging discreet meetings by the banks of the Betwa in spots hidden from the prying eyes of Bhopal spies. Eventually, the matter was taken up by the colonial rulers, who ordained that the marriage should go ahead.

The first child born to Iftikhar and Saijida was my mother, followed by Mansur Ali Khan—who would later captain India and be known and remembered as 'Tiger'. Cricket simply flowed down the genes to my elder brother and I, who grew up with the superstars of the sport. Test stars from different countries would often visit our home in Hyderabad. After a few drinks, they would ask my brother Aamir to get a tennis ball and bat. We would play alongside them but never had the urge to even take an autograph as we had none of the awe associated with fans and their heroes. These cricketers loved to tell their stories and we imbibed these with glee.

When I finally got the opportunity to play for Hyderabad, I wanted to live those stories myself. Sadly, it wasn't to be. M.L. Jaisimha had been a close friend of the family and would later become my godfather. However, during the time when Jaisimha and Tiger Pataudi played for Hyderabad, they never managed to win the Ranji Trophy despite having the likes of Sultan Saleem, Mumtaz Hussain, Abid Ali and Abbas Ali Baig. Hyderabad cricket had lost its golden generation.

During the year I played for Hyderabad, I was searching for something that I knew was no longer there. After that, an illness kept me in a two-bedroom clinic for over two years. In that period of recuperation, I realized that I didn't want to go back to Hyderabad. When I was well enough to play again, I decided to change teams to Haryana, where I had some friends.

I reported to Chandigarh in the freezing winter of 1983. Life in the north of India is so different from the south. Remaining oblivious to the politics of the Haryana Cricket Association at the time, I had a great time playing with people of real character. No story of my time in Haryana would be complete without a mention of my hosts. I lived as a paying guest with an Akali family. I have never seen such warmth, openness and trust as I did in their house—and they served such good food.

During net sessions with the Haryana team, the opening bowlers would gun for the batsmen in cold and misty conditions.

Instead of trying to get the batsman out, they would try to hit him. At times the ball would be delivered from well within 18 yards. After the quicks, we had to face Rajinder Goel, a left-arm spinner with amazing accuracy. To all those who have played with or against him, it was impossible to comprehend how a spinner of his calibre never played for India.

Our wicketkeeper knew that my younger brother, Omer, was studying at Sanawar in neighbouring Himachal Pradesh. He would take me on his scooter to visit Omer every weekend. After having been part of the dog-eat-dog world of cricket in the south, I was always touched by the sensitivity of the players in the north. Teammates here always cared about you and looked out for you.

I remember a game at Faridabad for which Kapil Dev joined us. We were put in to field, and I walked to my regular position at first slip. Kapil was at mid-off. A few overs went by and the big man still hadn't bowled. That's when I saw him nursing an injury. He would normally have stood at first slip but as I had already taken that position, he didn't want to ask me to switch. I ran across to him, apologized and offered to exchange places. Our team had an incredible camaraderie where we always helped each other in this way.

It was not surprising when we reached the semi-finals of the Ranji Trophy that year. That match against Bombay would turn out to be the last game I would ever play. I had already told the boys that I would be retiring. Somehow, I knew there was another calling, another life beyond cricket. After the season ended, I returned to Hyderabad. Later that year, I received a letter to report to Chandigarh for preparations for the next season. I declined politely. I am glad I did, for I was soon to discover my life in the bush, one that has only given me days of happiness.

I had found conservation and wildlife. Though it's been a tougher path to tread, it's given me untold joy as now I could change the lives of others along with my own. The basic understanding of conservation is missing in India. It would take nearly two decades of battling the inherent conflicts within our valley for me to imbibe the true essence of conservation, which is a means to maintain a perfect balance in nature.

One evening many decades ago, the Nawab of Pataudi Sr was down with a fever and I was sitting at his bedside, pressing his feet. We were discussing my life in the forest, our challenges and the need for change. That day we exchanged personal notes on cricket. He understood me and I knew that he too had shared a part of himself with me that he would never share with anybody else. I loved him then as I love him now.

I am so proud of the fact that I could walk on the same wickets that such great players have tread upon. I may not have done as much as them but merely walking the same path was enough for me. This helped me put cricket in perspective and move on from a sport that I so loved to other challenges and adventures in life. Today, at my age, all I can tell the readers is to go with your heart. There is nothing more pleasurable in this world than the pursuit of your passion.

37

HYDERABAD CRICKET

N. Jagannath Das

There is a romantic aura to Hyderabad cricket that makes old-timers' faces light up with delight. Since British troops introduced the game to the region, colourful cricketers and buzzing grounds have combined over the decades to give it a unique characteristic. The earliest of the Hyderabad cricket stars is perhaps Edulji Bujorji 'Eddie' Aibara. He played Ranji Trophy for twenty-five years before retiring to become one of the country's finest coaches. He was the first cricketer to get a diploma in cricket coaching from the National Institute of Sports in Patiala.

Ghulam Ahmed was a world-class off-spinner who played twenty-two Tests after making his debut against the West Indies in Calcutta in 1948. The tall bowler was a master of subtle flight and variation and would go on to captain India in three Tests against New Zealand and the West Indies. Ahmed was perhaps the first Indian cricketer to go on to play other roles after retirement when he became secretary of the Hyderabad Cricket Association (HCA) shortly after his retirement from active cricket in 1959. He held the post till 1976 and the game flourished under his stewardship. He was instrumental in reviving the Moin-ud-Dowlah Gold Cup as an all-India tournament.

Ahmed managed the Indian team on tours of the West Indies and Australia. On the West Indies tour—which was his first managerial assignment—he had to deal with a very difficult situation when skipper Nari Contractor was critically injured after being hit on the head by a Charlie Griffith bumper. The attention that Ahmed gave Contractor during that traumatic time won him many admirers.

Ahmed also had two stints as a national selector. During his second tenure, he was the chairman of the selection committee that picked the team that won the 1983 World Cup. He was appointed the joint secretary of the BCCI and later took over as secretary. M.L. Jaisimha—one of Hyderabad cricket's biggest icons—told me that he owed his career to Ghulam Ahmed. 'I used to play cricket, tennis and badminton,' he recalled. 'One morning, he called me and asked me to focus on one sport and not dabble in many. It was then that I decided to play only cricket, the sport I loved most.'

Jaisimha was one of the charmers of Indian cricket. Former Hyderabad all-rounder Jyothi Prasad says that Jai—as Jaisimha was popularly called—was a magnetic personality. 'Apart from his excellent leadership and reading of the game, he was a charming figure both on and off the field,' recalls Prasad. 'He drew crowds with his languid walk to the crease and his signature batting style. He excelled both as player and coach.'

In the book *I Adore Jai*—published by Jaisimha's wife, Jayanthi—there are many stories about this elegant Hyderabad batter. Bollywood actor Sharmila Tagore, the wife of former India captain Mansur Ali Khan Pataudi, mentions that Jayanthi's love for the man knew no bounds. 'You literally risked your life if you had the temerity to point out any flaw in her Jaisimha,' Sharmila recalls, while revealing that she too was one of the numerous female fans who considered Jai their idol. She mentions that Jai's upturned collar and signature silk handkerchief tied rakishly around his neck combined with his inimitable swag made him extremely dashing. According to her, Jai was her husband's closest friend. When Delhi stifled him, Pataudi had no hesitation to play under Jai as he immensely admired Jai's leadership qualities.

Hyderabad has an assembly line of stylish batters that have mesmerized the world. The on-drive is the signature shot of the Hyderabad batsman. Former India opener V.B. Chandrasekhar once said that batters from Hyderabad play the on-drive with ease and make it look simple. Famous Hyderabadi exponents of the stroke include Aibara, Jaisimha, Abbas Ali Baig, Mohammed Azharuddin and V.V.S. Laxman. The late Sultan Saleem, another stylish cricketer, said of Jaisimha's on-drive: 'I wondered how he could play that stroke so well, that too very late. He simply caressed the ball.'

The true successor to Jai as the representative of the Hyderabad school of batting was Azharuddin, who stormed into international cricket with centuries in his first three Tests. He used the lightest of bats, but it worked like a magic wand. Azhar's speciality was whipping the ball from off-stump to the mid-wicket boundary with his naturally wonderful timing coupled with nimble footwork and supple wrists.

Laxman followed in Azhar's footsteps, and when he was on a song, he was a purist's delight. 'Perhaps by playing in narrow lanes growing up, I learned how to play this stroke effectively,' he says.

Former India left-arm spinner Venkatapathy Raju says Laxman often sent the ball to the mid-wicket boundary with a simple turn of his wrists, finding the gaps with his excellent hand–eye coordination.

When it came to spin bowling, Hyderabad had a problem of plenty till the 1990s, with canny bowlers such as Mahendra Kumar, Mumtaz Hussain, Noshir Mehta, Venkatraman Ramnarayan, M.V. Narasimha Rao, Shivlal Yadav, Arshad Ayub, Kanwaljit Singh and Ananta Vatsalaya apart from Raju. Mahendra Kumar was a great exponent of leg spin and had a good googly too. Mumtaz was a mystery left-arm spinner and none less than Sunil Gavaskar felt that he had some unplayable deliveries. Raju was one of the finest left-arm spinners of the 1990s.

Today, the team is struggling to find a quality spinner. 'Hyderabad always had a rich tradition of spin bowling,' says Ramnarayan. 'It is sad to see off-spin bowling disappearing from Hyderabad cricket now.' Ramnarayan recalls that in the heyday of Hyderabad spin bowling there was stiff competition among spinners for berths in the squad. 'A few were lucky to get the big break, but others were not as fortunate,' says the veteran spinner. 'Kanwaljit had to fight for a place with Shivlal and Arshad and so had to wait for a long time to play for Hyderabad. That was a tragedy, as Kanwaljit was a classical off-spinner who could make the ball turn and bounce. He had a nice action but a clumsy run-up. Still, he impressed me very much. Shivlal could flight the ball and had a good straight delivery. His strength was sharp turn, whereas Arshad bowled faster, more in the Venkataraghavan mould.'

Hyderabad cricket has produced many talented cricketers over the years who have played for the country. In recent times, this includes the likes of Pragyan Ojha, Ambati Rayudu, Hanuma

Vihari and Mohammed Siraj. Despite this talent, it has won the coveted Ranji Trophy only twice. The first triumph was in the 1937–38 season under the captaincy of S.M. Hussain. They defeated a star-studded Nawanagar side—which had the likes of Vinoo Mankad and Amar Singh—in a thrilling final in Bombay. It was Eddie Aibara versus Nawanagar in that match. Aibara hit a spectacular unbeaten 137 to steer Hyderabad to the victory target of 310.

Former Hyderabad off-spinner Noshir Mehta has an interesting insight about Aibara, who was his mother's uncle. Noshir's father, S.R. Mehta, played in that final. 'I heard from my father that Aibara's pads were bolstered by bamboo,' reveals Noshir. 'He even took pains to go the U-Foam factory and insert foam into his pads. It could act as a thigh guard. Also, Aibara was one of the few Indian batters to have three Gunn & Moore bats.'

Hyderabad's second Ranji Trophy triumph came nearly fifty years after the first. In the 1986–87 final at Kotla, M.V. Narasimha Rao led Hyderabad to a win over Delhi in their own backyard. That season they had a well-balanced team with each member contributing to the team's cause. For Narasimha Rao, it was a dream come true. 'We won because we were positive and aggressive,' he revealed. The openers, Abdul Azeem and Vijay Mohan Raj, gave the team solid starts. If the openers had a rare failure, the middle order of Vivek Jaisimha, Khalid Abdul Qayyum, Arshad Ayub, V. Manohar and keeper Ehtesham Ali Khan rose to the occasion. Lower-order batters such as Rajesh Yadav and M.V. Ramanamurthy also made useful scores.

It is always puzzling to Hyderabad cricket fans how their teams of the 1960s and 1970s could never win the Ranji Trophy despite boasting of players of the calibre of Jaisimha, Pataudi, Baig and

Abid Ali. Prasad, who was one of the best swing bowlers of the 1970s, is among those who cannot fathom this. 'Somehow, the team faltered in important matches,' he says. 'It is strange that we had the best players but could not cross the final hurdle.'

The spiritual homes of Hyderabad cricket are the Gymkhana ground in Secunderabad, the Lal Bahadur Shastri Stadium (formerly known as Fateh Maidan) in Bashir Bagh and the Parade Ground in Secunderabad. Of these, the Gymkhana ground catered to cricket, football and hockey, among other sports. The likes of Jaisimha and Laxman developed their game on this ground. Former HCA Secretary P.R. Man Singh—who was the manager of the Indian team at the 1983 World Cup—says that in the 1930s, the nawabs and maharajas would play at this ground. 'The legendary hitting of C.K. Nayudu here is well known,' he says. Several successive governments attempted to convert this ground into a multipurpose sporting complex but the cricketers with fond memories of this ground are thankful that none of them succeeded.

Raju feels that the first-class careers of Hyderabad cricketers were made at either the Gymkhana ground or Fateh Maidan. 'There used to be huge crowds even for local league matches,' he recalls. 'Their banter was unique and in typical Hyderabadi dialect.' Fateh Maidan has now been renamed as Lal Bahadur Shastri Stadium. It was the venue for the Moin-ud-Dowlah Gold Cup tournament. The ground has hosted only three Tests, all of which were against New Zealand. Jaisimha remembers the 1969 Test in which India was saved from certain defeat by a sudden and heavy downpour that left the ground waterlogged. 'We were smiling and having a nice glass of beer,' he recalls. 'Tiger Pataudi had a cheeky smile as he watched the New Zealand team, including captain

Graham Dowling, helping the groundsmen to dry out the field. But it was a futile attempt. We were lucky to escape with a draw.'

The iconic Parade Ground was known for its numerous matting cricket pitches where dozens of teams played simultaneous matches in various HCA leagues. Man Singh gives an insight into the Parade Ground's history that started when three teams—Ethiraj, Azad Cricket Club and Risings—began playing there in 1959. By the late 1970s, five more teams were added and it became a regular ground with matting provided by the HCA. Every weekend, the ground would be a hive of activity with both professional and amateur cricketers playing matches.

Former Hyderabad and Bombay opener Vijay Mohan Raj says that playing on matting wickets is challenging as there is bounce for the bowlers. The batters can use them to improve their back-foot skills. He says that there are lot of similarities with the maidans in Bombay. Prasad feels the young cricketers enjoy the ambience. 'It is a noisy atmosphere,' he says. 'There are ice-cream carts and peanut vendors and many hotels and restaurants nearby where players gather before and after matches for lively discussions about the game.'

Hyderabad has also made big contributions to women's cricket. The city had a women's cricket league and knockout tournaments many years before other parts of the country, thanks to the initiatives by T.N. Pillay and Jyothi Joshi. Hyderabad women cricketers Purnima Rau and Mithali Raj went on to lead the national women's cricket team, while Rajani Venugopal and Sandra Braganza also played for the country.

38

INTERVIEWS WITH CHANDRASHEKHAR JOSHI AND KAILASH GATTANI

Srikant Kate

Chandrashekhar Joshi

How did you develop an interest in cricket?

I was eleven when my family moved from Bombay to Baroda. It was there that I started to get interested in cricket. When we were in the ninth grade, my friends and I made a 'wicket' on a nearby ground and started playing cricket. I used to cycle to school and pass a police ground on the way. We never had the chance to watch Test matches, so I would sometimes skip school just to watch the cricket match being played on that ground. There I saw great players such as Vijay Hazare, R.B. Nimbalkar, B.K. Gaikwad and J.M. Ghorpade and learned the game by watching them.

Later, I got a chance to play cricket for my school team because of M.J. Limaye. I remember that in the final he sent me in as an opener and I scored 130. Then I took 7 wickets while bowling. I got an award from Vijay Hazare for that performance. Even though I was good at studies, I wasted two years of school because of cricket. But my father always supported me. Finally, I got a letter from the Baroda Cricket Association inviting me to participate in net sessions for the Ranji Trophy.

I was fortunate to get a chance to practise with great players, but no one used to teach us technique. Hazare was a role model for us, so I started observing him closely and copying his style of bowling. That was how I developed my bowling. In university matches, I didn't get to bowl much but I made decent scores when batting. Later, in 1954, I was given the honour of captaining my university team. I remember we played in a final against Madras University that year and were so close to our first inter-university title—we lost the match by just two runs.

How was your first experience of playing on turf wickets?

The Baroda team visited Bombay in 1950 just to get the experience of playing on a turf wicket. We played our first match against the Cricket Club of India. Their team had a few good bowlers such as the Ashar brothers and Ali Abraham. I opened the innings, but no one could make big runs and from the non-striker's end I saw my batting partners being dismissed one after another. But after some time, the ball stopped swinging and I finished with 130. It was my first century on a turf wicket. In the second innings, I scored a half-century.

How was your experience of playing Ranji matches?

After good performances in club cricket, I finally got selected for the Baroda Ranji team for the 1951–52 season. I played my first match against Maharashtra at Kolhapur, batting at No. 3. Unfortunately, we lost that match and were knocked out of the tournament. The following year, we played our first match against Gujarat. I got Hazare run out and we were 49 for 4. From there, Ghorpade and I had a partnership of 176. I scored my first Ranji century, but eventually we lost that match too. I still wasn't getting a chance to bowl but my fate changed the following year. Ghorpade, who was a leg-spinner, injured himself against Maharashtra at Baroda. I grabbed the opportunity and took 6 wickets for about 70 runs. It was the first time I bowled in the Ranji Trophy. After that performance, I decided to pursue cricket full-time.

How did you shift to Rajasthan?

In 1956, I got a scholarship in fine arts from the Italian government. I visited the embassy in Delhi, where I met Raj Singh Dungarpur. As I was on holiday, he asked me if I would like to visit Rajasthan with him and I said yes. In Rajasthan, I met the king of Udaipur and that is when he told me that he wants to form a Ranji team. I also met the vice-principal of Mayo College and was shown around the institution. I received a job offer from him. After I returned from Italy, my father immediately wrote to the king of Udaipur and that is how I moved to Rajasthan to play cricket.

The first match I played for Rajasthan was in 1957 against Baroda. I took 5 wickets in that game. I remember I also took 10 wickets in a Ranji Trophy match against Delhi. Their score was 103 for 3 when I was given the ball. They ended up all out for 190. In 1958, I joined Mayo College as a teacher and was put in charge of cricket. After that, I practised batting only on Sundays, but I used to practise bowling daily. After bowling, I used to practise slip fielding. Eventually, I rose from playing Ranji Trophy matches to playing in the Duleep Trophy and then for Rest of India. Finally, I was called for trials for the Test team.

How was your Duleep Trophy experience?

I rarely played Duleep Trophy but whenever I had the chance to play in that competition, I used to perform well. I took 9 wickets against North Zone in my very first match, dismissing the likes of Prakash Bhandari, Akash Lal and Vijay Mehra.

What was the secret behind your bowling variations?

When I started playing cricket, I would turn the ball with my third finger. It was difficult to get wickets with such turn on coir matting, but with the same amount of turn, I could get wickets on turf. I realized that the ball skids instead of turning when I used my fingers while bowling on turf. The ball used to swing sometimes and that became another variation. Then eventually I started using my wrist and learned how to dip the ball. But whatever turn and bounce I used to get was all because of my fingers. I learned that the more spin you put on the ball, the more accurate you have to be. You can't give room to the batsman to cut the ball.

Who do you consider your cricketing guru?

It is definitely B.K. Gaikwad. He was my first captain at university. After practice, he used to call each one of us individually to the wicket and bowl to us. I remember he would tell me to come forward and drive. He taught us how to drive the ball outside the off-stump and how to play the square cut and hook. It is because of him that my foundation is very strong.

Who were the great players you played with? How was your experience with them?

The first name that comes to mind is C.K. Nayudu. At the age of sixty, he hit two sixes off Vinoo Mankad. I have seen D.B. Deodhar play, but didn't get a chance to play with him. I was a fan of his batting. I also thought highly of Vijay Hazare, Gul Mohammad, C.S. Nayudu, Vinoo Mankad, Subhash Gupte, G.S. Ramchand, Hanumant Singh and Mushtaq Ali.

How was your experience playing in the Central and East Zone Combined XI in the match against the West Indies?

That match was played in Indore in 1966. On the Indian side were players such as Hanumant Singh, Ambar Roy and Subrata Guha. It was very memorable for me not only because we won the match but also because I took five catches.

Kailash Gattani

How was your experience of playing with the legends of Rajasthan cricket?

I consider myself very fortunate because I got a chance to play with the great Subhash Gupte when I made my debut for Rajasthan while still a schoolboy. It was a rare opportunity to witness first-hand how wonderful this leg-spin googly bowler was. I saw the Vidarbha team collapse facing him in a match that we won by an innings in just two days. I would never hesitate to call him a magician. It was very difficult to anticipate what type of ball Gupte is going to bowl. If only India had had outstanding fielders when he played, I am very sure he would have many more wickets to his name and would have won more matches for India than he did.

Everyone knows about Hanumant Singh's talent and exceptional performances as well as his love for coaching. He was a person who bought life to Rajasthan cricket. I remember him saying to me, 'I see this team as champion within two years.'

And that's exactly what happened. Unfortunately, by the time we became champions, he had already passed away. We paid a tribute to him as we all knew that the win was only because of his efforts.

I was also fortunate to play with the great Vijay Manjrekar. Believe me, it made no difference how much pace and skill the bowlers had or whether the wicket was helpful for them—he made the bowling look ordinary. You certainly had to be a top-class player to play on a spinning or seaming wicket and still manage to hit every ball off the middle of the bat.

When I started playing, Raj Singh Dungarpur was very quick, an outstanding fast bowler. I also remember how C.G. Joshi mesmerized the best batsmen in India with his bowling, but it was very unfortunate that we didn't have any good wicketkeepers at the time. It was my privilege to play with these legends of Rajasthan cricket.

Who were the opponents you loved facing?

To be honest, Bombay was the toughest side during my playing days. Even if we took early wickets, they had so much depth in their batting line-up that they would end up with a huge total. But that was also because we had ordinary fielding. In those days, there were hard-fought battles on the ground but friendship off it. We never sledged each other. Regardless of the result, both teams would go for dinner after the match. That's how cricket should be.

During your time, the Rajasthan team played several Ranji Trophy finals but couldn't win any. What were the reasons?

The main reason was that we couldn't get enough practice on turf pitches. For most of the year, we used to practise on jute matting, with only two or three weeks of practice on turf pitches in Bombay. Also, since we got fewer days for practice, we used to practise for almost the entire day. So, I think fatigue took over very easily and that ultimately impacted our performance in the finals.

What would you like to say about Chandu Borde and Ajit Wadekar?

I would describe Ajit Wadekar as an absolutely outstanding cricketer. His batting didn't look very attractive, but he could accumulate runs and was known for his shrewdness. Chandu Borde was a great all-rounder and played attractive strokes. There were very few players of his calibre at that time.

What are your thoughts on your best performance, which was 7 for 13 against Railways?

I think that was a very awkward performance. They scored nearly 200 runs in that innings while I picked up 7 wickets even though I was unwell with a fever and could not bowl more than three overs in a spell. It was so bad that I couldn't even walk after bowling a couple of overs. Despite the weakness I felt, I could still get movement from the ball and captain Hanumant Singh used me beautifully. I take pride in saying that even under such circumstances, six out of my seven dismissals were either bowled or LBW.

Vinoo Mankad was your cricket guru. What would you like to share about him?

Whatever I have achieved in cricket is only because of Vinoo Mankad. I consider myself very fortunate to have had his guidance. I met him at Hindu Gymkhana when special coaching was arranged for junior cricketers. Vinoo Mankad was to be my coach. It has been an amazing journey since the day he picked me after my trials.

He used to be very particular about my training and make me bowl non-stop for an hour with a new ball. To increase the difficulty of my training, I was asked to hit the top 6 inches of the stumps. The new ball was always moving, so I had to land it at the right length from where it would hit my target after bouncing and moving. That was a big help in building my accuracy.

What differences do you notice between earlier and current batting techniques?

Earlier, batting was considered good only when you played along the carpet. In those days, the likes of Manjrekar, Vijay Merchant and Vijay Hazare only played along the ground. They rarely hit in the air as it was also not considered to be correct cricket. But today, you can hit the ball in the air and as long as you are not caught, you'll score runs and people will applaud you for the shot.

What are your views on seam and swing bowling?

It's easier to play swing than seam because if the ball swings in the air, you can anticipate the direction. With a lot of practice, you can judge where the ball will end up. But when it comes to seam, you cannot know how much it's going to move off the pitch.

Why do you arrange England tours for young cricketers?

It has always been my ambition to help young cricketers. When I was playing, I saw many senior Test players go to the UK to play professional cricket. But they never helped me even when I asked them. This is my way of giving back to cricket.

39

BOMBAY CRICKET

Hemant Kenkre

One of the reasons Bombay cricket has prospered for many years is the system that the founding fathers of cricket in the city had laid down. The genesis of cricket in the city (and in India) began in a vast tract of open land that was called the Esplanade and is presently referred to as the Maidan. The open area housed the European Club—as the present-day Bombay Gymkhana was then known—which was a local retreat for resident Englishmen. They had brought with them recreational cultural activities from their homeland, including games called polo and cricket.

These activities aroused the curiosity of the locals, especially among the Parsi community. They tried to emulate the British and began playing cricket after forming their own team. The success of the Parsis had Bombay's Hindus and Muslims following suit. Eventually, this led to the birth of tournaments among these local teams that were to become the foundation of Indian cricket. The Presidency matches between the Parsis and the British became the Triangular when the Hindus team was added, and then were renamed again as the Quadrangular with the addition of the Muslims. When a Rest of India team joined, the tournament finally became the Pentangular.

Various other city tournaments followed. School cricket had the Giles and Harris shields and corporate cricket was contested in the Times Shield. The Kanga League was played during the infamous southwest monsoon and honed the talent of many a Bombay cricketer—from Vijay Merchant and Sunil Gavaskar to Sachin Tendulkar and Rohit Sharma. I studied the history and heritage of Bombay and India cricket as a young wannabe cricketer learning the intricacies of the game in the city's maidans. Here I will introduce some stalwarts of Bombay cricket.

The Merchant of Runs

Vijaysingh Madhavji Merchant was born in Bombay on 12 October 1911 to the Thackersey family of industrialists. His surname was changed to Merchant through a curious incident: the young Vijay was asked what his father does by the principal of J.D. Bharda High School when interviewing the boy for admission to the school. 'Merchant,' he replied, and this was recorded in his school records as his family name. All future documents were based on this record and Merchant became his official surname.

Merchant was one of the first Indian batsmen to adopt the English batting philosophy of technique, patience and perseverance. However, he never had formal coaching, instead learning by watching his seniors. He played for two years with the stylish L.P. Jai in the Bombay team and believes that he owes more to Jai for his cricket success than to any other individual. He was obsessed with perfection and would bat in the nets with the same intensity as he did in a Test match.

But why is someone who played only ten Test matches considered to be one of the greatest Indian cricketers? Merchant's Test record of 859 runs in 18 innings at an average of 47.72 with only three hundreds is nothing exceptional. However, if we look at his first-class record, his status as an icon becomes easier to understand. Merchant played 150 first-class matches, scoring 13,470 runs at a phenomenal average of 71.64. This ranked him behind only the legendary Don Bradman and ahead of other legends such as George Headley and Bill Ponsford.

Despite being an ardent admirer and diligent follower of English cricket, Merchant did not tour England in 1932 as a mark of protest against the colonial rulers who had jailed distinguished Indian leaders such as Mahatma Gandhi. When he did play in England for the first time on India's next tour in 1936, Merchant scored 1,745 runs at an average of 51.32. His 203-run opening partnership with the stylish powerhouse Mushtaq Ali in the second Test match at Manchester made the cognoscenti take notice of the slim batsman who put a heavy price on his wicket.

His performances in England that year saw him named Wisden Cricketer of the Year. Merchant did even better on the 1946 tour of England, amassing 2,385 runs at the phenomenal average of 74.53 with seven hundreds. Fabled cricket writer and commentator John Arlott stated that Merchant's 148 at Lord's in overcast conditions that year was one of his best performances.

Merchant retired from Test cricket in 1951 after scoring a memorable 154 against Nigel Howard's Englishmen at the Kotla in Delhi. Saying goodbye to the game at the highest level is never easy for a player still capable of big performances. When asked why he was stepping away, the genial opening batsman said that it is better to retire when people are still wondering why he would and not when they are wondering why he doesn't. After retirement, Merchant went back to his family business but continued to serve the game as an administrator and selector.

In the 1969–70 season, he spearheaded a mini revolution as chairman of selectors by giving young hopefuls a chance to represent India. The players included Chetan Chauhan, Eknath Solkar, Ashok Mankad, Mohinder Amarnath and the brilliant Gundappa Vishwanath, all of whom went on to play important roles in Indian successes. As the chief selector in 1971, Merchant cast his vote in favour of Ajit Wadekar replacing M.A.K. 'Tiger' Pataudi as captain for the tour of the West Indies. That tour would lead to one of Indian cricket's greatest triumphs and shape the future of the game in India. A young Sunil Gavaskar made his India debut on that tour. As chairman of selectors, Merchant had watched Gavaskar bat in the final of the Purshottam Shield, a premier local cricket tournament. Gavaskar scored a triple century that led to his team, Dadar Union, lifting the trophy. Merchant had declared then that Gavaskar was the future of Indian cricket.

Merchant urged the Bombay cricket authorities to start a tournament to get local cricketers fit before the start of the cricket season. This led to the establishment of the Kanga League that is played from mid-June till September each year, which is when the annual monsoon descends on the city. It challenges cricketers to play in difficult, wet and humid conditions. He also served as the president of the Cricket Club of India (CCI) when I was captain of the side. I remember that he used to visit the dressing room occasionally but never interfered in matters such as team selection.

Merchant also had stints as a commentator and even hosted a popular show called *Cricket with Vijay Merchant* on All India

Radio. A committed philanthropist, Merchant headed the National Association for the Blind for many years. He also served as the sheriff of Bombay. Arlott wrote in *Indian Summer*, his book on the 1946 Indian tour of England: 'It is impossible not to like Vijay Merchant; his manners are polished to the last degree, his consideration for others impeccable and he looks you in the face when he talks to you. His honesty is unmistakable—he speaks out the truth, but never crudely.'

The Prince Among All-Rounders

Vinoo Mankad was born Mulvantrai Himmatlal Mankad on 12 April 1917 in Jamnagar, Gujarat. He is considered to be one of India's greatest all-rounders and perhaps the country's first professional cricketer. The ambidextrous all-rounder batted right-handed and bowled left-arm spin. Mankad became the first Indian to achieve the double of 1,000 runs and 100 wickets in Tests. His final tally of fourty-four Tests, 2,109 runs and 162 wickets do not do justice to his immense talent.

Mankad represented nine teams in Indian first-class cricket. After making his debut for Western India in the 1935–36 season, Mankad played for Nawanagar, Hindus, Maharashtra, Gujarat, Bengal, Saurashtra, Bombay and finally Rajasthan until his retirement in 1961–62. His Test debut came against England at Lord's in 1946. Mankad opened the innings with his friend Vijay Merchant and scored an aggressive 63 in the second innings. However, it was in 1952 that Mankad created history at Lord's by becoming the first Indian to get on the hallowed ground's famous honours boards. He scored 72 and then a scintillating 184 in the second innings after taking 5 wickets. Though India lost the match, it became known as 'Mankad's Test'.

Developments before that Test at Lord's demonstrated Mankad's importance to the Indian team. Leading up to the tour, Mankad had asked the selectors for a guarantee that he would be included in the Indian squad for England. The BCCI's refusal to give him this assurance led to the all-rounder signing up for the season with Haslingden Cricket Club in Lancashire as an overseas professional. He did not play in the first Test of the tour at Leeds, which England won by 7 wickets. The Indian team management desperately recalled Mankad to the squad for the second Test. The rest is history. Wisden rated his valiant efforts as the greatest ever in a Test by a member of the losing side.

Mankad toured Australia under the captaincy of Lala Amarnath in 1947–48 to battle against Bradman's Invincibles. The hosts won the five-Test series 4-0 but Mankad shone with the bat and the ball, scoring 306 runs with two centuries and taking 12 wickets. After struggling against the pace of Ray Lindwall in the first two Tests, Mankad sought the advice of his nemesis. Lindwall told him that his back-lift was so high that his bat came down 'all the way from Sydney Harbour Bridge'. After that, Mankad had scores of 116 and 111 in subsequent matches and was praised by Bradman and Lindwall, as well as the Australian media.

An incident during the second Test at Sydney put Mankad in the limelight. He ran out Australian opening batsman Bill Brown for leaving his crease before the ball was delivered. This was not the first time Brown was guilty of this—he had been warned, and then run out the same way, during an earlier match on that tour against an Australian XI at the same venue. However, the Australian media made no note of Brown's repeated offences when blaming Mankad for not playing in the spirit of the game. Bradman backed Mankad and declared that it was wrong to question Mankad's sportsmanship as the laws of cricket make it quite clear that the non-striker must keep within the crease until the ball has been delivered.

The lion-hearted Mankad played a stellar role in India's first-ever Test victory—against England at Madras in 1952—taking 12 wickets in the match. In the 1955–56 season, the same venue saw him post a world-record opening partnership of 413 with Pankaj Roy against New Zealand. His 231 in that game remained the highest individual Test score by an Indian until Gavaskar made an unbeaten 236 against the West Indies in 1983.

Mankad dedicated his post-retirement life to coaching across India. Among the players he coached were Madhav Apte, Salim Durrani, Eknath Solkar, Sudhir Naik, Umesh Kulkarni, Dilip Doshi, Padamkar Shivalkar, Diana Edulji and his own son, Ashok Mankad. I too was fortunate to have learnt the basics of cricket under his tutelage at the P.J. Hindu Gymkhana in Bombay.

Though an aggressive batsman himself, Mankad did not like young players playing fancy slog shots. He would chastise any errant youngster that employed such tactics by saying, 'It will take me just five minutes to teach you how to attack the bowling but more than five years to teach you how to defend.' It reminded me of what famed cricket writer Raymond Robertson-Glasgow had written about Mankad in 1952: 'Mankad in attack is instantaneous, timeless in defence; in both, most courageous. He is the cat that springs and the cat that waits.'

The Third Vijay

Many young cricketers in Bombay grew up on cricketing stories about the 'third Vijay' (after Merchant and Hazare). Vijay Laxman Manjrekar grew up in the Shivaji Park neighbourhood and, along with the legendary leg-spinner Subhash Gupte, started the famed lineage of Shivaji Park cricketers who bought glory to Bombay and India. Known for his prodigious talent and sublime technique, Manjrekar was a thorough professional who represented six states (Bombay, Andhra Pradesh, Bengal, Maharashtra, Rajasthan and Uttar Pradesh) in first-class cricket.

He made his Test debut at Eden Gardens against England in 1951–52, scoring a sound 48 till he was bowled by the off-spin of Roy Tattersall. This led to Manjrekar being nicknamed 'Tat'. Not long after, Manjrekar scored a flawless 133 at Leeds in his first match in England against a top-notch English attack. He shared a 222-run stand with skipper Hazare, who wrote about Manjrekar's innings: 'Neither the pace of Fred Trueman and Alec Bedser nor the spin of Jim Laker could hold him on a leash. I shared with him the longest Test partnership of my career. Under trying circumstances, it was an invaluable display of fortitude and skill.'

Commenting on Manjrekar's technique, Hazare noted that there were similarities in the way they played the cover drive. Hazare wrote, 'He stepped a little away from the wicket to execute the cover drive, as I did. Because of his quick footwork, he could tackle spin with the same ease as pace.' To Hazare, it appeared that Manjrekar's style was a combination of Vijay Merchant's and his own. Comfortable while playing pace—a rare skill for an Indian batsman in that era—Manjrekar's next ton came against the West Indies in 1953. He scored 118 in the second innings at Kingston, Jamaica, sharing a record partnership of 237 for the third wicket with Pankaj Roy to draw the match.

Among his best performances were the ones against the touring New Zealand team of 1955–56 (he amassed 386 runs in that series at an average of 77.20) and against Ted Dexter's English tourists in

1961–62 (586 runs at an average of 83.71). The Brabourne Stadium in Bombay saw Manjrekar contribute 59 and 39 in India's Test victory over Australia in 1964–65. The last of Manjrekar's seven Test centuries came against New Zealand in Madras in what turned out to be his final Test innings. He scored an unbeaten 102 and then retired in a huff, much to the surprise of cricket fans across India. He played fifty-five Tests and finished with 3,208 runs at an average of 39.12, which was an underachievement if one considers his tremendous talent.

The Safe Bank of Bombay

Narendra Shankar Tamhane was born in Bombay on 4 August 1931 and developed a reputation with his performances as a wicketkeeper in the local cricket circles. He first appeared on the radar of the state selectors when playing for Combined University against the MCC in 1951 and was eventually fast-tracked into a strong Bombay team at the age of twenty-two. Tamhane was soon keeping comfortably to the spin of Vinoo Mankad and Subhash Gupte. What made Tamhane stand out was his approach to keeping. Sticking to the 'body behind the ball' technique—considered an old-fashioned style by modern keepers—he kept in the way made popular by the past masters such as Don Tallon.

The slightly built Tamhane became known as a keeper who was as dependable and safe as a bank. He became the first to reach the mark of 100 dismissals as a keeper in the Ranji Trophy. When he eventually made his Test debut against Pakistan in Dhaka in 1955, it marked the start of a period of stability in the keeping position for India. Until Tamhane, no wicketkeeper could keep his place for long in the Indian side.

Sports journalist Raju Bharatan wrote in *The Times of India*: 'Tamhane fulfils, in many ways, one's image of the ideal stumper. One observes that he is always careful to get his body well behind the ball in collection. We have, since the war, never had a "specialist" for the post, and have tested and discarded so many aspirants that the advent of Tamhane, reliable without being showy, has given our cricket a much-needed injection of youth.' After Tamhane was eventually dropped from the team, he graciously gave his personal keeping gloves to his replacement, Budhi Kunderan, for the latter's debut. Tamhane ended his career with 51 dismissals (35 caught and 16 stumped) in only twenty-one Tests.

Tamhane remained quick and proficient behind the wickets even past the age of forty, which I found out when playing against him in club cricket. In 1975, Bombay University was playing against Tamhane's Tata Sports Club in the semi-final of the Mahindra Shield at the Parsi Gymkhana in Bombay. The university team's star batsman was Dilip Vengsarkar, who was batting on 98 when he nicked one. Everyone thought the thick outside edge would fly to the vacant third-man fence. But the next thing we knew was that Tamhane had the ball comfortably ensconced in his outstretched glove. His anticipation meant that he did not even have to dive. Vengsarkar couldn't believe he had missed out on a well-deserved hundred.

That catch had left me wondering what Tamhane's reflexes would have been like in his twenties.

Many years later I asked him why he didn't need to dive for the catch despite the ball being far from his initial position. He replied, 'Anticipation was always my forte. My hero Wally Grout never dived either. I knew the delivery was an outswinger and also knew Vengsarkar would attempt a cover drive. So I moved to the right in anticipation of an edge.'

After retirement, the genial, soft-spoken Tamhane became as an administrator and selector, also serving as chairman of the national selection committee. When the teenaged Sachin Tendulkar's name was discussed for a possible first national call-up for the tour of Pakistan in 1989, the other selectors were worried about the youngster having to face the likes of Imran Khan, Wasim Akram and Waqar Younis. 'What if he fails?' asked a selector. 'He may lose his confidence.' Tamhane insisted on his inclusion and backed the prodigy to succeed. Tendulkar went on that tour and the rest is history.

The Palm-Tree Hitter

The sleepy town of Sholapur saw the birth of a colossus of Indian cricket on 28 March 1926. He went into the birth registry as Pahlan Ratanji Umrigar, but became known across the cricketing world as Polly Umrigar, one of the finest captains in the history of Indian cricket. Tall and robust, Umrigar was skilled with both bat and ball and had quicksilver reflexes on the field. Having made his first-class debut for Bombay in the 1944–45 season, he came into the national spotlight when he scored an unbeaten 115 for Combined Universities against the West Indies in 1948–49. He made his Test debut against the same side shortly after that.

A hard-hitting, aggressive batsman, Umrigar made his mark in unofficial Tests against the visiting Commonwealth team in 1950–51. He scored centuries in Bombay and Madras, batting with a flair not associated with Indian batsmen of his era. Vijay Hazare captained the Indian side against the strong Commonwealth team and later wrote about Umrigar's display against them: 'The calm and assured manner in which he tackled the pace of (Fred)

Ridgeway and the wiles of (Jim) Laker and (Frank) Worrell would have done credit to a far more assured campaigner.'

On the England tour of 1952, Umrigar struggled against the sheer pace of the English attack—which included Fred Trueman—and the experts began to doubt his ability. Despite scoring a mammoth 1,645 runs in the tour matches, he could not carry the same form into the Tests—in which he managed only 43 runs in four matches. However, he came back into form against a strong English attack later that year, cracking an unbeaten 130 at Madras that played a crucial role in India's victory.

It seemed like Umrigar was determined to succeed against the quicks and make people forget his dismal show against England because he continued the assault against the West Indies in their own backyard. He scored 560 runs at an average of 62.22 with two centuries and four fifties on that tour of 1952–53. His tremendous efforts earned him the sobriquet 'palm-tree hitter' because of the mammoth sixes he hit.

The Caribbean was a happy hunting ground for Umrigar. In 1962 at Port of Spain in Trinidad, he became only the second Indian (after Mankad at Lord's) to score a century and take 5 wickets in an innings in the same match. Before that, he had become the first Indian to make a double century in Test cricket when he scored 223 against New Zealand at Hyderabad in 1955.

Umrigar was an astute captain who was removed from the India captaincy under strange circumstances. However, he had no problem playing under others and was captained by ten different individuals in Test cricket. When he retired from Test cricket, Umrigar had scored 3,631 runs at an average of 42.22 in 59 matches. After retirement, he worked as an administrator for the Bombay Cricket Association (BCA) and also served as the executive secretary of the BCCI and as a state and national selector.

Umrigar's biggest contribution to cricket after retirement was curating the pitch and outfield of the Wankhede Stadium in the mid-1970s. Until then, the BCA did not have its own stadium and held domestic and international matches at the CCI's Brabourne Stadium. However, the BCA got into an imbroglio with CCI after the 1972 Test match against England and decided to construct their own venue. A vacant plot of land a short distance from the Brabourne was earmarked for the project and Umrigar was tasked with developing the pitch and grounds. He carried out his duties with distinction, using the famed local red clay to build good pitches that helped batsmen and bowlers alike.

The fifth match of the 1975 series against Clive Lloyd's West Indians was the first Test to be played at the new ground. With the series tied at 2-2, the West Indies were expecting a turner, which would effectively seal their fate. The sight of a brown wicket was not particularly encouraging and the tourists' team management declared that the wicket would not last for more than a couple of days. This was eagerly lapped up by the media and Umrigar's credentials as a curator were immediately questioned. However, not only was the pitch not a rank turner but also it lasted for six days. Umrigar proved that he had the skills of an expert curator.

When working for the BCCI, Umrigar was treated with disrespect by the elected members of the organization despite being one of India's all-time greats. Resigning from his position, he dedicated the rest of his life to Bombay cricket.

The Tiny Dynamo

Ramakant Bhikaji Desai was born in Bombay on 20 June 1939 and was nicknamed 'Tiny' due to his short stature and slim physique. But as a fast bowler he was bestowed with natural rhythm and an indefatigable spirit. Any batsman who underestimated him after seeing his size did so at his peril because Desai could make the ball skid off the pitch and crack the batsman's stumps—or his ribs. Desai started out as a tennis-ball cricketer until spotted by the scribe G.K. Menon, who convinced the committee of Shivaji Park Gymkhana to include him in their team.

I remember watching Desai bowl for the Bombay team in the Ranji Trophy at the Brabourne Stadium in the late 1960s. The footprints on the dew-kissed grass from his seemingly innocuous but perfectly angular run-up lasted all day. The Bombay bowling attack of the era was dominated by spin stalwarts such as Bapu Nadkarni, Sharad Diwadkar, Baloo Gupte and Padmakar Shivalkar. Former Bombay and India seamer Umesh Kulkarni recalled that the spinners used to monopolize the bowling after only ten overs had been bowled by the pacemen. But despite this, Desai could make his mark on that team.

Desai generated a lot of pace from his wiry build. His contemporaries attribute this to his perfect run-up. He also had a lethal 'slippery' bouncer in his repertoire that surprised most batsmen. Bowling on a nasty rain-affected wicket in a Kanga League fixture to future India openers Gavaskar and Ramnath Parkar, he sent the latter back to the pavilion with a bruised head in his third over. Desai made headlines after taking 50 wickets at the measly average of 11.10 in 1958–59, which was his debut season in the Ranji Trophy. He made his Test debut against the West Indies in Delhi shortly thereafter.

Bowling his heart out on a placid pitch, he took 4 for 169 including the wickets of Rohan Kanhai and Garry Sobers. On the tour of England later that year, Desai added his name on the honours board at Lord's by taking 5 for 89. He will also be remembered for performances with the bat, such as his valiant 85 at the Brabourne Stadium as the ninth-wicket partnership with P.G. Nana Joshi added 149 runs against Pakistan in 1960. In that series, he had made life miserable for Hanif Mohammad, dismissing the Pakistani great four times in nine innings.

Desai had a never-say-die attitude and was willing to bowl for as long as required by the captain. Captains at various levels over-bowled him, leading to burnout and early retirement. He was only twenty-eight when he played his last Test in 1968, finishing with 78 wickets from twenty-eight matches. In first-class cricket he ended with 468 wickets in 150 matches. He continued to play inter-office cricket for his employers, Associated Cement Company, until the early 1980s.

After retirement, Desai served on the managing committee of the BCA and also as chairman of the national selection committee. He did not enjoy the role as he was a man of few words and not one who could take the aggressive approaches often required for a person in his position. His shy demeanour made him extremely uncomfortable while facing the media, and things became worse each time the BCCI spokesperson made comments that contradicted Desai.

Ramakant Desai belonged to the generation of cricketers who put honour, prestige and pride in their performance above all else. He will be remembered as a cricketer who shattered the myth that one had to be big and burly to be a fast bowler.

40

SERVICES CRICKET

Probir Sur

The Services cricket team is different from the other teams participating in the Ranji Trophy, as it does not represent an Indian state. Rather, the team represents the armed forces—the Indian army, navy and air force. The core profession of the members of the Services team was military, though this has changed in recent times. In my playing days, we would play cricket in our spare time because of our passion and love for the game. This meant that Services cricketers would not get many opportunities to practise and play when compared to the professionals from the state teams, who were able to play cricket throughout the year and participate in a variety of tournaments.

Services players would be released from their military units just before the Inter-Services tournament, which was held a month before the Ranji Trophy. Some units are posted in far-flung border areas and inhospitable terrains. Players from such units required not only proper environmental adjustment but also the feel of bat on ball as they may not have seen cricket gear for months. These circumstances mean that any good performance by a Services cricketer against professionals must be lauded and recognized.

The Services cricket team plays under the Services Sports Control Board, which is headquartered in Delhi. Its present home ground is the Palam Air Force cricket ground, but it also has registered cricket grounds in Secunderabad and Udhampur (in Jammu & Kashmir) where Ranji Trophy matches have been played. The Services Sports Control Board oversees not just cricket but also all the sports played by the Armed Forces—including hockey, soccer, basketball, archery, shooting and boxing, among others. In fact, these sports are given more importance than cricket as they build physical fitness, self-confidence, team spirit and aggressiveness—and could thus be considered as a part of military training.

Physical fitness is of immense importance in the armed forces. All ranks are expected to be physically and mentally strong to survive a tough, hazardous and challenging military career in harsh climatic conditions and dangerous situations. From that point of view, cricket is seen as a game of luxury, both in terms of monetary costs and time. Thus, it was included only in officers' training. All the other sports have year-round training available at the Army Sports Institute in Pune, where the most talented military sportspersons are groomed for representing India at the Olympic Games and other international events. Cricket has no such facilities and gets neglected in the world of Services sports.

The Services team played in the Ranji Trophy for the first time in the 1949–50 season. Its golden period was in its early days, when it dominated North Zone cricket in the 1950s. Services reached the semi-finals of the Ranji Trophy six times that decade and played two consecutive finals in the 1956–57 and 1957–58 seasons. During this period, several Services players went on to represent India in Test cricket. Among them were Hemu Adhikari, Bal Dani, C.S. Gadkari, Narain Swamy, Surendra Nath, Apoorva Sengupta and V.M. Muddiah.

Adhikari even captained the Indian team against the West Indies in 1958–59. He later served the Indian team as coach and manager. Though he was very tough on the field, he was liked by all. Surendra Nath was known for his prodigious swing and will be remembered for the dismissal of Peter May at Lord's. The ball pitched outside the off-stump, swung back at an absurd angle and uprooted the leg stump. As a schoolboy, I remember Nath bowling inswingers with a packed on-side field that included three leg slips! His regiment, 16 Cavalry, has a silver memento displayed in the officer's mess commemorating his incredible delivery to May. I also recall Sengupta visiting our house in Dehradun in 1959, fresh from scoring a hundred against the mighty West Indies at the NDA grounds in Pune. I was in the seventh grade at the time and felt thrilled to have him autograph my cricket scrapbook.

The wars in the 1960s—against China in 1962 and Pakistan in 1965—totally changed the Indian armed forces. They became more professional, acquiring sophisticated arms and putting more emphasis on military training. This adversely affected Services cricket, which could not even field a team in the Ranji Trophy for the 1962–63 season. Despite still having talented cricketers in the ranks, the various units could not afford to give them time for cricket training and matches. This led to a notable decline in Services cricket.

However, even in this difficult period, there were some heroes worth mentioning. The first such individual was Joginder Singh

Rao, who took a hattrick in his debut match against Jammu and Kashmir with his medium-pace bowling in the 1963–64 season. He followed it up by taking *two* hattricks in his second match, which was against Northern Punjab. Rao took both hattricks in the second innings while bowling in tandem with Surendra Nath. He is the only bowler to have taken three hattricks in his first two first-class matches.

Unfortunately, Rao fractured his foot in a para jump and had to give up playing competitive cricket. In 1970, I had the opportunity to play with him for the Army team in a friendly match in Indore against Holkar. I remember that he troubled some of the opposition's best batsmen with his off-cutters in that match. That day, Rao told me that I have the potential to play for the Services team in the Ranji Trophy. His words are still vivid in my mind.

The second star player of that generation was Gokul Inderdev, who was my first captain in Services. An all-rounder, Gokul was one of the best leg-spin bowlers in the country. He took 302 wickets and scored 3,485 runs in ninety-three first-class matches. He was a happy-go-lucky person, always ready with spontaneous witty comments. In a match against Punjab in Delhi, he was about to bowl to Test player Yashpal Sharma when the batsman pulled out at the last moment because the sightscreen had fallen. Gokul promptly quipped in Punjabi: '*Edda vada screen twade samne si, fir twanu ki problem* (You have such a big screen in front of you, so what is your problem)?' He was pointing at umpire Swaroop Kishan, who was a rather large individual. Everyone on the field had a good laugh.

The 1971 war further impacted the Services cricket team and it was not until several years later that it could finally put in some good performances. Reporting on a Ranji match between Services and Haryana in 1978, *The Times of India* wrote: 'The Services team, which has been reduced to a nonentity in recent years, is showing signs of looking up.' They were referring to the 151-run partnership between R.K. Ohri and me against a strong bowling attack spearheaded by Kapil Dev and Rajinder Goel. Thereafter, the team produced good performances in the Ranji Trophy. In the 1979–80 season, Services nearly made it to the knockout stages. They were on 20 points and thought they had qualified for the next round when the abandoned match between Delhi and Punjab was replayed and Delhi qualified with 21 points.

During this era, Services cricket continued to do well and produced very good players such as Bhaskar Ghosh, Ajay Jha, Gajendra 'Gajju' Shaktawat, Chinmay Sharma, M. Subramanayan and M.V. Rao, among many others. I rate Chinmay's double hundred against Himachal Pradesh as a Test-quality innings. M.V. Rao bowled at close to 150 kilometres per hour and posed a real threat to any batsman. However, Services were always the underdogs and often became victims of biased umpiring. Rao had told me about an episode in a match against Delhi. He had Test player Gursharan Singh plumb in front of the wicket, but his confident appeal was turned down. The very next ball, a vicious off-cutter again hit the batsman's pads. This time, to escape the LBW, Gursharan made a gesture to indicate that the ball had touched his bat. However, the umpire could not save him—because the ball had flown off his pad and directly into the hands of the fielder at gully.

My article would be incomplete if I failed to pay tribute to Services cricket legend Mahindra Singh, popularly known as Bob. Memories of this devoted all-rounder is etched in gold in the minds of our generation of cricketers. He played against Bombay in the 1957–58 Ranji Trophy final, and later became an administrator.

He was instrumental in establishing the Northern Command cricket team to further improve the level of Services cricket. There was a unique event in the 1979–80 season that showcased Bob's wholehearted passion for cricket that I will share here.

The Northern Command team was sitting pretty at the end of the first day in a two-day match at Udhampur. But as luck would have it, it rained heavily overnight. As the captain of Northern Command, I rushed to the ground early in the morning to assess the situation only to find the pitch well covered. The groundsmen informed me that Bob had arrived at midnight in the heavy rain with an umbrella and a torch to supervise the laying of the covers himself. I was amazed that a brigadier—the operational head of the entire Northern Command army—would do such a task himself instead of simply delegating it. His exemplary dedication to the game really had no bounds.

Fortunately, the rain stopped, and the outfield dried up. However, at 3 p.m., the umpires still thought that the pitch was unsuitable for play as there were wet patches at both ends. What followed was a unique and amusing turn of events—probably the first such instance in cricketing history. Bob sought the assistance of the air commander, who was his friend—and fifteen minutes later, the players and spectators saw to their amazement and glee that a giant MI-8 helicopter was roaring towards them.

For the next ten minutes, the big bird hovered 10 metres off the ground over the pitch with the rotor blowing a heavy blast of air on the wet areas. This unique method was successful in drying the wet spots enough for us to resume playing, and we went on to win the match. Incidentally, this method of drying the pitch by helicopter was later used in an international cricket match at Guwahati in 2006. Other countries have also tried this method—

for example, in Melbourne in 2017 and then in Lahore and at a venue in Namibia the following year.

Due to the modernization of the armed forces and the increasingly heavy operational commitments of the officers, it became very difficult for the Services Sports Control Board to field a good cricket team at the national level. Thus, in 2000, a nationwide recruitment drive began for hiring junior-level cricketers who had found it difficult to push through to senior levels. They would be hired under the sports quota and directly given the rank of havildar or naib subedar in the army (or the equivalent rank in the navy or the air force).

Despite having to go through basic military training, these aspiring cricketers were lured by the good pay and the opportunity play a higher grade of cricket. This system allowed the Services team to play cricket throughout the year and resulted in a tremendous improvement in performances. Some recent Services cricketers such as Rajat Paliwal, D. Pathania and Rahul Singh have played for India A, while more than half a dozen others have represented North Zone. Services even reached the semi-finals of the Ranji Trophy in 2012–13. In 2022-23, the Services team defeated a strong Mumbai side by 8 wickets in the Vijay Hazare trophy.

Times have changed, but it is worth remembering that the original generation of Services cricketers played for the sheer love of the game. We still do so by arranging matches for veteran Services cricketers at various venues every year. I always look forward to these great reunions.

41

THE CHENNAI SINGHS

A.G. Satvinder Singh

I come from a cricketing family. My father, A.G. Ram Singh, was a left-arm spinner par excellence who batted left-handed. He learnt the rudiments of the game at school and later perfected his skills by watching the English cricketers at the nets or during matches for the Madras Cricket Club in Chepauk. My father was in the Madras (now renamed Tamil Nadu) team in the inaugural Ranji Trophy match against Mysore (now Karnataka) in November 1934. The match finished within a day with Madras winning by an innings. My father claimed 11 wickets in the match.

In those days, there were no live broadcasts of matches, and newspapers were available only at the railway station. Cricket lovers in Bangalore rushed to the station the next day to check the score after the first day's play. To their surprise, they saw the Mysore team emerge from the station. The players themselves told the fans the scores!

My father played first-class cricket for over twelve years and took 164 wickets in twenty-seven Ranji matches, once taking 14 in a match. His best was 8 for 14 in an annual match between Indians and Europeans. Only the legendary Amar Singh had achieved the double of 100 wickets and 1,000 runs in Ranji Trophy cricket before A.G. Ram Singh, who was unlucky not to have played for India. He did play in a couple of unofficial 'Tests', but despite scoring an unbeaten 125 and taking 2 wickets in a selection match for the Indian team to tour England in 1946, he was not selected.

After his playing days were done, my father began coaching. He successfully developed many cricketers, not only in Tamil Nadu but also nationwide. Eventually, he became the chief national coach at the National Institute of Sports in Patiala, where he worked with other famous coaches such as Vijay Hazare and even Dhyan Chand, the hockey wizard. Salim Durrani spent a few years in Madras playing in the local league tournament and fondly recalled the coaching sessions with my father.

No one else in our family was a left-arm bowler. Even though I was naturally right-handed, my father tried to get me to bowl left-arm spin like him. He used to place a four-anna coin on the batting pitch at the good-length area and challenge me to hit the coin as many times as I could. One tip he gave me was to flex the wrist like when you reel in a yo-yo. This would help to impart spin on any wicket. My father continued coaching at various schools in Madras and other districts of Tamil Nadu even when he was approaching eighty. It showed his enduring love for the game.

The eldest of Ram Singh's sons was Kripal Singh, who was an all-rounder. He batted right-handed and bowled off-spin. Kripal achieved what our father was denied—an India cap. In his first Test, he played as a batsman against New Zealand and scored a century on debut. In 1959, Kripal toured England with the Indian team under the captaincy of D.K. Gaekwad. He played one Test and scored 41 in the second innings. On the domestic circuit, Kripal had many memorable matches in the Ranji Trophy. He won the trophy in 1955 with Madras. In the final against Holkar, Kripal scored 75 and 91 and took wickets in both innings. As a schoolboy, I watched Kripal score a 50 against West Indian greats Wes Hall and Roy Gilchrist at their terrifying best. An immaculate cover drive off Denis Atkinson is still etched in my memory.

Kripal was a shrewd captain who led Tamil Nadu and South Zone for many years. His prowess as captain was growing and there were even rumours that he may lead India soon. However, a controversial incident at Calcutta led to Subhash Gupte and Kripal never playing for India again. Kripal later served as a national selector and his sons, Swaran and Arjan, went on to represent Tamil Nadu in the Ranji Trophy. Kripal Singh passed away in 1987, a couple of weeks before what would have been his fifty-fourth birthday.

A.G. Ram Singh's fourth son was Milkha, better known as Micky, who made both his first-class and international debuts while still in his teens. In the inaugural Duleep Trophy match, he hit the tournament's first-ever century—151 for South Zone against North Zone. Micky was a graceful left-hand batsman and his strongest shots were the cover drive and hook. Spin legend B.S. Chandrasekhar said that Milkha was one of only two players who could play his bowling comfortably—the other was former India captain Ajit Wadekar.

In a match for South Zone against the touring West Indies side, Micky batted well against the scorching pace of Gilchrist, and eventually his performances led to a national call-up. He made his Test debut on his home ground of Chepauk against Australia in 1960. He stepped out to the first ball he faced—from Richie Benaud—and drove it to cover, but was soon bowled by Alan Davidson for 16. We once played together in a match in Sri Lanka and built a good partnership. The next day a newspaper published a photograph of us walking to bat with the caption, 'When the Sikhs go marching in.'

I am Ram Singh's youngest son, and played sixty first-class matches in my career. I cherish my Ranji Trophy debut—for Madras against Kerala in Salem in the 1963–1964 season—as Kripal was the captain and Micky was also in the side. Us brothers were playing a first-class match together for the first time. I enjoyed my cricket playing with great players in the Tamil Nadu side.

A couple of Ranji Trophy matches remain particularly vivid in my memory. One was in 1972, when Tamil Nadu played against Maharashtra in Poona. Maharashtra had stalwarts such as Chandu Borde and Chetan Chauhan in the side. Despite Maharashtra needing only 150 to win, great bowling by Tamil Nadu on the final day led us to a great win. The other game I remember well is the 1973 final, played at Chepauk against a formidable Bombay side featuring the likes of Wadekar, Sunil Gavaskar, Dilip Sardesai, Ashok Mankad and Eknath Solkar. The wicket was underprepared and it ended up as the shortest Ranji final, the match finishing on the first ball of the third day.

One of my regrets is that I couldn't represent India. I felt this regret the most during a felicitation ceremony before the start of a Ranji match at Chepauk between Madras and Hyderabad. Test cricketers from Madras were having a group photo taken, and among them were my father and my brothers Kripal and Milkha.

Abbas Ali Baig, who was playing for Hyderabad, strolled up to me and said, 'Wouldn't you love to be in that photograph.'

There is another member of my extended family who played for Punjab and India—Sarandeep Singh, an off-spinner, whose grandmother was my father's sister. His father, Mohan Singh, also played for Punjab. Until recently, Sarandeep was a selector for the national side under the chairmanship of M.S.K. Prasad. Overall, ten members of our family played first-class cricket, out of which three played for India—Kripal Singh, Milkha Singh and Sarandeep Singh.

Of the rest, Kripal's children—the two sons mentioned earlier and a daughter, Malvika—played for the state side. Apart from Mohan Singh and myself, another cousin, Harjinder Singh, played for Tamil Nadu and Railways. Ten first-class cricketers from one family—the Chennai Singhs.

Our family had a special relationship with Bishan Singh Bedi. I first met Bishan during the Madras trials for an all-India university team that would play against the touring Ceylon team. I invited Bishan for dinner at our house, which was close to the Chepauk ground. It was there that Bishan met my father and brothers. It was the start of a lifelong relationship with one of India's finest left-arm spinners.

I once visited him in Amritsar and he invited me to join the nets where some of the North Zone players were practising. It was very good batting practice for me to face the likes of Bishan, Madan Lal and Mohinder 'Jimmy' Amarnath. I went on to get some substantial scores in the Ranji matches I played that season. Bishan had great respect for my father and very often sought tips from him. When Ram Singh passed away in 1999, Bishan flew down to Chennai to pay his respects.

During my school days in the late 1950s, cricket coaching would be held at the Chepauk nets. There were four nets at the far end of the ground, and practice would be from 3 p.m. to 5.30 p.m. We were thrilled and honoured when we heard that we would be coached by the great Col. C.K. Nayudu. Even after he arrived, we continued our practice in the nets as usual. But Col. Nayudu then decided that we young cricketers needed match practice. He divided the players into two groups and conducted regular matches of two innings at the adjoining MCC B ground from 3 p.m. to 6 p.m.

We soon understood that practising in the nets could never give us the experience that comes from playing in a match with spectators around. All of us gained a great deal from this experience. Col. Nayudu did not frown when the batsman hit a ball over the bowler's head. In fact, he encouraged it. According to legend, in his heydays the colonel had hit a six that broke the clock hanging in front of the pavilion at Chepauk.

In my playing days, Tamil Nadu had various cricket competitions such as varsity games, league matches, junior state matches and the Buchi Babu Tournament. Of these, two tournaments were unique. One was the Sport and Pastime Trophy (later called the Hindu Trophy after *The Hindu* newspaper took over its organization), which was a thirty-overs match played between major corporate organizations in the state. Many a famous cricketer participated in this tournament and the final attracted large crowds. It was indeed a forerunner to the T20 tournaments being played today. The other tournament is the Gopalan Trophy, an annual fixture played alternately at Chennai and Sri Lanka. Before Sri Lanka obtained international status, the matches were between Ceylon and Madras. Later, it became Sri Lanka President's XI versus

Tamil Nadu. It was a premier tournament and both sides had international cricketers.

It was always a pleasure to play against such high-calibre opponents, who were great hosts in the years the tournament was held in Sri Lanka. Madras had to wait many years to win the Gopalan Trophy in Sri Lanka, finally lifting it in 1968. During one of our visits, the Sri Lankan sports minister hosted a dinner in our honour. One of our teammates had spent some time with his secretary and had collected various details about the minister. He then went up to the minister and introduced himself as a very good palm reader. Based on the information collected from the secretary, he gave an accurate account of the minister's past, besides mentioning something about his future. The minister was flabbergasted. We all had a good laugh about it in our room later.

Cricket can be addictive. It builds character and makes one physically and mentally strong. Playing a game over three to five days in front of thousands of spectators helps a cricketer to learn focus and enables him to counter the vagaries of fortune in his life. During a history lesson in school, I had read the famous saying by the Duke of Wellington: 'The battle of Waterloo was won on the cricket fields of Eton and Harrow.' Having played the game, I now understand the true meaning of his statement.

42

A BOMBAY CRICKETER'S STORY

Sulakshan Kulkarni

I consider myself fortunate that I could enjoy the beautiful game of cricket right from my childhood. Since then, it has given me so much. I have learnt so many things from cricket, both on and off the field. It has taught me how to overcome tough situations and bounce back after failures. Through playing the game, I have made hundreds of good friends and found a coach, philosopher and guide in former India Test cricketer Naren Tamhane. So, I always remain grateful to this sport.

Early Days

I started out by playing tennis-ball cricket matches from the age of eight. The games were played on Sunday in a 'play-to-finish' format without any over restrictions. Senior players would send me to open the innings because they were confident that I could remain unbeaten for at least thirty minutes and frustrate the opponent's bowling attack. I think that concentrating on staying at the wicket for hours in my early days as a player helped me to become a good cricketer. That foundation played a major role in shaping my career in school and age-group cricket.

When I was around ten or eleven, while fielding during our tennis-ball games I observed that the fielder standing behind the stumps got the most attention and was regularly in action when compared to outfielders, who may have nothing to do for most deliveries. That was when I was first attracted towards keeping. The most senior player of our team was a wicketkeeper and his style was appealing to me. He encouraged and guided me to follow his methods and that was how I became a wicketkeeper.

Eventually, I began playing in tournaments. In those days, tennis-ball cricket tournaments were quite popular in Bombay. League games were of twenty to twenty-five overs and the final was a two-innings affair. Even Ranji Trophy players—and on occasion Test cricketers such as Ajit Pai and Ramnath Parkar—used to play in those games. The matches were competitive and were watched by thousands of spectators. These games helped me develop my match temperament.

Junior Cricket

I studied at Shardashram Vidyamandir school in Dadar. In 1980, Ramakant Achrekar was the coach there. Our team had very good players such as Pravin Amre and Naresh Churi and we would practise at Shivaji Park. When I would see the other players competing for the school team, I always used to ask myself whether I would even get a chance in the playing XI. But most people are not aware that I had been selected for the West

Zone Under-15 as well as a junior India camp even before I had represented Shardashram at school cricket. How I got the chance to represent Bombay even without playing for my school is an interesting story—I was selected after keeping to just four balls in the selection trials.

I still remember the day I entered the Wankhede Stadium for the first time. I was starstruck after seeing the famous ground, the pitch at the centre and the dressing rooms. At the nets in the corner, the Bombay Ranji team—which had stalwarts such as Sunil Gavaskar, Dilip Vengsarkar, Sandeep Patil and Ravi Shastri—were practising for their next game. It was the best experience of my life until then to see them playing from such close quarters. I was speechless and almost forgot that I was there to attend selection trials! Those trials were being held at the opposite corner of the stadium.

As I mentioned, I got only four balls to show my wicketkeeping skills in the trials. However, by then the tennis-ball cricket matches had helped me become a fearless and street-smart cricketer who was able to make quick decisions. Because of that background, I did not feel any pressure during the trial. It was perhaps this confidence that led me to be selected after such a short trial.

The person who selected me was none other than Mr Tamhane, whom I call 'Tamhane Sir'. I still remember that after watching those four balls, he had declared, 'This boy will probably play for India in the future.' I don't know what he saw in me, but from among the fifty aspirants it was me who was selected for the Bombay Under-15 team. From there I represented the West Zone age-group team, and after performing well for the zonal team I was selected for the India Under-15 camp.

At the Under-15 national camp in Bangalore, our head coach was Colonel Hemu Adhikari. Helping him were five specialist coaches: Ramakant Desai for fast bowling, Bishan Singh Bedi and Erapalli Prasanna for spin bowling, Dilip Sardesai for batting and Tamhane Sir for wicketkeeping. During one practice session I gathered a throw near my toes. Immediately Tamhane Sir tapped me on my head and said that if I had taken a step forward, I could have easily collected that throw at waist height. Then he told me that it is the keeper's duty to convert a bad throw form a fielder into a good one. On another occasion, when I was trying to collect a ball moving towards my left, my initial movement was slow and as a result I collected it by the left side of my body instead of in front of it. Tamhane Sir immediately told me I was being lazy by not using my footwork to gather balls in front of my body. I think these small but important things made a huge difference to my abilities as a keeper.

I was even further motivated when I read Tamhane Sir's article in a Marathi magazine called *Kridangan*, in which he wrote that Sulakshan Kulkarni could be a future India wicketkeeper if he keeps performing well. At that time, I had no idea of my abilities, but Tamhane Sir always gave me a lot of self-belief. Today, as a coach, I try to do for junior cricketers what he did for me.

After my experience with the state and zonal junior teams and even attending a national camp, I returned to school cricket. My teammates and coach were proud of my achievements. I was eventually selected to play for my school team, and really enjoyed my school cricket days.

Ranji Debut with Railways

Making my first-class debut for Railways instead of Bombay was the result of superb advice from Tamhane Sir. It was the 1985–86 season and the Bombay side had two senior wicketkeepers in

Zulfiqar Parkar and Chandrakant Pandit. Because of this, it was difficult for me to get a chance in the playing XI. That was when Tamhane Sir suggested that I play trial matches for Railways and, if I get selected, play for their side instead. It would give me a season's first-class experience and help my Bombay prospects. The plan was successful. I scored around 800 runs in five trial games and was selected to play Ranji Trophy for Railways. Next year, Zulfiqar retired from first-class cricket and Pandit was called up to the India team. That is how I got the chance to represent Bombay.

Playing for Bombay

Sharing the Bombay dressing room with stalwarts of the game was a dream come true. When I entered that dressing room for the first time, my heroes—just the sight of whom had amazed me at my Under-15 trials—were there to welcome me. At that time, there were eleven India players in the Bombay squad. It was my destiny to share a dressing room with them. That day, I learnt that if you are optimistic and ready to chase your dreams with sincere hard work, you can achieve them.

My first game for Bombay was against Baroda at the RCF ground in Chembur. It was a memorable match for me as I took seven catches in the game. I remember being in awe that the likes of Gavaskar, Vengsarkar and Sanjay Manjrekar were standing in the slip cordon next to me. I batted as a night watchman and had a big partnership with Vengsarkar. Both Gavaskar and Vengsarkar gave me a jersey after that game in acknowledgement of my efforts.

Apart from Gavaskar, my idol in cricket is Gundappa Vishwanath. I will always remember the match when I finally got to play with both idols—for Bombay alongside Gavaskar against Vishwanath's Karnataka. It was a turning track at their home ground, the Chinnaswamy Stadium in Bangalore. Despite the ball almost turning square, I scored 175 in that game against very strong opponents.

The Bombay team had some tough times in the years from 1985 to 1994, when we couldn't win the Ranji title. But we finally broke that jinx when we beat Bengal under Ravi Shastri's captaincy in 1994. In the years that followed, Bombay were Ranji champions ten more times until 2016. I was part of the Ranji-winning team three times and won the Irani Cup when we beat the Anil Kumble-led Rest of India in 1998. That year we were Ranji and Irani champions and also beat the visiting Australian Test team inside three days at the Brabourne Stadium. That Aussie side was led by Mark Taylor and included legends such as Shane Warne, the Waugh brothers and Ricky Ponting.

In my opinion, that 1990s Bombay side had our best-ever bowling attack. Among the pacers was Salil Ankola, Paras Mhambrey and Manish Patel and in the spin-bowling department there were Nilesh Kulkarni and Sairaj Bahutule. It was a well-balanced attack, which gave us the belief that even if we conceded a first-innings lead, we could bounce back in the second innings and always take 20 wickets in the match. The batting too was of high quality. In that era, our top six batsmen were all-time Bombay greats: Wasim Jaffer, Sanjay Manjrekar, Vinod Kambli, Sachin Tendulkar, Amol Muzumdar and Ravi Shastri.

Representing Other Teams

I got an opportunity to play for the India Under-25 team against the great West Indies side that dominated world cricket in the 1970s and 1980s. Our team was led by Chandrakant Pandit and that match was vital for us players because the Indian squad for the West Indies series would be selected after that game. The opposition's top six batsmen were all legends: Desmond Haynes, Gordon Greenidge, Carl Hooper, Richie Richardson, Viv Richards and wicketkeeper-batsman Jeff Dujon.

I kept wickets for 150 overs, and despite 600 runs being scored against us there was not a single bye conceded in that total. That still gives me a lot of satisfaction. When it was our turn to bat, I faced their skilled fast bowlers—including Patrick Patterson, Courtney Walsh and Winston Davis—but still batted for over ninety minutes. After the match, I got a compliment on my glovework from Dujon, who came to our dressing room and said to me, 'Well done, young man. Keep it up.'

People have always asked me whether I have any regrets in narrowly missing the opportunity to represent the country. After all, I was a probable for the 1987 ODI World Cup. But I have no regrets. On the contrary, I am happy and satisfied that I got a chance to play alongside and against so many greats of the game.

Later in my career, I played for Assam, Vidarbha and Madhya Pradesh as a player-cum-mentor. I would represent the team only in first-class games. When I played for Vidarbha, I found that both individual players as well as the team as a whole lacked a professional approach to the game and instead demonstrated a laidback attitude. It was a challenging task to motivate them and get better results. After captaining Madhya Pradesh, I returned to Bombay (then renamed to Mumbai) and played for several more seasons until retiring from playing.

As a Coach

My journey as a coach started with the Indian Oil team in 2003. Then I completed the BCCI Level-2 coaching course the following year and was offered the post of coach for the Mumbai Under-19 team. It was a very different challenge for me, but we emerged champions in the Vinoo Mankad Trophy in my very first year. I think Under-19 cricket is at the heart of every state team and if you work on developing it, the bench strength of the first-class team becomes stronger. In my tenure of three years as coach of the Mumbai Under-19 team, the side produced cricketers such as Ajinkya Rahane, Rohit Sharma, Dhaval Kulkarni and Aditya Tare, among others, who would perform at the highest level for the next fifteen years or more.

When I became the coach of Mumbai's Ranji team in 2011, there was a lot of pressure because we had not performed well in the previous two years. In my first year in the job, Mumbai lost in the semi-finals. It was not a great season but there were reasonable performances. In the next season, we struggled even at the league stage and were in danger of not qualifying for the knockouts. It was because of our inability to get 20 wickets in a match. However, in a close finish, we beat Madhya Pradesh by just 6 runs. That win gave us some momentum. In the next match, we beat Gujarat outright and qualified for the quarter-finals.

I must give credit to Ajit Agarkar, who led the team extremely well. In my time as a player and coach I have observed the work of nearly twenty-five captains and strongly believe that a good captain can understand the bowler's mind and plan accordingly. Ajit set the perfect example of how to get the best out of each bowler according to the situation. I think he is the finest captain I have ever seen.

Unfortunately, Ajit led the team in only that one season. I was expecting him to lead Mumbai for a few more years. He had the quality and potential to even captain India. Ravi Shastri is the only captain I have known who can match Ajit Agarkar's leadership qualities. Shastri got only one opportunity to lead the country—in a Test against Australia—but he had the potential to have been the all-time greatest captain of India.

I was given the opportunity to coach the Indian team to compete in the inaugural T20 Physical Disability World Series in England. It was altogether a different coaching experience for me. Under Vikrant Keni's captaincy, India went on to lift the trophy. I learnt a lot from the disabled players. Despite their physical limitations, their quick adaptation to match situations was remarkable. The Indian team's fielding standard set us apart from the other teams. I gave the team a target of getting at least two run-outs in each game. We managed to get nine run-outs in five games, each of which were turning points in the match. We beat hosts England three times in the tournament, including in the final.

Presently, I am the head coach of the Tamil Nadu first-class team and also enjoy coaching kids at the grassroots level. I always remind them to be optimistic, to keep putting in their best efforts and to be ready for any opportunity that comes their way.

43

SARKAR TALWAR

Vijay Lokapally

For Sarkar Talwar, cricket was best learnt in the searing heat of Chandigarh. His brother Swami was ten years older and was already playing first-class cricket, making him an idol worthy of emulation for the young Sarkar. Swami had made his first-class debut in 1957, and Sarkar eventually followed in his brother's footsteps a decade later. By 1972, when Swami retired, Sarkar had started to make his presence felt in the cricketing circuit as an off-spinner.

Sarkar was one of the many accomplished domestic players who were denied the national team cap. He bowled best in the company of Rajinder Goel, forming a lethal pair that skittled out famed opposition. However, they lacked the support of their own batsmen, who could not make the most of the advantage taken by the bowlers. 'It was fun to snare the batsmen, but it hurt when we could not bat well,' recalls Sarkar.

Sarkar had a relaxed bowling grip and could toss the ball high and skid it through to rattle the batsmen. He was difficult to read. Chetan Chauhan described him as a 'versatile performer' and said that the batsman had to be alert as Sarkar could produce a variety of deliveries with little change in his action. Sarkar could bowl the regular off-spinner, a quicker one and a floater. This variety made him an intriguing bowler.

'I loved to test the batsmen,' says Sarkar. 'There were times when I felt clueless when attacked but I believed in never giving up. I respected the good batsmen.' The good batsmen respected him too because he played the game with distinction. Sarkar was a good sportsman, never crossed the line and came for praise even from the opposition.

'I remember my debut for Southern Punjab against Services vividly,' recalls Sarkar. The match was played at Patiala. 'I was the first player from Chandigarh to play in the Ranji Trophy. It was a cold morning and our captain, M.P. Pandove, tossed the ball to me. I bowled with the almost-new ball. It was baptism by fire, as they say. But Pandove encouraged me a lot and I never looked back.' He played one more match for Southern Punjab and one for Punjab in 1970 before joining Haryana, which had obtained BCCI affiliation the same year.

The backyard cricket lessons from Swamy went a long way in helping Sarkar stay focused. He was a student at Senior Model School when a good performance in an inter-school match caught the attention of local coach Jaidev Chauhan. Sarkar had taken just two wickets but Chauhan, who had also given lessons to Kapil Dev early in his career, saw his potential. He convinced Sarkar to move to DAV School, which had a better infrastructure for cricket.

Sarkar knew the disadvantage of playing for a weak team like Haryana, but he also gave importance to loyalty. It was imperative that he performed consistently, and that he did even against the toughest opponents. Bombay was the opposition that got the best out of Sarkar. Matches against Bombay have always been a special part of his cricket career. The Ranji match against Bombay in Rohtak in 1980 particularly stands out in his memory, as at the time Bombay had a strong batting line-up with Sunil Gavaskar at the helm.

'Bowling to Gavaskar was a huge honour,' recalls Sarkar. 'I had not seen a batsman like him, so sure of his off-stump and equally at ease against pace and spin. Of course, it was also challenging to bowl to Vishy (Gundappa Vishwanath) and I am blessed to have taken their wickets.' Sarkar picked up 4 for 42 and 5 for 63 in the two innings. The treasured wicket was of course Gavaskar. He had him caught at short leg by Ravinder Chadha for 32. 'I beat him in flight and he edged to Chadha, who took the catch nicely,' reminisces Sarkar. 'It was a big boost to my career. I added the wicket of Dilip Vengsarkar in the second innings. We lost the match, but I gained a lot of experience and thought that I had passed the test against two of the best batsmen in India.'

Sarkar said that getting the wickets of these superstars was as good as receiving an international cap and claimed that he did not feel hurt when they hit his bowling all over the park. It was after that game that Gavaskar made Sarkar an offer to play for Bombay. 'It was a surreal feeling when he invited me to his dressing room and said I could get a job with Nirlons and play for Bombay,' says Sarkar. 'But I was not prepared to leave Haryana.'

Sarkar learned a harsh lesson a year later in Jammu in a match against an England XI. Kapil Dev was the original captain, but he withdrew from the match, citing a niggle. Sarkar was one of the spinners in the side along with Maninder Singh, Rakesh Shukla and Deepak Chopra. To Sarkar's misfortune, stand-in skipper

Yashpal Sharma decided to give his own bowling ambitions some wings. All Sarkar got was two overs in the first innings and five in the second. Yashpal bowled fifteen overs. It was heartbreaking for Sarkar. 'It really rattled me,' he says of the incident.

Three years later, Sarkar produced a scintillating show with the ball in the Ranji quarter-final match against Hyderabad in Chandigarh. He returned figures of 5 for 66 and 4 for 63 as Haryana won the match by 158 runs to make it to the Ranji semi-finals for the first time ever. He had done justice to his potential and Haryana was now considered to be one of the top teams in the country. Apart from Sarkar, the team had the likes of Kapil Dev, Rajinder Goel, Ashok Malhotra and Chetan Sharma playing for them at the time.

Sarkar was loving his new-found stature, ranked among the top first-class spinners of the time—names such as Arshad Ayub, Shivlal Yadav, Rajinder Singh Hans and Maninder Singh. 'I was aware that the competition was intense but I was concentrating on playing for a long time,' says Sarkar. Once again, he broke the back of Bombay in the Ranji quarter-final at Faridabad—but again ended up on the losing side. Sarkar had claimed the wickets of Lalchand Rajput, Ghulam Parkar, Sandeep Patil and Chandrakant Pandit to help Haryana gain the first-innings lead. But Bombay hit back in the second innings to assert its supremacy. His haul of 7 for 107 may not have prevented Bombay from winning but the respect for his art grew manifold.

Haryana taught Bombay a lesson when they next met—in the semi-finals of the Ranji Trophy at the Wankhede Stadium in 1985. Inspired by Chadha's unbeaten 159, Haryana made 423 and took a big first-innings lead. Sarkar's 6 for 103 set up the game for Haryana in the first innings, and his 3 for 94 in the second saw

Haryana cruise into the final with a 150-run win. 'I remember Raj Singh Dungarpur talking of an India cap for me when he took us to a Lata Mangeshkar concert,' recalls Sarkar. 'Many years later, Chandu Borde told me that I was unlucky to not have earned a national team call-up for the 1985 season's performance. It was then that I realized that I had missed the bus.'

Sarkar recalls moments of both sadness and happiness in the cricket field. A disappointing memory was from 1974, when Bishan Singh Bedi was the captain and he named Sarkar as the twelfth man for a match against a Sri Lankan side. Another was in 1985, when he was dropped from the Duleep Trophy North Zone side led by Mohinder Amarnath and replaced by Mahesh Inder Singh. In contrast, a standout moment from the field was when he got Vishwanath to edge to the keeper in a Ranji Trophy match against Karnataka. Salim Ahmed took the catch, but Vishwanath stood his ground. The umpire ruled him not out and the Haryana team was hugely disappointed. However, even as Vishwanath hung around, Kapil called him from the slips: 'Come on, Vishy, you are our idol.' And Vishwanath walked.

Sarkar fondly remembers the first-ever knockout match he played for Haryana in 1975. It was against Madhya Pradesh at Indore. On that occasion, it was the bat that he sparkled with. The home team had posted 383 and was on the verge of taking the first-innings lead as Haryana struggled at 346 for 7. Sarkar, batting at No. 7, hammered 143—his only first-class century—to kill Madhya Pradesh's hopes of a win. 'We won the match on the first-innings lead and it was great to have won the match with my batting,' Sarkar says with pride.

Sarkar bid farewell to the game in 1987 in a Wills Trophy match against Karnataka in Jamshedpur. 'I was not going to get a chance to play for India and it would not have been good to just hang around and block a youngster's place in the side,' states Sarkar. 'I made the right choice at the right time.' After retirement, he worked as the deputy director of the Nahar Singh Stadium. He held regular coaching clinics and continued his association with the game when he was asked to be the coach of the Haryana team.

Sarkar played one Ranji final as a player (in 1985) and one as a coach (in 1991). He played the role of a mentor and coach exceptionally well in 1991, a season in which Haryana beat Bombay by 1 run at the Wankhede Stadium under Kapil Dev's captaincy. 'An unforgettable moment,' recalls Sarkar. 'We won a thriller. The Irani Cup triumph was equally sweet.' His glorious moments as a coach were recognized in 1996 when he was asked to guide the India Under-15 team at the Lombard Junior World Cup held in England. Sarkar handpicked the boys—including Mohammed Kaif, who had not been selected initially. He worked magic with the team and led them to victory in the final at Lord's against Pakistan.

Sarkar retired from government service in 2007 and within a year joined Manav Rachna University as director of sports. The Dronacharya Award in 2021 was a much-deserved recognition for Sarkar. 'I am grateful to Mr S.K. Misra and Mr Ranbir Singh Mahendra at the Haryana Cricket Association for their support. My family—Chandrika (wife), Agam (son), Nidhi (daughter), Albha (daughter-in-law) and Upendra Kalakoti (son-in-law)—has supported me all the way,' says Sarkar.

Sarkar Talwar did not play for India, but he served the game with dignity and distinction. He is considered one of the finest spinners in the history of Indian cricket, one who was distinctly unlucky to miss wearing the India cap.

44

CHALLENGING THE CHAMPIONS

Milind Gunjal

The Ranji Trophy championship in 1989 was special for Maharashtra cricket, as Prof. D.B. Deodhar was in his hundredth year. Maharashtra was facing their arch-rivals Bombay, and the latter had piled up a mammoth first innings total of 515. I endured one of my worst days in the field. A couple of edges fell short while some went too high, and then I dropped a difficult chance off Lalchand Rajput. Thankfully, it didn't turn out to be a costly mistake as he was out not long after that.

However, to add insult to injury, the media blamed me for five dropped catches. No one talked to me that evening, which really hurt me. People who understand cricket will agree that chasing 515 is not easy on any wicket, especially against Bombay. Coming in at 89 for 3, I remained not out on 43 at stumps on the second day.

As the proverb goes, it never rains but it pours. That evening, on my worst day in the field, my elder daughter, Manasi, then all of six months, became unwell. She wouldn't stop crying. Although she was used to me putting her to sleep every night, she was too unwell that evening to fall asleep. It was 1.30 a.m. before she finally dozed off, but I couldn't fall asleep, what with the prospect of chasing a 500-plus target also weighing heavy on my mind. Tired of worrying and tossing and turning, I got out of bed at 4.30 a.m. and went to the ground early.

I kept mostly to myself and avoided talking to people there. The first session of the third day got underway, and I was happy to be out in the middle doing my thing without having to worry about what everyone was thinking of me. I reached my century just before lunch and remained unbeaten with Surendra Bhave when the first session ended. I pulled on a fresh pair of gloves that my father had thoughtfully brought with him to the ground and walked out with Bhave for the second session.

Bombay decided to take the second new ball, with Salil Ankola and Prasad Desai raring to go. But by tea, I had scored my first double hundred in first-class cricket. I fell soon after at 204. However, my effort was enough to ensure Maharashtra went on to score 525 and win the match. I was under so much pressure and so eager to do well for my team. Even now, in my mind, I can hear the sound of my bat meeting the ball and the ball rebounding off the boundary wall.

In the 1985–86 season, Maharashtra chose to bat against Bombay on a fresh Wankhede pitch. We were soon reeling at 44 for 5 in the tenth over. The ball was swinging and the Bombay bowlers bowled beautifully. Three wickets fell in Pradip Kasliwal's fifth over as I stood at the non-striker's end. I just closed my eyes and told myself that there is no option for me but to get a hundred today. That made me concentrate more, and with the help of Azim Khan and the tailenders we managed to post a total of around 300. My score of 125 that day was one of the best innings of my career.

In 1988–89, it was important for Maharashtra to win our last league match against Bombay. They scored 467 in their first innings after winning the toss. I inspired the six batsmen to rise to the challenge. It was a test of character. Raju Kulkarni, Anup Sabnis, Kiran Mokashi and Ravi Thaker formed a formidable Bombay attack. However, Maharashtra managed to put up a score of 470 for 7. Riaz Poonawalla, Shrikant Kalyani, Shrikant Jadhav, Nandan Phadnis and Shantanu Sugwekar all contributed. I scored 120 that day, and it was so satisfying and heartening to chase down 467 against Bombay away from home.

These three centuries against a champion Bombay team gives me immense satisfaction and a sense of fulfilment.

BEYOND THE PAVILION

45

COMMENTATING ON CRICKET

Narottam Puri

The first match that had cricket commentary broadcasted in India is believed to be the Parsis versus Muslims game at Bombay Gymkhana in 1934. The commentator was Ardeshir Furdorji Sohrabji 'Bobby' Talyarkhan, with additional comments by Joe Birtwhistle. History is silent, however, on which airwaves this was broadcast, as All India Radio (AIR) came into existence only in 1936! Was it done through the Indian Broadcasting Company (later renamed Indian Broadcasting Service), which was established in 1927? However, this company was liquidated in 1930.

It was only in 1935 that an office of 'Controller of Broadcasting' was established. The first person to hold the office was Lionel Fielden, and broadcast began as AIR on 8 June 1936. The following year, a radio station was established in Lahore and in 1938, a shortwave transmitter was installed at Bombay. Thus, 'Bobby' Talyarkhan could not have been broadcast by AIR in that match in 1934! However, what is not in doubt is that Talyarkhan was not only the first cricket commentator in India but also the first to commentate on hockey and football. He is also credited as the first contributor to the first-ever sports page in an Indian newspaper (*The Free Press Journal*).

Talyarkhan was a very gifted orator and a devotee of sports. Blessed with fluent diction and eloquence and boasting a comprehensive knowledge of the game, he was a true giant of the world of sports broadcasting in India and is remembered with affection and respect. He continued broadcasting until a tiff with AIR resulted in him being dropped. I was told by some journalists and commentators of that era that his insistence on doing Test commentary alone and his stubbornness about who could potentially share the mic with him led to his dismissal.

Like the sport itself, radio commentary on cricket had started in England. Inspired by similar live commentary on baseball in the USA, Lance Sieveking of the British Broadcasting Corporation (BBC) first experimented by doing real-time commentary on rugby. Buoyed by this experience, the BBC appointed the Reverend F.H. Gillingham and 'Plum' Warner as the first-ever cricket commentators in 1927. On 14 May, the Essex versus New Zealand match featured the world's first broadcasted ball-by-ball commentary. However, Australian historians dispute this and believe the first such broadcast was Lionell Watts's commentary in Charles Bannerman's testimonial match in 1922. Whichever claim is accurate, the die had been cast.

The popularity and quality of broadcasts and commentators only grew. In England, Howard Marshall and John Arlott emerged as favourites, and in Australia, the leading commentators of the time were Alan McGilvray and Johnny Moyes. The 1940s saw the first popular voices from India—the likes of Berry Sarbadhikari, Vizzy, Pearson Surita and Devraj Puri. They followed in the pioneering footsteps of Talyarkhan.

When all five Tests of the 1948–49 series against the visiting West Indies were chosen for live radio commentary, these four covered the matches for AIR and their voices were broadcast all over India. Of these early Indian commentators, Vizzy was popular with a certain type of audience but was more of a raconteur or storyteller rather than a ball-by-ball commentator. Incidentally, Devraj Puri was still playing Ranji Trophy when he made his commentary debut.

The popularity of cricket in India owes a great deal to the AIR cricket commentary broadcasts. From the 1950s to the 1980s, names such as Balu Alaganan, Ananda Rau, Dicky Rutnagur, Anant Setalvad, Suresh Saraiya, Raj Singh Dungarpur and J.P. Narayanan, along with others such as Kishore Bhimani, Ashish Roy and I, took the game from the stadium to the streets and schools. They were joined by the 'experts'—former players such as Lala Amarnath, Vijay Merchant, Tiger Pataudi, M.L. Jaisimha, Abbas Ali Baig and Bishan Bedi.

It was the introduction of commentary in Hindi and other regional languages that led to the growth of cricket in smaller towns and villages. The early stalwarts included the popular Ravi Chaturvedi and Jasdev Singh and their good work was carried forward by Sushil Doshi and Manish Deb, amongst others. Whilst AIR cricket commentaries are still broadcast today featuring knowledgeable voices, the popularity of radio has gone down tremendously in a world where media is dominated by TV and the internet.

Television broadcasts in India began in September 1959 when Doordarshan was inaugurated by President Rajendra Prasad. However, Doordarshan remained under AIR's wing until 1976, when it became a separate and individual entity. In 1966, India saw its first live telecast of a cricket match. It was the touring West Indies side under Garry Sobers taking on the Board President's XI at the Kotla in Delhi. The commentary team with the honour of becoming the first to do live TV commentary in India comprised Joga Rao (Hindi), Devraj Puri (English) and Fatehsinh Rao Gaekwad (as an expert). I was involved as a statistician.

In those early years until the 1980s, matches were covered by only three to five cameras. TV commentary was often done from temporary positions in the pavilion, the press box or even amongst the spectators! The commentary box was reserved for radio commentators, as AIR had the widest bandwidth for transmissions. Things started changing when more cameras were installed and TV broadcasts started having better quality images and wider transmission. In the early 1980s, popular commentators were still doing both radio and television commentary even though the requirements and techniques for the two are quite different.

The basic principle of television commentary is to let the picture speak. The commentator can embellish it if needed and provide technical or statistical insights—although with the addition of computerized graphics, statistics are now easily superimposed on the screen. However, with commentators nowadays working in groups of threes and with limited-over games moving far more rapidly than Tests, it is difficult if not impossible to not speak a lot. It is here that some manage to convey more in fewer words whilst others talk virtually non-stop and even after the bowler has started his run-up.

In radio commentary, through knowledge of the game, command over the language and the use of voice modulations and pregnant pauses, the commentator is expected to paint a picture in the minds of the listeners and transport them to the action. This was why AIR used the services of professional broadcasters for cricket coverage, despite many of them not being well-versed with the nuances of the game. Some of them became popular cricket commentators—Jasdev Singh and Murli Manohar Manjul in Hindi come readily to mind, as do Saradindu Sanyal and V.M. Chakrapani in English.

One of the reasons why some of the outstanding cricket commentators of India did not rule the airwaves to the extent they should have was AIR's overly democratic processes, which distributed assignments amongst its roster of commentators regardless of performance or ability. This was in contrast to national broadcasters in other countries, where the leading commentators were nurtured, developed, marketed and branded. Some of the names who benefitted from supportive policies include Rex Alston, Christopher Martin Jenkins and Jonathan Agnew of England, Jamshed Markar and Omar Qureshi of Pakistan and Tony Cozier of the West Indies.

As the popularity of Doordarshan grew, AIR's cricket coverage following dwindled. Some of the commentators kept doing a good job but the overall standards had dipped by the mid-1980s. Several commentators who had come through the ranks of AIR switched over to Doordarshan. The introduction of colour broadcasts gave TV coverage a further boost, and when Doordarshan covered India's win in the 1983 World Cup, television commentary came of age in the country.

Kerry Packer's innovative but controversial World Series of Cricket in Australia had opened a new chapter of television coverage in the world. Several new camera angles were used, games were played at night and in coloured clothing and the traditional red ball was replaced by a white one. All of it made for great television. However, in India, Doordarshan was slow to adapt to technology and continued the 'democratic' rather than merit-based assignments of commentary work. And when the BCCI won coverage rights to international cricket from Doordarshan in court, the national broadcaster took a blow from which it never really recovered.

Over the past twenty-five years, TV coverage in India has greatly improved and now features commentators from all over the world, usually legendary former players. Broadcasters use twenty to thirty cameras and advanced acoustics and technology. These developments mean that the viewer hears the snick almost at the same time as the umpire does and sometimes sees a phase of action more clearly than even the players on the field. This has led to many die-hard fans no longer watching matches at the ground and preferring to sit comfortably in front of their TVs at home.

It would be safe to say that the phenomenal popularity of the game in India owed, and continues to owe, a tremendous debt to radio and television broadcasts. Today, cricket coverage is big business, and the money is welcome as it has improved the lot of not just the international players but also that of first-class cricketers, both current and retired. Commentators are rightly very well paid now, unlike in my time—if memory serves me right, the pay for commentators when I started in the field in the 1970s was

Rs 250 per day ... but if a day was rained off in a Test match, you didn't get paid!

The advent of the internet has provided another dimension to cricket coverage. It means that the modern follower no longer has the need to ask someone in the street, '*Bhai, score kya hai* (What is the score)?'—a practice someone from my generation grew up with. Yes, it a far cry from the early days, but many connoisseurs still miss the legendary television commentators such as Richie Benaud, who was perhaps the greatest commentator of all.

Let us pause and salute the coverage of cricket that began in India with 'Bobby' Talyarkhan and rejoice in the high standards of broadcasts that we can enjoy today while remembering and appreciating all those who have brought viewers and listeners closer to the glorious game of cricket over the past hundred years.

46

MY UMPIRING JOURNEY

V.K. Ramaswamy

I joined Hyderabad Cricket Association as a club-level umpire in 1970 after accepting that, given my level of skill, I had no chance to even be a first-class cricketer. I took up umpiring just for the fun of it without any big aspirations. With the support of P.R. Man Singh, the joint secretary of the association, I got the opportunity to stand in the All-India Moin-ud-Dowlah Gold Cup tournament in my first year. In those days, Moin-ud-Dowlah was a three-day affair, with participation by almost all the national team cricketers as well as many prospective ones. Umpiring in such an atmosphere was challenging. The tournament was often affected by rains—in fact, Gundappa Vishwanath would refer to it as 'Rain-ud-Dowlah' and Yajurvindra Singh would jovially say that he wanted to host the tournament in Saurashtra where rains are scarce. But it motivated me to aim higher.

I became a first-class umpire in 1973 and stood in my first international match in 1983. After officiating at both the domestic and international level for eleven years, I was inducted into the ICC umpires' panel in 1994. I remained part of the panel until 1999, the year I stood in my last Test match. I continued umpiring in one-day internationals until 2002 and in domestic matches until 2004. Even after my umpiring career ended, I remained associated with the BCCI for another fourteen years in various capacities such as match referee, umpiring coach and performance review committee member, until I retired from all aspects of the game in 2018.

My debut as a first-class umpire was memorable. Andhra beat Tamil Nadu by 1 run, with the last wicket falling to what is referred to as a 'Mankad' run-out. Unlike the present, in those days we used to officiate in only one Ranji Trophy match per season. We had to keep ourselves fit by standing in local club matches. The present-day umpires get to officiate in around eight to ten first-class matches per season.

Despite not getting many opportunities to umpire, I stayed motivated through my determination—much like the cricketers who played the game because of their passion and not for money. In fact, my fees for standing in a Ranji Trophy match when I started out was fifty rupees per day! For my first Test match in 1985 I received 1,000 rupees in total for all five days. The earnings for the Indian cricketers were similar, and this resulted in comradery between cricketers and umpires. They laughed away our mistakes and appreciated the good decisions.

The BCCI was not rich enough back then to afford more facilities for cricketers, leave alone umpires. Except for some cricket associations such as Bombay, Tamil Nadu, Karnataka, Bengal and Delhi, domestic cricket was not financially sound. As a result, cricketers from some associations had to travel by train to matches.

Some travelled in sleeper classes or sometimes in the unreserved compartment. But I never saw them complaining.

In those days, umpires too had to travel by train. Sometimes the journey took longer than twenty-four hours. Accommodation was another ordeal. Initially, host associations used to make boarding and lodging arrangements. But after a few years this was dispensed with and a 'dearness allowance' system was introduced. This caused more discomfort as the allowance was not sufficient. This was the case with cricketers too. I remember Erapalli Prasanna once telling me that even while representing the country, the allowance was meagre. When they were on tour to England, the players used to avoid breakfast in the hotel and eat toast with butter at the ground! Will the present-day players and umpires believe these stories?

However, the situation improved considerably over the years. I can say that I enjoyed the comforts provided by the BCCI in my later years. The inconveniences in the earlier days did not affect our morale—be it umpires or cricketers. We were simply looking for more matches in which to officiate or play. In the present day, umpires travel by air and stay at accommodation provided by the BCCI while receiving match fees of 30,000 to 40,0000 rupees per day. This means that for them, umpiring can be a full-time job.

Measuring the performance of an umpire is tricky, as it is not always possible to do a self-assessment. When I started out, there were no match referees, so the only assessment of the umpire was the captain's report—which may be biased. But in the 1980s and 1990s, nearly all captains were sincere in their reports. I remember umpiring a Ranji Trophy semi-final in which I declared Sunil Gavaskar out in both innings. Each time, he stared at me before leaving but never showed dissent. His captain's report at the end of the match helped me to understand my mistakes and improve. Similarly, in one of the one-day international games that I officiated, Kapil Dev was the captain. In that match I did not have an extraordinary performance. However, the captain's report was good.

Later, I came across an incident where a captain had remarked about one of my colleagues that 'his LBW decisions are not good'. Interestingly, of that umpire's three LBW decisions in the match in question, one was against that captain! I am mentioning this to highlight the plight of the umpire if the captains are not sincere. In a lighter vein, there is the time when Parath Sharma, then the captain of Rajasthan, wrote a positive report about an umpire who had committed many mistakes during a match. His teammates were shocked and asked why was giving such a report. Parath smilingly said that the ordeals they had faced should be faced by other teams too!

The latter part of the 1990s saw the introduction of the self-assessment system and the position of the match referee. This led to a more formal performance review of umpires. The BCCI too adopted the match referee system for domestic cricket. This considerably eased the pressure on umpires as there was an independent evaluation of their performance. In addition, the 'umpire coach' system also came into existence in 2007. The coach independently monitored the performance of umpires and guided them where necessary. Once domestic matches began to be telecast live, the third (TV) umpire also began to be appointed.

The evolution did not stop there. All domestic matches were recorded by video analysts and every appeal and decision was reviewed by a panel of former umpires to assess the performance of the match umpires. Based on this assessment, the panel could make recommendations for their promotion to higher-level matches. This system worked well, and many young umpires got the opportunity to become a part of the ICC panel and also umpire IPL matches. Despite this, for reasons unknown, this system is no longer used.

The question that arises then is: with all these innovations, has the performance of umpires improved? This is a debatable point. No doubt, the pressure umpires feel has decreased because of better evaluation systems. In the days when proper monitoring systems and match referees did not exist, umpires faced some unpleasant situations. The main grievance in international matches those days was not as much about performance but a perceived home bias. This perception was not true. Mistakes do happen in umpiring but not due to bias.

I categorize mistakes into three types. The first is a momentary lapse of concentration. This should be avoided as this is not acceptable. There are various methods to maintain concentration levels that umpires are trained in. The second type of mistake happens in difficult decisions with fine margins—such as when the bat and pad are close together or when the ball takes a very thin edge of the bat. For such cases, following the ball closely will help. The third type is the unavoidable mistake. This happens when the umpire doesn't have a clear view of the incident, such as when the bowler ends up in front of the umpire in his follow-through or the ball comes off the gloves after the batsman had turned his back. As umpires, we hope and pray that such situations do not arise during a match.

The use of technology to assist umpires on the field has increased over the years. Many improvements have been made over time to cover different types of situations. I will not dwell on whether technology is always accurate; instead I will discuss its impact on umpires. While technology certainly assists the umpires, it also has some psychological side effects for them. There is always the possibility that an on-field decision is reversed by the TV umpire. If it happens a few times in a match, even umpires with great mental strength may struggle to overcome the impact of these incidents. I have known a few elite-panel umpires who quit after finding themselves unable to bear the mental pressure.

The overuse of technology also means that the unpredictable element of human error will be missing from the game. Backed by technology, umpires may also inadvertently relax, due to which mistakes may occur. Many a time I have seen umpires using the referral system for run-outs even when the batsman has crossed the bowling crease by the time the stumps are broken. They did not get into the proper position to judge the run-out because of the availability of technology. I would suggest limiting the use of technology when it comes to umpiring.

My journey as an umpire from 1973 to 2004 has been rewarding not in monetary terms but in developing new friendships and seeing new places both within the country and abroad. An umpire must possess the motivation and commitment to do well at all levels of the game. Only then will his journey be smooth.

47

CRICKET FANDOM

Shashi Tharoor

I was introduced to Test cricket one sunny afternoon in Bombay by an indulgent father. It was late 1963, I was seven, and we were in the lovely Brabourne Stadium watching a depleted English side that was touring under Mike Smith. The Englishmen were so ravaged by an assortment of maladies that they played both tour wicketkeepers and enlisted the fielding of the Indian twelfth man, Hanumant Singh—who would score a century on debut against them in the next Test.

Whatever the strength of the visitors, though, the cricket on the third day of the Test was marvellous. I watched with enthralled seven-year-old eyes as Budhi Kunderan, India's opening batsman and wicketkeeper—who looked like a West Indian and played like one—pulled John Price, England's fastest bowler, for six over square leg. The ball landed practically at my feet. He repeated the shot the next ball, this time just failing to clear the rope. In less time than the difference between a four and a six could be explained to me, Kunderan had reached 16; but he tried his shots too often and sent up a skier that swirled in a gigantic loop over mid-on. As the ball spiralled upward, Kunderan began running. Even when it was caught by a relieved Fred Titmus in the deep, Kunderan continued running; but then he hurled his bat skywards with an exuberant war whoop and caught it by the handle as it came down before running into the pavilion. It was exhilarating stuff, and I was hooked for life.

Cricket fandom is an intensely personal experience, but it has certainly evolved over the years in India. Initially, as everywhere, it was Test cricket that fans were obsessed with. Specific moments of fan exhilaration stand out. Who can forget the excitement stirred by Abbas Ali Baig's dream debut in England in 1959, when he was conscripted out of Oxford University by an Indian team in the doldrums and promptly hit a century both in his first tour match and on his Test debut? Or that magical moment when, as Baig walked back to the pavilion in Bombay after a brilliant 50 against Australia, an anonymous sari-clad lovely ran out and spontaneously greeted him with an admiring (and scandalously public) kiss? The episode is part of national lore; it has been immortalized in Salman Rushdie's novel *The Moor's Last Sigh*. Who in the screaming crowds that welcomed Salim Durrani's appearance thought of his batting statistics when they cheered themselves hoarse over that green-eyed inconsistent genius with the brooding movie-star looks? I will never forget the outrage that swept the country when he was dropped from the national team during an England tour in 1972; signs declaring 'No Durrani, No Test' proliferated like nukes. Fan pressure worked, and Durrani was indeed recalled for what turned out to be his last Test series.

But now Test matches have gone a different route: they play to depleted audiences as the emanations of 'serious' cricket, to be endured only by the true believers. I felt this most strongly during the 2011 India–West Indies Test series in the Caribbean, which marked the return—unwelcome to many—of cricket as an exercise in attrition. Run-rates below 2 runs an over for long periods of time, batsmen's strike-rates in the low thirties, half a session without a single boundary—all these, and more, were on display. To see a batsman nicknamed 'The Wall' obdurate in defence, and players of lesser talent barely pushing the ball off the square, seemed both to explain and justify the largely empty stands in famous cricket grounds that had previously been the sites of many a crowd-pleasing act of derring-do.

Though there have been exceptions—such as the last two India–Australia Test series played Down Under—Test cricket suffers by comparison with the alternatives. With the throbbing, pulsating, time-bound and cheerleader-inflected joys of T20 cricket on offer around the world, Test cricket looks in danger of failing the viability test that any activity depending on public support must pass.

In my high school years and on visits thereafter, I watched Test cricket in Calcutta, which prided itself on its knowledgeable crowds; 93,000 filling the stands for each day of a Test match was a common sight. Today, with the arrival of T20, that era is over. The unfolding of a five-day match, like the narrative of an intricate novel; the tension of watching a master spinner tie a gifted batsman in knots, even if few runs are scored in the process; the sight of a willow-wielding talent asserting his mastery over the fire and brimstone of an aggressive fast bowler, again whether or not a fusillade of runs results; even two tailenders holding out against the clock in the gathering gloom to snatch a brave draw from the snapping jaws of defeat—all these are unavailable in the shorter formats of the game, and they all offer pulsating tension and satisfaction unrelated to the hitting of sixes or the cavorting of cheerleaders.

To love cricket is to appreciate the sheer joy of the highest forms of sport—the elements that stretch human talent to the limit, that transform mechanical skill into beauty, that assert the pleasures of complexity over those of instant gratification. No form of the game showcases these qualities better than Test cricket. But few Indian fans are left with the time or the inclination to see this magic unfold over five days. Not even in Calcutta, where the West Indians played its last Test before largely empty stands.

Of course, it is fair to appreciate the obvious advantages of white-ball cricket. Sport is, after all, a form of mass entertainment too. It is one thing to see a good batsman struggle to keep out a brilliant tweaker, another to watch players of less than incandescent talent patting ordinary bowling straight to a fielder. The former offers the spectacle of skill rising to a challenge; the latter inflicts mediocrity on those who rightly feel that they are entitled to watch something better and more enlivening. Players who, in ODIs or T20s, would thump short-pitched deliveries heading down leg or smash widish balls outside the off-stump, leave them alone in Test matches. Worse, they are applauded by the discerning for this show of discretion and temperament. This is why most Indian fans today would also rather spend three hours on some run-of-the-mill IPL game than spend the same amount of time watching a dull session of indifferent cricket that seeks to justify itself through its Test label.

The salvation may lie in what the English have been doing recently, in an approach dubbed 'Bazball' after the nickname of their coach, Brendon McCullum. They have so dramatically increased run rates with their daredevilry that they have brought a level of heady excitement to Tests that the format had lacked for decades. Sometimes this has led purists to sniff in disapproval, but for the most part, the results—and the crowds—have vindicated their approach.

Over the years India has had no lack of cricketers who approach Test matches imbued with the spirit of the limited-overs game. Virender Sehwag was emblematic of the tribe. He had an uncomplicated approach to batting—if he felt a ball was there to be hit, he hit it, often successfully (having brought up several of his landmarks with a six), and sometimes unsuccessfully (having famously perished going for his shots at 195 and 293, when lesser mortals would have pushed and nudged their way into the record books). Today Rishabh Pant is his spiritual successor—the one player who brings Indian fans in even to watch Tests. Perhaps he will leave his legacy in the kind of performance that a Kunderan turned in, but at a higher level of accomplishment —and that will keep a new generation of fans enthralled for life.

EPILOGUE
Arunabha Sengupta

Brisbane, January 2021. Josh Hazlewood's delivery angled across Rishabh Pant. The mid-off area was vacant. With a cool head and dextrous wrists, Pant creamed the ball to the left of extra-cover and started running. It was the climax of the deciding Test of an epic series between India and Australia. The ball rolled over the ropes, and the fortress of 'Gabba had been conquered. Australia had been defeated in their own backyard by India for the second tour in succession. India had to wait for over seventy years to win their first series Down Under. But it took them only two years to win their second.

The 2020–21 win was more than a miracle. India had been blown away in the first Test, being bowled out for 36 in their second innings. After captain Virat Kohli had left the tour on paternity leave, other senior members of the squad started to succumb to injuries. But their replacements—mostly youngsters and debutants—more than held their own against the might of the

Aussies playing at home. They were the new face of Indian cricket, a side that played without fear.

A shot that exemplified this spirit was debutant Shardul Thakur hooking Pat Cummins—one of the best bowlers in the world today—over fine leg for six. It showcased assertiveness with none of the meekness that seemed to perpetually accompany the Indian cricket teams of yesteryears when they travelled overseas. Times have changed. India can now be reduced to a third-string side in the hostile home environment of one of the strongest sides of the world, and yet they can emerge victorious.

Indian cricket fans celebrated M.L. Jaisimha's courageous innings at the 'Gabba on the 1967–68 tour of Australia because even in defeat India could put on a heroic performance. On that same tour, we celebrated M.A.K. Pataudi's valiant 75 at the MCG, batting with an injured leg after walking in at 25 for 5. However, despite these moments of bravado from India, Australia won all four Tests in that series.

In the 1977–78 Indian tour of Australia, the home side had been devastatingly shorn of talent due to the Packer desertions. Led by Bobby Simpson, who had been asked to come out of retirement, the hosts still won 3-2. Despite the series loss, the two Indian wins had been celebrated because India seldom won abroad.

Today, we don't need to fantasize about the fairy-tale finishes that did not quite transpire. It is now India that wins playing away from home with a third-string side. There are plenty of incredible stories that the champion modern-day Indian side is now scripting. In fact, Australia have won only one series in India over the past fifty-four years. At the time of writing, Australia have lost ten of the last twelve Tests they have played in India—and twelve of the last sixteen. They have won only one Test on Indian soil in the last fifteen years.

Pakistan and the West Indies have similar records in Australia and are often rudely told by former Australian cricketers to not waste everyone's time by touring Down Under. They wonder aloud in print and on air whether these countries should even be invited to tour. Yet, India is now in a position to ask the same question to Australia.

This is in stark contrast to our fortunes back in 1991, when an event was held to celebrate the twentieth anniversaries of the famous Indian triumphs in the West Indies and England. The papers of the day remarked that Indian overseas accomplishments were so sparse that the next celebration would likely be the anniversary of our 1983 World Cup win. Today we no longer celebrate every overseas win like in those days, as wins abroad have become frequent. This is reflected in the statistics.

In its first eighty years of Test cricket, India won thirty-seven Tests away from home. In the past ten years alone, they have won twenty-one. The overall win-loss record for India was 116-149 in the first eighty years, in contrast to 56-25 over the past ten years. Now the Indian team is free from the fetters of the past. We are far removed from the days when our team used to visit nations where cricketing infrastructure was more advanced with only the hope of learning from them.

Now India is a major power in the game. In every series we contest, home or away, we are favourites to win. Only South Africa remains an unconquered land as India is yet to win a Test series there. However, even there our win percentage is steadily improving. But this growth into a cricketing superpower owes a lot to those triumphs of yore, when success was rare. From Ajit Wadekar's team winning in West Indies and England in 1971 to Kapil Dev's boys lifting the ODI World Cup in 1983—and even the backs-to-the-wall resistance of Jaisimha and Pataudi in losing causes in Australia ... all these moments need to be celebrated even more. They were the stepping stones—laid with painstaking effort over the detritus of a complicated past—on the way to the top. Belief had to be built in the psyche of an emerging nation when success was pitiably scarce.

In 1986, Dilip Vengsarkar notched up his third hundred at Lord's as India took the lead in the Test series against England. At Leeds in the next Test, he seemingly batted on a different surface from the rest of the players, scoring 61 and 102 not out while the next highest from either side was 36. India won the series 2-0. Later, Vengsarkar revealed the inspiration behind his performances.

Vengsarkar was just fifteen when Wadekar led India to the memorable triumph in England in 1971. He recalled, 'We huddled around a radio, willing India to get the runs on the final day. When Ajit Wadekar was run out we started praying ... we kept praying till the last run was scored. When I played in 1986, I *knew* that it could be done. We had been shown that it could be done.'

Similarly, Vengsarkar's heroic deeds of 1986 showed the future generations what was possible for Indian cricket. That was how belief has been built into the Indian cricket psyche, and how India has emerged as one of the most powerful cricketing nations.

Every story that is covered in this book played a role in this journey.

INDEX

ABOUT THE CONTRIBUTORS

Abbas Ali Baig is a former India Test cricketer. He scored a hundred for India on debut against England in 1959. He was the coach of the Indian cricket team in Australia on the 1991–92 tour and during the 1992 Cricket World Cup.

Prakash Bhandari has been a journalist for fifty years. He was editorial consultant, *The Times of India*, and a correspondent for *The Free Press Journal* and *South Asia Times*, New York. He was awarded by the Rajasthan government for his contribution to sports journalism.

Aditya Bhushan is a cricket writer and the author of three published books.

Rituraj Borkakoty is deputy sports editor at *Khaleej Times*, Dubai.

Michael Dalvi is a versatile cricketer who played first-class cricket for Delhi, Tamil Nadu and Bengal, and for South and East Zone. He manages a resort in Dehradun.

Navroze D. Dhondy is a nephew of former India captain Nari Contractor. He has been a pioneer in sports marketing in India, including the Hero Cup in 1993 and the co-creation of the Wisden Awards and other brand partnerships.

N. Jagannath Das is a sports journalist based in Hyderabad. He has worked with *Newstime*, retiring as deputy editor, *Telegana Today*.

Rahul Dravid is a former India Test captain and the current coach of the Indian cricket team.

Aunshuman Gaekwad is a former India Test player who captained Baroda in the Ranji Trophy. He has worn many hats as a player, coach of the Indian team, commentator, member of the Apex Committee of the BCCI and now president of the Indian Players' Association. He hails from a distinguished family: his father was former India captain D.K. Gaekwad.

Milind Gunjal played eighty-six first-class matches for Maharashtra and West Zone. He was an accomplished batsman and has authored a book.

Vijay Hazare was a former India captain and a prolific batsman. He was the first Indian to score a hundred in both innings of a Test match, at Adelaide in 1947.

Saad bin Jung played cricket for Hyderabad and Haryana, and South Zone. A scion of the renowned Pataudi and Bhopal families, he is a conservationist, a published author and a television personality.

S. Kannan is a senior sports writer with thirty-six years of experience.

Srikant Kate played first-class cricket for Services and North Zone, and is presently chairman of the Ranji Trophy selection committee for Maharashtra.

R. Kaushik has been a cricket writer for over three decades. He started his career with *Newstime* in Hyderabad and has worked with *Deccan Herald* and *Wisden India*, and has reported on more than 100 Test matches. He is the author of several books and the co-author of V.V.S. Laxman's and G.R. Vishwanath's autobiographies.

Hemant Kenkre is a communications professional and cricket columnist. He has played cricket in England, Australia, Kenya and Singapore.

Shubhangi Kulkarni is a former captain of the Indian women's cricket team and has played nineteen Tests. She has seen the rise of women's cricket at close quarters and is currently the players' representative on the BCCI Apex Committee. In 1985, she was presented with the Arjuna Award.

Sulakshan Kulkarni is an experienced first-class cricketer who has represented five teams—Mumbai, Railways, Assam, Vidharbha and Madhya Pradesh. He is a qualified coach who has worked with the Nepal national team and is currently head coach of the Tamil Nadu Ranji Trophy team.

Vaman V. Kumar is a former India Test player who took 599 wickets in first-class cricket with his leg spin.

Vijay Lokapally is a noted journalist, author and former deputy editor of *The Hindu* and *Sportstar*. Starting as a freelance writer in 1981, he has covered six limited-over World Cups and more than 150 Tests and ODIs. He has authored several books.

Suresh Menon is an author and columnist. He has reported from all cricket-playing countries over a period spanning four decades. He is the founding editor of *Wisden India Almanack* and is the author of several books.

Vijay Merchant played for the Bombay and India teams. In 1936, he was the second Indian to score a Test century and was associated in a then-record partnership with Mushtaq Ali at Old Trafford.

Ramaswamy Mohan has been a journalist for over fifty years and has reported extensively on Test and ODI cricket live from around the world for *The Hindu* and *Sportstar*. He has been editing the *Deccan Chronicle*, Chennai, since 2005 as its resident editor. He has authored several books.

Raju Mukherji is a former first-class cricketer who played for and captained the Bengal team, and also represented East Zone. A classy batsman, he has a penchant for writing. He has authored several books on cricket and is an authority on the early days of Indian cricket. He was the first non-Test player to be nominated to the ICC Match Referees panel.

Clayton Murzello is sports editor, Mid-day Group. He has been a journalist for thirty-five years and covered cricket all over the world. He has co-authored two books and is a recipient of two Sports Journalists Federation of India (SJFI) awards for excellence in journalism.

H. Natarajan is a former all-India deputy sports editor of *The Indian Express*, senior editor of Cricinfo/ Wisden and executive editor, CricketCountry.com. A prolific writer, he has contributed to some of the biggest newspapers, magazines and websites across the world.

Vijay Nayudu is a grandson of the first India Test captain, C.K. Nayudu. He played first-class cricket for Madhya Pradesh and Central Zone and was vice-president of the Madhya Pradesh Cricket Association.

K.N. Prabhu was a renowned journalist who was sports editor of *The Times of India* for nearly two decades. He co-authored Sunil Gavaskar's *Sunny Days* as well as Tiger Pataudi's *Tiger's Tale*.

Dr Narottam Puri is an acclaimed sports commentator, quiz show host, presenter and television and radio compere. He is the author of several sports books.

V.K. Ramaswamy umpired in twenty-seven Test matches and fifty ODIs, and one women's Test. In 1986, he was invited as one of the first neutral umpires for a Test match featuring Pakistan and the West Indies.

Partab Ramchand has had an illustrious fifty-five-year-long career, starting with *The Indian Express* in Chennai as a sports reporter. He has worked at senior positions in various organizations, making the transition from print to electronic to internet journalism. He has authored ten books on cricket.

Milind Rege is a former Mumbai cricket captain.

Pranab Roy is a former India Test player. Like his father, Pankaj Roy, he played for Bengal in first-class cricket. An accomplished opening batsman, he was a stylish player who played over seventy first-class matches.

Arunabha Sengupta is a cricket writer who is based in the Netherlands. His latest book, *Elephant in the Stadium,* was shortlisted for the Cricket Writers' Book of the Year Award 2022 and was named by *The Times*, London, as the best cricket book of the year for 2022.

A.G. Satvinder Singh represented Tamil Nadu and South Zone in first-class cricket.

Yajurvindra Singh is a former India Test cricketer and a prolific writer.

Ramji Srinivasan is one of India's most acclaimed biomechanic specialists. He was with the Indian team as a fitness expert. He was instrumental in ensuring that a physical fitness regime was established in Indian cricket at the highest level.

Col. Probir Sur is a former Services cricket captain. He commanded a battalion of the Special Frontier Force at the Siachen Glacier, the highest battlefield in the world. He has commented on cricket on television and radio.

Shashi Tharoor is a third-term Member of Parliament, a former undersecretary-general of the United Nations and a former minister of the Government of India. He is also the author of twenty-four books and innumerable commentaries in Indian and international media. As a child he always wanted to play cricket very badly, and that's exactly what he did when he grew up—he played cricket very badly. He wisely chooses now to write about it instead, occasionally.

Dilip Vengsarkar, nicknamed Colonel, is a former India Test captain and a member of the 1983 World Cup-winning team; he led India to victory in the 1988 Asia Cup.

ABOUT THE EDITOR

Venkat Sundaram is a former first-class cricketer who played in and captained the Delhi and North Zone teams. He has worn many hats: a commentator on television and radio, a manager of the Indian cricket team, a coach, and chairman of the BCCI Grounds and Wickets Committee. He has authored *The Cricket Coaching Handbook* and edited *The Sardar of Spin*, an anthology of writings on Bishan Singh Bedi.

30 Years *of*
HarperCollins *Publishers* India

At HarperCollins, we believe in telling the best stories and finding the widest possible readership for our books in every format possible. We started publishing 30 years ago; a great deal has changed since then, but what has remained constant is the passion with which our authors write their books, the love with which readers receive them, and the sheer joy and excitement that we as publishers feel in being a part of the publishing process.

Over the years, we've had the pleasure of publishing some of the finest writing from the subcontinent and around the world, and some of the biggest bestsellers in India's publishing history. Our books and authors have won a phenomenal range of awards, and we ourselves have been named Publisher of the Year the greatest number of times. But nothing has meant more to us than the fact that millions of people have read the books we published, and somewhere, a book of ours might have made a difference.

As we step into our fourth decade, we go back to that one word – a word which has been a driving force for us all these years.

Read.

Harper Collins · 4th · HARPER PERENNIAL · HARPER BUSINESS · HARPER BLACK · हार्पर हिन्दी

HarperCollins *Children's Books* · HARPER DESIGN · HARPER VANTAGE · Harper Sport